Juliana Datry Most is from Decatur, GA. She lives with her spouse on the Chattahoochee River, north of Atlanta. They have four children, and are Momsie and Popsie to five granddaughters.

She graduated from Emory University and was a librarian, special ed teacher and German teacher. She attended the University of Freiburg in Germany.

She taught for the Dekalb County School System. She does story telling in costumes and has original characters like "Candy Lauper," "Holly Parton" and "Cleana Turner".

She enjoys expressive arts, domestic arts and loves to Zumba dance, swim and travel.

She is the author of the children's picture book *"The Princess and the Sneeze"*.

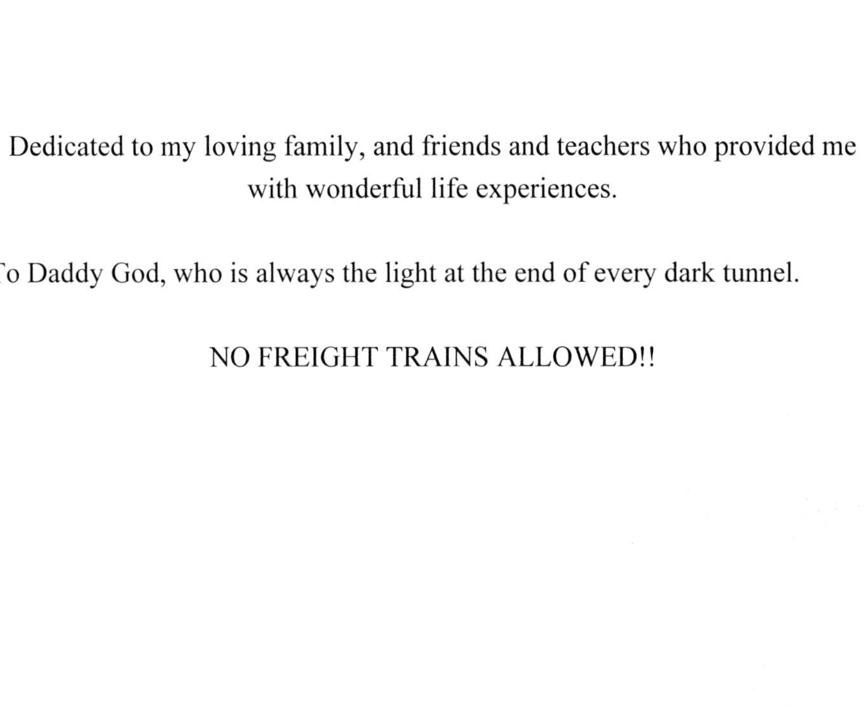

Dedicated to my loving family, and friends and teachers who provided me with wonderful life experiences.

To Daddy God, who is always the light at the end of every dark tunnel.

NO FREIGHT TRAINS ALLOWED!!

Juliana Datry Most

ME, MYSELF & I REMEMBER DECATUR (AND BEYOND)

AUSTIN MACAULEY PUBLISHERS™

LONDON * CAMBRIDGE * NEW YORK * SHARJAH

Ordering Information
Quantity sales: Special discounts are available on quantity purchases by corporations, associations, and others. For details, contact the publisher at the address below.

Publisher's Cataloguing-in-Publication data
Most, Juliana Datry
Me, Myself & I Remember Decatur (and Beyond)

ISBN 9798891551923 (Paperback)
ISBN 9798891551930 (ePub e-book)

Library of Congress Control Number: 2024900374

www.austinmacauley.com/us

First Published 2024
Austin Macauley Publishers LLC
40 Wall Street, 33rd Floor, Suite 3302
New York, NY 10005
USA

mail-usa@austinmacauley.com
+1 (646) 5125767

DEEPEST THANKS for your kind, willing, helping hands & hearts to
April Fallaw
Crystal Lash
Pat Nichols

Chapter 1
Gloria Steinem, Eat Your Heart Out!
Will the Real Feminist Please Pull Up in Your Crib!

World War II ended. David Everett Dattelbaum came home to Decatur, Georgia from the Marine Corps in the Pacific on Midway Island. He had been a stance gunner living in a fox hole and was trained also in bomb disposal. A few days before the war ended, he and his buddy were bored and requested to be sent to the front lines. I am probably pretty lucky to be alive, or? Daddy met Mama when he was on leave in Washington, DC where she had been working in the fingerprint division of the Federal Bureau of Investigation. Mama was there to support her sister Sara who was having special facial burn surgeries from a childhood accident. My parents wrote to each other for over a year. Mama went back to Decatur after the war. She was an excellent writer and secretary and was working in Atlanta for Travelers Insurance with her friends Frances and Minnie. Daddy's family was also in Decatur.

During the war, Daddy's very pretty baby sister, Judy, was photographed at the Venetian Pool in a red bathing suit, and the picture was put on the front of the Atlanta Journal Sunday magazine section. A Decatur lady mailed it to her son overseas, and he taped it to his locker. So many young soldiers fell in love with her that they named a B-52 bomber after her. It was called the Judy Dattelbaum. My little brother, Eric, thought for many years that Judy was Marilyn Monroe. Mama and Daddy married in the Decatur Methodist Church that September. The church had dark wood and beautiful old stained-glass windows and dark, wine-colored carpet. At the altar were lush, dark green leather leaf ferns and three arches of seven candles the color of Mama's ecru satin and Chantilly lace dress. The reception was at Mumsie and Grandaddy's house on Adams Street. Mumsie had antique family tablecloths and truly knew how to cater such events so beautifully. Daddy's sister Judy and Mama's sisters Sara and Kitti were bridesmaids along with a couple of other close girlfriends, Jo Anne and Minnie. They were the perfect couple: smart, ambitious, hard-working. They both had impeccable character and were from fine families of salt of the earth type people.

Daddy soon enrolled at Emory University, wanting with all his heart to be a physician. Mama said he was so tender-hearted and gentle-spirited that when they rode on a bus, little children came and climbed up in his lap. Neither of my parents were overtly physically demonstrative with their affection. Nonetheless, we decidedly knew how much we were loved and cared for. They provided everything we needed at any given time and made us the priority and center of their lives. Daddy worked part-time at Monroe Nursery digging holes and planting shrubbery. Gardening became a life-long family hobby. We forever had an abundance of lush shrubbery. Through the years the scent of lilacs, gardenias and tea olive bushes wafted through the screen into my bedroom window on summer evenings. I loved the roses and blue hydrangeas and ate rose and gardenia petals often.

By Thanksgiving Mama was in a family way with child Juliana and stayed home making pastel, flannel baby blankets as were customary in those days. They were edged with matching embroidery thread done with the blanket stitch. Maternity clothes consisted of skirts with a cutout for the blossoming tummy. It had a fabric tie at the waist that could be loosened more and more. The long matching tops were huge and boxy with buttons. People called them "hatching jackets." Pregnancy was not discussed openly, and women stayed fairly close to home. Instead of saying you were pregnant, you said, "PG." Of course, moms chatted among themselves about their labor and delivery experiences and the day-to-day routines of being young mothers. Morning sickness was handled with saltine crackers and ginger ale.

Nine months later I was born somewhere around six pounds and about nineteen inches long. My abundant head of hair was jet black, later turning toe-head blonde. Mama said my big eyes were always wide open and seldom closed. My parents really got me with a 100% off coupon in the bargain baby basement, so to speak. Since Daddy was in premed at Emory University, the obstetrician, Dr. Matthews, did not charge even a penny for the prenatal care or delivery. Mama had Chantilly lace, perfume, china, silver and crystal. They actually considered naming me Chantilly. Not a joke! My parents named me Juliana for my Uncle Julian Moore who died in a plane crash during World War II in Saskatchewan, Canada. He was the oldest sibling and a civil engineer from Georgia Tech helping to build the 1,390-mile Al-Can Highway that connected the United States to Alaska through Yukon territory in Canada. It was a tragic loss. Julian was such a fine son and brother. He was a brilliant scholar and Eagle Scout. He always shepherded his little sisters with great care. He had started college at Emory at Oxford in Oxford, Georgia.

Mama often called me "Dooley Annie Jane" as she was so poetic. When little brother came along six years later, he could not pronounce a J, so he called me "Shooey, and Shoo Shoo" which, ironically is the French nickname for Chantelle, or Chantilly!

Mama diligently tried to breast feed me, and I was growing and gaining normally and was a very content baby. After six weeks the pediatrician, Dr. Leslie, asked Mama for a sample of her milk. We know that the first milk of a feeding is thin and more like skim milk. The creamy milk comes at the end of the feeding and is called the "hind milk." The doctor told Mama that her milk was too thin and no good. He put me on a bottle of canned evaporated milk mixed with water and corn syrup. I got horrible tasting cod liver oil and iron supplement drops. What a formula fiasco! Thankfully today's mothers have gone to La Leche type support groups and worked with qualified lactation consultants.

Sadly, the pediatricians were brainwashed by the formula companies and uninformed then. They insisted on strict four-hour feeding schedules. That meant that a hungry baby had to cry until four hours had elapsed. Didn't anyone attend the Institute of Logical Living, for Pete's sake! Medical school did not cover all the bases regarding nutrition. The milk companies were labeling breast feeding as old fashioned. Shame on them for putting corporate profits above the needs and welfare of babies! What a travesty! I was allergic to orange juice. Mama stopped giving it to me, because it came right back up like a little Italian fountain!

When I was born, Mumsie was in Los Angeles helping her Uncle Will. His wife, Aunt Marguerite, had dementia. She had been the pianist for the San Carlos Opera Company, and Uncle Will had made a small fortune with oil wells. They were in a car wreck which killed Aunt Marguerite and put Mumsie in the hospital in traction with two pelvic fractures. Aunt Kitti flew out to help them. In that bed Mumsie made little four-inch samples of her tatted lace and mailed them to Mama to choose her favorite. Mama was making me pastel pink, yellow, white and blue dresses with smocking on the bodice. The lace was for the sleeves and collar. When I was old enough to treasure Mumsie's lace, I asked her to teach me the art. Sadly, her eyes were too far gone from macular degeneration.

This was an era before disposable diapers or cloth diapers with rubber pants or plastic pants. We wore thick layers of diaper that were called "soakers." When a baby was born, someone in the family or the godparents probably gave a set of sterling silver diaper pins with the child's initials engraved on them. They usually were connected with a silver chain to help the mom keep up with them. Now that was a silver polishing nightmare! Yes, we had small silver drinking cups, hair brushes, combs, rattles and piggy banks. We southerners love our silver. It's a cultural thing since people had to bury their silver to keep Yankees from getting it during the War Between the States. I would say that it was also snobbery to pretend that we were more regal than the folks from up north. Long ago, southerners were predominantly English/Scotch/Irish protestants. I suppose it is nice to pretend that you are the king and queen!

We lived with Papa and Grandmother, Myron William and Hazel Elsey Dattelbaum, on Glenn Circle in Decatur. Papa was from Cleveland, Ohio and had run away to Halifax, Nova Scotia to join the British Army in World War I. He was a chaplain's assistant in London and never saw a day of combat. He was there to entertain officers with his superb tennis, golf, poker, and billiards skills. He told me he had to stomp grapes to make jam for the officers. Now I think he was pulling my leg on that one! Grandmother was from Austin Texas by way of Ashgrove, Missouri, Kansas and Oklahoma. She was born when her parents were pushing fifty years old. They lived above the family store, so her birth certificate was written on a small brown paper grocery bag. Again, I am lucky I made it to planet earth.

Papa met Grandmother's brother in the war. They wrote to each other and fell in love. He got on a train to Austin, Texas in New York on a Friday. By Sunday they were married. Grandmother's father was a Methodist circuit rider preacher. He painted houses during the week until he fell off his ladder and broke both arms. Then he became a photographer. Her much older siblings already had children when she was born. Her brothers owned a mattress company. They built her a tiny stage beside the barn and her mother made little curtains out of mattress ticking fabric. Grandmother remembered when her much older brothers were making beer in the bathtub during prohibition. The revenuers came and poured all that beer into the gutter.

She had worked as a hosiery buyer and bought her own car and taught Papa to drive. She and Papa lived in New York City. She was a bona fide Roaring 20's flapper and taught me the Charleston dance when I was knee high to a keg in a speak easy! Papa was in investing and sales, and Grandmother sold hosiery at a department store. One of her customers was Rudolph Valentino the film star. When Daddy joined the planet as a five-pound preemie, he was born in a cousin's medical office on 5th. Avenue. He was a colicky baby, so Grandmother took the train to Ohio. Papa's mother, Gramma Fannie rubbed whiskey on his belly. Apparently, the fumes soothed his digestive system or something. She spoke no English, but she and Grandmother adored one another.

My Aunt Judy was seventeen years old and lived with us there also while finishing Decatur Girls High. At my birth at Crawford Long Hospital in Atlanta she proclaimed to the doctor that she was going to have six babies someday. She made it to five.

Our attic room was hot and stuffy, but Daddy sprinkled baby powder every day for the pleasant scent. This was probably not the best idea for Mama's nasal allergies. Our family friends, Lloyd and Virginia, gave me a very nice, black baby carriage. It was cumbersome and probably three-quarters the size of a baby crib. Moms did not run very many errands in a car, and there were no malls, so it was sturdy and suitable for strolling around the neighborhood. When we were older, my siblings and I rode in it down the long, steep hill of our driveway, and that was loads of fun, especially when we hit a bush and crashed and rolled over.

We all attended the old gray granite stone First Methodist Church on Sycamore Street. Grandmother's father had been a Methodist circuit rider preacher in Austin, Texas. Along came Christmas when I was four months old. The boy babies were born much earlier in the year. I was the youngest baby, so I was cast in the part of Baby Jesus in the live nativity scene on the front lawn of the church. Now, that is about as feminist as one can get, playing the part of Baby Jesus. Of course, that is also a good way to have the devil on your trail trying to use you as a dartboard forever ad infinitum. Put that in your SMOKE and PIPE it, Ms. Steinem!

I was christened at that church. My godparents were Mr. and Mrs. Dennis, owners of the Covington News in Covington, Georgia where Mama grew up. They had wanted Mama to marry their son, Bill, but were delighted to finally have a baby girl in the family. My other godparents were the Stantons. When they moved to Texas, they gave me their beautiful, blonde cocker spaniel, Bonita My Silversheen. Bonnie was a show dog. She survived a copperhead snake bite at our creek and had two litters of puppies.

We moved to Mumsie and Granddaddy's house on Adams Street to have a larger ground floor room. Mumsie was from Hogansville and Covington. She was a fifth-grade teacher and had once been a social worker. She was a graduate of Wesleyan College in Macon, Georgia and had roomed with Mai Ling who later became the world-famous Mrs. Chiang Kai-Shek of Taiwan.

Granddaddy's family from North Carolina had prospered selling mules to pull barges on the inland waterways. They moved to Winder, Georgia and had a general store and lived next to Senator Richard Russell's family. Mama's sisters Sara and Katherine (Kitti) lived at home while attending Georgia State University downtown. Sara was majoring in education, and Kitti was studying home economics. Being the first grandchild and niece, I had no shortage of adoring family members to dote on me, take me places and spend the most quality kind of time with me. Granddaddy never really got over Julian's death, but I did bring a lot of joy and laughter into his life that helped to displace some of the grief and loss.

I got into my share of mischief as a toddler. Poor Aunt Kitti's ruby ring was accidently flushed down the commode, and I got red nail polish on her new white chenille bedspread. My teddy bear had Mama's pink lipstick on his chest, so I called him "Lipstickedy Pinty". Mama hid him up in the closet and I said, "Poor Pinty, runned away!" I got him back when she figured out how to clean his white, sticky chest.

Papa often took me riding around Decatur in his big, shiny blue Buick. It distinctly smelled of fine Cuban cigars. When Papa was a boy, his father owned a cigar and candy store with tables in the back for playing Pinochle. Papa's job was to roll the tobacco leaves from Cuba into cigars.

There were no children's' safety car seats or seat belts back then so, horror of horrors, I stood up at the steering wheel when Papa drove. He taught me all the names of all the automobiles. Once a car pulled out in front of Daddy, and I shouted, "Watch out Buddy, Cadillacs wreck too!" It was indeed a Cadillac, and my parents were very flabbergasted that I knew cars backwards and forward from Chevys to Fords, Plymouths, Chryslers and so forth.

My baby book states that I was potty trained and eating with knife, fork and spoon at six months. I am not sure I believe that completely if at all. My Mommy was in the "Mom Overachiever's Club", (probably the president) and she may have exaggerated a bit and fudged on the facts. It seems that Baby Boomer parents had delusions of grandeur with the need to believe their offspring were exceptionally advanced and brilliant. This was in keeping with the pride of America winning World War II. I think the proof literally lay in my white Buster Brown high top shoes. I had a habit of standing and letting the tinkle run down in my shoes to the point that they called them "tinkle pots." Many parents took their children's baby shoes and had them dipped in bronze for preservation. They kept them on coffee tables or had them made into book ends. My mom and dad did not do this. I imagine my shoes were too ratty-rotty! Truthfully, I really have vague memory of these events.

I was a long-term thumb sucker and rubbed my lips with my top sheet. If we were away from home and my own cotton bedsheets, and I needed a nap, I asked for "white cover." Resourceful Daddy would just pop a white handkerchief out of his pocket and give it to me. Thankfully, I never needed braces on my teeth.

I have also heard that I loved to chase Papa and Grandmother's Boston terrier named King. I liked to play Mumsie's piano standing up on the bench in my little white training pants. They say I touched the keys thoughtfully without banging. My ears are literally hyper-occlusive, so I am categorically allergic to noise. My eyes are photophobic and cannot tolerate bright lights. I walked around their house saying, "Where Granddaddy's shoes? Where Granddaddy's shoes?" That was because like all toddlers, I wanted to clomp around the house in them.

I was told that Mama and Daddy once went out with some friends and left me with the lady's mother. I had never known anyone other than my grandparents and aunts. So, the lady said I was sobbing the whole time inconsolably, and thus she locked me in the bathroom. I am not sure how long I was confined in there, but that was the beginning of my severe, debilitating "closet-phobia". It is a shame that there were no cell phones in those days. She was certainly not likely a mean, sadistic monster, and I feel sure she would have called Mama and Daddy to come and get me.

I walked at twelve months and soon became a very loquacious little chatter box. There was no need for a playpen to keep me safe. I mean, come on, someone was watching me almost every minute of every day. I remember my wooden high chair, shiny with varnish. There was a bunny rabbit decal on the back of the seat. I named the brown bunny with blue overalls "Bubba" and turned around backwards to try to feed him carrots. I had a small ball with a face on it, a Dutch boy doll and some rattles. There was a small, round rubber pool. Plastic had not made its debut on the world stage where it was christened and bar mitzva-ed to plague the seven continents and the seven seas and the landfills and all biology phylum of animals from lepidoptera to homo sapiens. My eyes are not microscopic, but I venture a guess that the one-celled amoebas and paramecium were carrying protest posters and singing: We are the world, we are the creatures…

There were not so many toy companies, so toddlers played with household items like pots and pans and spoons. We had metal and wooden toys and rag dolls and hard as a rock rubber dolls. There were electric-powered horses here and there in public places. You held the child on tight, put a dime in the slot and got about a one-minute ride.

Chapter 2
Pranks of A Preschooler

Aunt Judy around age seventeen married Mr. Shackelford, who was called Shack. I recall riding around with them in a shiny, yellow Cadillac convertible. Shack kept it immaculately waxed and vacuumed. They moved to New York. Aunt Judy worked at Saks Fifth Avenue, and they had a black cocker spaniel named Saksy. When Uncle Shack grew tired of New York, they split up, and he moved back to Decatur. He married a widow with two children, and Judy married Uncle Ted Lash.

Aunt Kitti fell in love with Uncle Truman. I was three years old, and truthfully, not really old enough to be a flower girl in their wedding. Nonetheless, they were convinced that I was so precocious and brilliant and cooperative that I could pull it off. My adoring family was positive that I would be the next Shirley Temple. They said I had her vivacious personality and talents with natural curls. They believed that I was "Super-preschooler." I am surprised they did not make me a superhero cape!

Mama sewed me a long, white Swiss organdy dress. It was sleeveless and the neck had gathering that would remind you of smocking but without any embroidery. My skin was fair and sensitive, and I remember that it felt scratchy and snug on my midriff. To this good day I cannot abide anything tight around my middle. My complaint was always, "It twitches, it twitches!" Thankfully by the time I was a teen, long waisted Roaring 20's flapper style dresses were in style: no sash, no belt, no elastic, no zipper or waist band.

The bridesmaids, clad in rose colored satin waltzed down the aisle gracefully in time to Lohengrin's 'Wedding March.' Then it was my turn to scatter pink rose petals from my little white wicker basket. One problem, I was a very precise, persnickety little girl that liked my ducks in a row in full dress military uniforms. In this scenario it had to do with roses in a row. I carefully placed one petal next to a pew on the left and then one petal next to a pew on the right, slowly and thoughtfully with great purpose while the organist repeated the bridal march more times than she had agreed to for that paycheck she received. Finally, Granddaddy and Aunt Kitti had to pass me to get to the altar before Uncle Truman gave up hope of having a bride that day or year. I did finally reach the altar and stood quietly and politely next to my aunts.

That little white flower girl dress got a lot of mileage that year and the next. I was constantly standing in front of the mirror playing pretend wedding with an imaginary groom and a lace curtain over my head. At the end of each ceremony, I pronounced me husband and wife and kissed the mirror. Eventually I could read the wedding ceremony out loud from the old dark green Methodist Hymnal.

Daddy was doing well traveling Georgia and Florida peddling dresses with Papa. He and Mama started building a house off South Candler Street on Midway Road on three acres of land with lots of woods and a creek. It was white clapboard siding and had a living room with fireplace, two bedrooms, one bath with bright, light mint green tile, a living room, a kitchen and a screened porch. There was an unfinished basement with large laundry sink and electrical receptacles. Later, as our family grew, they turned the living room into a bedroom with half-bath and built a huge brick living room/dining room/den addition and enclosed the porch. We had a patio outside the living room, and the chimney opened on both sides for outdoor grilling or cozy indoor fires. Later when Mama was the Civil Defense chairman for my school's PTA, we built a bona fide, Class A great bomb shelter in the basement. It was fully stocked with ample food, water, medicines, cots and first aid supplies to survive part of an atomic bomb attack. There was an abject terror madness roaring across America due to the weapon competition with the Communist Soviet Union.

In those days of the late 1940's young families regularly went to a farmers' market to buy in bulk and save money on fruits and vegetables. You could purchase a nice size Christmas tree for less than $3.00. My parents usually went with their close friends Buck and Evelyn. Their son Ralph was my best friend. He liked me even though my August birthday had gotten me the part of Baby Jesus in the live nativity scene. Ralph was born into the world in April that year.

It was Summer so our parents had bought a bushel of cantaloupes and a couple of watermelons. The adults were busy in the living room talking and listening to radio. (That is correct. We had no TV yet.) All of a sudden, they heard us laughing with the greatest delight. They ran to the kitchen and saw us at the top of the basement stairs rolling melons down the steps one at a time. When a melon landed at the concrete bottom and smashed open, we squealed at the top of our lungs with complete joy.

Once at Ralph's house the adults heard me crying and gasping for breath. They found me under a child's rocking chair with Ralph rocking on top of me. Ralph's parents were horrified, but he had a perfectly rational explanation that eliminated the word sociopath: She was trying to kiss me! So much for the idea of childhood sweethearts, right? We remained friends all the way through the school years and even started Emory College at Oxford together, but I can promise you, there was never even the first bit of romantic ideas or feelings. You might call it "Rock and Run."

I was a tiny petite lass for a three-year-old, but my little yellow Easter duck was just the right size for me. I put him in my backyard rubber swimming pool. I would spend hours chasing him all over the yard. However, little ducky grew up and was almost taller than me. Ducky seemed to realize that he suddenly had an advantage over me. Ducky learned to chase me around the yard and snap my hand with his orange beak. I really did not like Ducky all that much anymore and avoided the yard. It was probably my first experience with fear. One day I was looking out the window for Ducky. He was simply gone, nowhere to be found. I asked Daddy about Ducky. He said Ducky had gone to dance with Dan. Somehow that explanation satisfied me and was actually, a relief. Years later I found out that Dan was the owner of the butcher shop where my Papa bought steaks and prime rib. So, it became clear that Ducky had danced right from the oven onto the plate of someone who lived in Decatur, Georgia in 1950.

My blond, wavy hair grew to shoulder length, and I had the typical bangs on my very tall forehead. Yes, my three-year-old portrait from Olin Mills Studio shows that I had cut those bangs a wee bit crookedly. The giant silver scissors came out of Mama's sewing basket. I think most preschoolers do that at some stage or another. Some kids might even give their siblings or playmates a wacky haircut also. It is a thousand wonders that children do not poke an eye out doing these stunts.

Mama enrolled me in The Decatur School of Ballet across from the railroad depot when I was three and a half. I do not remember a lot about it, but the teacher was strict and abrupt and I thought she was scary and mean. Being such a little golden child wherever I went, I was not used to scolding or disapproval. She thought my ballet was seriously lacking. I think it was because I did not understand her instructions, and I had become fearful of making a mistake. Thus, she made me sit down, and I spent much of the lesson time sitting on the hard, cold brown floor with my knees pulled up against my chest and my face buried in my knees from shame. Mama quickly realized this was not a good experience for me, and since she was having a difficult pregnancy with my little sister, Davilyn, she was happy to stop taking me to ballet lessons.

There was also a veterinary office in the ballet school building. That is where we took my boxer, Hans, that Papa had bought as a watch dog when Daddy went on the road with him selling dresses. Daddy and Papa worked for Forest City Manufacturing in St. Louis. Papa's ladies' dress line was called Martha Manning and came in sizes 6-18 for more mature figures. Daddy's line was called Shirley Lee. It was for junior sizes 5-15. Sadly, Hans got loose and died. The vet on the farm up the street, Dr. Von Grimp, said that Hans had been given rat poison. My parents always suspected the very grumpy elderly lady at the bottom of the hill. Not wanting to stir up trouble, they never said anything to the neighbors. She was known to dislike children and pets. She worshipped her flower garden. Perhaps playful Hans took a pounce on her petunias.

My Granddaddy had a small upholstery and furniture refinishing shop in the ballet school building on the left side lower level. One had to step down two steps to get into the shop which had a bumpy concrete floor and Granddaddy's work bench, tools, rags and jars of various kinds of tacks and nails. I loved to go there. There were colorful velvet fabrics. Granddaddy used more burgundy velvet, but I especially loved the bright sapphire blue and the emerald green colors. He also had solid and floral and geometric patterned brocades in pastel colors. I liked the smell of wood stain but not so much the varnish that irritated my throat. Granddaddy's fingernails were often brown from the wood stains, and at home his shirts smelled like his shop. I still have two small brocade cushions that Mumsie made me from his fabrics. One is soft gold, and one is burgundy.

Mumsie and Granddaddy lived right up the street from us with Aunt Sara and Aunt Kitti. I could walk to their house every day if I walked down our very long driveway, crossed the field of bottomland, crossed the creek and walked up Midway Road a bit. Daddy and Granddaddy had built that bridge out of railroad ties and telephone poles. It was very sturdy and had benches on the sides. It was pleasant to sit there and watch the Shoals Creek rush under the bridge. However, when they first built it and painted creosote on it to prevent insects, that odor made me feel very queasy and light headed. Creosote is now banned due to its carcinogenic properties. I was always under foot when they built Abraham Lincoln split rail fences or gardened or planted camellias, gardenias, tea olive bushes and so forth.

Our fence was lined with ilia gnus bushes. They produced small, sweet sour reddish berries that I liked to eat. Good that they were not poisonous since I never told Mama I was eating them! Children do act like little bunny rabbits and eat clover and chew on pine needles and such. Usually, they have a really good instinct of what is toxic and what is not. For example, I ate gardenias and roses but never touched a poisonous daffodil. Daddy had espaliered pyracanthas bush on our front stoop on the outside of the gray granite chimney. I can tell you that it's tiny reddish orange berries were awful tasting. Many years later I read in the 'Georgia Farm and Home Journal' that one can make delicious pyracantha jelly by adding plenty of sugar.

My dearest mom was always a wonderful birthday party fairy. For my fourth it was a circus party. She cut the tops off of big brown cardboard boxes from the grocery store, turned them on their sides. She put stuffed animals inside the boxes and made cage bars from crepe paper strips. She fed the children circus food including little bags of popcorn, peanuts and hotdogs. A man came with a cotton candy machine. Wow! That was a hit! We drank lemonade and chocolate milk. The children in the neighborhood came and had a blast. My cake was decorated to look like a merry-go-round with a circus tent-like top and red poles. Back then sweet treats were reserved for special occasions. Our diets had far less cookies and cake and ice cream and candy. Sugary cola was for special times and for headaches and upset stomachs.

Our family liked to take trips together. Granddaddy was frail and stayed home, but Mumsie took me on my first train ride to Covington, Georgia to see my great grandmother, Carrie Sockwell Mobley and her sister, Sallie Mae Sockwell. They were both brilliant scholars, and Grandmother kept the Covington Library two days a week as one of her lady's society volunteer duties. She was a well-known historian. Now and then writers came to interview her. Usually, we had Thanksgiving dinner at their house in the huge dining room with twelve-foot ceilings and dark, mahogany antique furniture. Some pieces went all the way back to the American Revolution such as the federal chest and the Martha Washington dressing table. The food was very traditionally southern roasted turkey, cornbread dressing, gravy, candied yams, fruit cake. We did not stuff our turkeys. That was considered Yankee. The most memorable flavor was Auntie's orange charlotte dessert. It was fluffy, and I can still taste the delicate orange flavor.

If you spent the night with Grandmother and Auntie, you slept on a screened sleeping porch, weather permitting. Grandmother taught you the names and history of all the ancestor portraits and tin type photos on the walls. Breakfast was always poofy, mouthwatering cheese omelet. There were fireplaces in every room. Grandmother put magnolia blossoms in each fireplace every day when they were in bloom. She was very British and had a formal English garden with very definite red brick borders. Mumsie's brother, Marvin, had despised working that garden for his mother when he was a boy and teen. Next to the free-standing garage that housed their dark green Plymouth, there were fig trees. I found it magical to eat fruit right off the trees!

Mama, Daddy, Papa, Grandmother and I went to Florida to Tarpon Springs. We went far out from shore on a sponge boat. The deep-sea diver clad in a full-body diving suit, went way down in the water and surfaced many times with armloads of sea sponges which we could purchase. Most of the adults were hanging over the edge of the boat upchucking sicker than dogs and pale as ghosts, but I was sitting on the deck eating pimento cheese sandwiches on whole wheat bread. Thankfully, to this day I have never suffered from seasickness or carsickness.

A couple of summers we drove to Cleveland, Ohio to see Papa's family. His parents, Fannie Englander and Friedrich Joachim Dattelbaum were from Nagy Vitez Austria-Hungary. I never met Grandpa Friedrich who died when hit by a motorcycle walking home from his cigar and candy store. Grandma Fannie barely spoke any English, and she was disabled from a stroke, but she was always smiling and gave warmly loving hugs. She sat in a chair all day in her long white granny gown with a colorful crocheted Afghan on her lap. Her long white hair was braided with the braids wrapped around her head. She had such kind, gentle eyes. Grandpa was well-known for buying shoes for immigrant cousins' children so they could look nice in public school and learn

English. They both had very generous, warm hearts and were always prosperous from believing in the Blessings of Abraham.

The summer that I was four, when we were in Ohio. Aunt Judy came from New York and met us there. We watched men play bocce ball there by the lake. That is an Italian game, and we definitely did not have that in Atlanta which was still pretty WASPY. Up north there was wide-spread diversity of a plethora of ethnic groups. I walked on the shore of Lake Erie in a royal blue bathing suit with white polka dots. I tried to walk pretty lady style just like my glamourous Judy with my long blonde wavy curls blowing in the breeze. After seeing one dead fish I refused to go in the water anymore. Papa's youngest widowed sister, Aunt Ellie, lived right on the lake. She was a dental hygienist and had a case of not so tasty sugar free gum on a floral chair in her upstairs bedroom. Help! I probably swallowed fifty pieces of gum that summer.

Aunt Hilda had long ago been in a "ballet" with the Vaudeville star, Fannie Bryce. The attic was filled with white and pink ballet costumes and pink toe shoes plus very old dresses and black button-up pointy-toe shoes. The whole family had such fun dressing up in the attic. I remember all the laughter so vividly. Mildred played the piano, and we all sang. During the Depression, Gramma Fanny had paid $1,000.00 for a Steinway grand piano. She proclaimed, "My children will have music." They all loved the opera, theater and the symphony and attended regularly. They volunteered as ushers to get free tickets.

We took Daddy's baby cousin, thirteen-year-old Ruthie, home with us for a visit. Her dentist dad had died suddenly the previous year, and she was very sad. When it was time for her to fly back home, Mama and Daddy dressed her like a child in rolled up jeans with bobby socks and a plaid shirt. She had braids and a stack of comic books so she could pass for twelve years old and get a cheaper ticket on Eastern Airlines. I know she thought I was a little pain in the butt. I was often whapping her on her backside to get her attention. Once we were both grown, we became the best of cousin/friends and have often spent happy times together with our children. We even go on long trips together to visit cousins in distant states. Her husband, Woody was a nuclear physicist. His father was the editor of the Merriam Webster Dictionary in Boston, and he sent us a giant library edition signed by him. Mama put it on a proper library dictionary stand in our family room that had copious built-in bookcases.

Mama loved to take me on the trolley from Decatur to downtown Peachtree Street. I was fascinated by the bright, fiery sparks that bounced off the overhead cable. There was the large department store called Davison's which later became Macy's. From Davison's we could take the shoppers bus down to Rich's, another large, local department store. One day at Rich's a lady was admiring herself in a mirror while trying on dresses. She abruptly moved backward and fell over me and got injured. She filed suit against my parents, claiming I was a wild, out of control child. However, the sales ladies testified that I was quietly standing still holding my mom's hand like a perfect little lady. So that was the end of that even though it had frightened me a lot and made me shyer.

Across from Davison's was the S & W cafeteria. Mama and I always ate there when on a shopping trip. I adored the red Jell-O with abundant, sweet whipped cream on top. The only problem was that I had not learned to pronounce the letter "J", so I always asked for red "Dello".

Shopping trips included a trip to the Penny Arcade, a large three-story recreation area with a kind of honky-tonk carnival atmosphere where the smell of fresh popcorn and roasted peanuts would knock you over. There were ice cream and candy vendors and little stalls that sold cheap trinkets and costume jewelry. The game machines were called pin ball machines and cost a nickel. Bubble gum and lollypops were a penny. Though I was a gutsy, fearless child, one day I met my match. Here came Mr. Peanut, a man from the Planter's Peanut stand dressed up like a giant peanut with a top hat and cane. He was probably close to eight feet tall, and I grabbed my mom's skirt and held on to her leg and hid behind her. She quickly assured me there was no danger whatsoever, so I boldly went up to him and shook his hand.

Mama and Daddy took me to Sunday School every week. My teacher was Mrs. Paul Graves, a kind and gentle woman who made The Old and New Testament come alive for me. She told my parents that I asked her deep questions about God and The Holy Bible that she could not answer. She declared that I was "a child of God." And that will also get Beelzebub after you! Probably in the south we should call him "Beelzebubba!"

My bedroom was painted a soft, sky blue. Mama made valances out of pale-yellow woven placemats. She stenciled animals like Peter Rabbit on them. My parents realized how much I loved to draw, so they bought a large blackboard and gave me a nice supply of white chalk and an eraser. I was such a typical first-born child, very obedient and parent pleasing. Mama was horrified to find me one day with a pencil drawing all over the walls. Before losing her temper and scolding me or giving me one swat (my parents' limit) with the piece of linoleum rubber tile (Boy, did that sting!) she sat me down and asked me why I was drawing on the walls instead of on the blackboard. I told her in no uncertain terms: Mommy, I was drawing angels. They need to be blue like the color of the sky in Heaven. Needless to say, I was forgiven without stingy rubber tile touching my angelic derriere!

By the time I turned four, Mama was very frail and sickly before the new baby came. She spent a lot of time in bed. With Daddy traveling during the week, I needed to be my mommy and hers. I recall being an early riser as soon as the light hit my window each morning. I popped up, got dressed and went to the kitchen to fix breakfast. I could reach the stove by standing on a sturdy brown, wooden chair. Mama got a fried egg every morning plus buttered toast and juice. I had no clue how to make coffee in the aluminum percolator pot. The strange thing was her egg always had a hole in the white part. She found this mysterious and wondered and wondered how I fried eggs that way. Then, voila, one week 'Life Magazine' had a photo taken by one of their photographers of his little girl frying an egg. Same dilemma! The dad's egg had the same hole. Time lapse photography revealed that the culprit was a giant lump of butter. When a child cracks an egg over a huge lump of butter, it leaves a hole in the egg. Neither Inspector Poirot nor Miss Marple was needed for that poultry problem.

Mama also often drifted off to sleep in the daytime sitting on the sofa. I decided to be a big girl and surprise her with a manicure. We had gone to the beauty salon. I saw how the manicurist filed Mama's nails. Little Miss Self Confidence was sure she was up to the challenge. When Mama woke up, she was very surprised to find that each one of her nails was a different length and had different angle edges. She tried to hide it, but I could tell she was a bit upset. I decided that would be my last attempt at filing nails for a while. Aren't we thankful that Mama was not a lady that loved to have colored polish on her nails in those days?

When Davilyn was born, Mama and Daddy hired an ambulance to drive us home so that I could experience that. I remember the baby was in a little brown wicker bassinet with skinny silvery metal legs that were bolted securely to the floor for safety. My parents were always so good about providing us with lots of hands-on life experiences. They took us to visit many senior citizens also. This is the way a child develops divergent thinking which is in many ways a true sign of giftedness. That is every bit as important as the results of an IQ test since there are actually thirty-four different kinds of intelligence. Well, they must have overplayed their hands with me, because when people tell me I am out of the box, I say: Box? What box? I never saw a box!

Chapter 3
Who Knew Five Years
Old Would Be This Fearsome?

Five years old like three and seven is supposedly one of those magical years where a child's physical, mental and emotional development are all in sync. The child is content and has it all together. Five was very hard and challenging for me in other ways. I had a best friend right down the hill to the left of the creek across from Mumsie and Granddaddy. Her name was Anne. We spent a lot of time together. One week in the summer Anne, Davilyn and I came down with a fever. My fever went away quickly as was always the case with me, but Anne wound up in an iron lung in Warm Springs, Georgia, and my little sister became profoundly disabled. Yes, it was the polio virus before the Salk vaccine came out.

I loved having a baby sister. Dede was such a beautiful baby with large eyes and soft curls and the sweetest little face. I helped Mama bathe her and feed her and folded dozens of cloth diapers every week. Her illness brought a sadness to our home that could never really go away. Dede's birth, unlike mine, was planned. That's why they say, "Life is what happens after you make your plans." Perhaps broken things or breaking things bothers me because I had a broken sister that could not run and play with me or talk to me.

There were several other children in our neighborhood that had polio, but the cases were mild. One boy had a slightly withered arm but managed fine. At age sixteen he drove with one arm, no problem. The other boy had no really bad residual damage that was visible, but he could not participate in contact sports.

I was around fifteen years old when we got the vaccine. On a Sunday afternoon we went to Briarcliff High School and were given a pink sugar cube. The vaccine was soaked into the sugar. Anne walked with crutches and a leg brace for many years. She still has the brace but gave up the crutches when we were in our thirties. She taught Kindergarten, married and had two beautiful children.

Kindergarten for me was a real bust! In those days there were no public kindergartens, so older women had kindergarten classes in their homes and the structure and schedule were kind of com si com sa. My Kindergarten was at Mrs. Yancey's home, and she was a grumpy lady around sixty years old who did not seem to like children very much. One day I came to school with a rash on my arms, and she overreacted and called my mother to come get me. She said I was a danger to the other children and needed to stay home and have medical treatment. I felt frightened and humiliated. The rash was really only poison ivy. We lived in three acres of woods and I spent countless hours in the trees and creek. Of course, there was poison ivy. In those days before cortisone cream all we had for treatment was calamine lotion. It did help relieve some itching, but the healing was slow and uncomfortable. You best believe that I learned to recognize that dreaded "leaves of three." I became an expert at avoiding the plant.

I remember learning at Kindergarten the Hokey Pokey and pledge to the flag. We sang familiar nursery rhymes. We played on a swing set and had juice and cookies for snack, and then the day ended, and we went home for lunch. I think the main objective was for us to learn to be social and to be away from our mother. I don't recall anything academic happening to do with the alphabet or numbers, days of the week, months, holidays or such. There was a tiny bit of painting with tempera paints on newsprint standing at an easel. My best friend was Shelly. She wore white high-top lace-up shoes and claimed that was the reason she could climb so well on the monkey bars.

Nonetheless, my Granddaddy Moore had once been a teacher. When Mumsie was gone teaching fifth graders in a public DeKalb County school, Granddaddy sat me down one afternoon and literally (pun intended) taught me to read. Mumsie's college roommate from Wesleyan College in Macon, Georgia, Miss Odille Ousley, had written first grade readers similar to the Dick, Jane and Sally primers. Miss Odille's books featured Tom, Betty and Susan. I still have copies of her books: The Red Book, The Blue Book and the Green Book.

Granddaddy taught me sight recognition of all the words. There were no phonics involved. The first word he taught me was "the". Eventually by second grade, I could somewhat read the 'Atlanta Constitution' newspaper with certain limitations. One afternoon Daddy came home. I was sitting on the floor with the newspaper all spread out. He asked me what I was reading. I said: the AB U TERIES. Yes, you figured it out, the Obituaries.

The happy thing that year was my birthday party. Mama had a Storybook Party for me. All of the children came dressed as their favorite character from Mother Goose or Disney. I was Alice in Wonderland. I remember a Little Boy Blue, a Little Jack Horner, a Little Bo Peep and a Mistress Mary. We played pin the tail on the donkey. There was a clothes pin game. You tried to drop wooden clothes pins in a glass milk bottle. Someone gave me a Disney book 'Alice in Wonderland.' I really played that part and pretended to be Alice for many months. It was probably good practice for all of the "Mad Hatters and White Rabbits" I would have to deal with and survive! Many a rabbit hole have I visited!

Daddy still traveled with Papa, so Mama had the use of our Ford automobile. It was the color of cappuccino coffee. Daddy was so good to send me little surprise boxes. We had such a long driveway up a steep hill, but I would walk down to the mailbox every day to look for a package. The favorite one ever was a little striped sundress. It had a pastel candy stripe pattern the color of those old-fashioned peppermint sticks made of a candy that melted in your mouth quickly. I was sad when I outgrew that dress, but the memory is sweeter than candy canes.

A very frightening thing happened to me that year. Our back yard was not fenced, and it backed up to a yard that was the home of a teen boy. I wandered over into his yard, and he got a little bit too curious about my little girl body. I instinctively knew something was very wrong and scary. So, I ran home as fast as my little legs could carry me and dashed into the house and told Mama. She was horrified and called the boy's mom. I remember the lady sitting at our kitchen table, and she was sobbing. He was her only child. Of course, in a childlike way, I took all the guilt on myself and blamed myself for being near their yard. My parents swept it under the rug and never really talked to me about it, so they had no idea how I felt. At that point they did fence in our yard. Sometime later that boy was killed on a motorcycle, and again, I blamed myself and had a terrible guilt feeling. If I had not told my mom, maybe all those bad things would have never happened.

Mama's Kappa Theta sorority sisters from Georgia State University had lovely Easter egg hunts and Christmas parties for the children. I loved those ladies and their sons and daughters. We had the adult married couples over for dinner from time to time. I remember their names and faces so vividly. Mama was their president one year. I have the square sterling silver candy dish they had engraved for her that says Kappa Theta with the year she served.

Chapter 4
School Girl Now:
World, Here I Come!

We lived on Midway Road in the Winnona Park district of the Decatur City Schools. Thankfully it was a small school system and school. In graduate school I read a study of large systems in New York City. The basic premise was that they could never meet the needs of schools, children and neighborhoods down on the local level. My mom was expecting my brother Eric that year, so I rode to school with a lady named Mrs. Fuller. She had a dark green Plymouth and took a load of children to school every day for a reasonable sum. There were no seatbelts in those days, but we were so tightly crammed in the seats it was doubtful that anyone could have fallen or been thrown out. We sat one up and one back to get more children in the seats. I was embarrassed to ride with Mrs. Fuller for reasons I cannot explain. Due to my own little girl feelings, it somehow seemed degrading. I wanted to ride with my parents.

Our principal was Mrs. Burgess. Her baby sister, Minnie was one of Mama's dearest friends. The funny thing about Minnie was that when we had family birthday parties and sang the Happy Birthday song and sang, "May you have many more", I thought they meant may "Minnie Moore" come to the party. Since she was Minnie Foster, I could not figure out if she used to be a Moore or what was going on. Mrs. Burgess had complete authority over our school, and that was good. She ran it like a well-oiled machine with great wisdom and love for the children and the community. My first-grade teacher was Mrs. Moore. She was very fond of me since she and Mumsie were in a teacher sorority together. School work was totally easy since I already knew how to read thanks to Granddaddy. I understood numbers and math very well because Grandmother and Papa sat on the rug with me at their house and taught me to count and add and subtract with Papa's red, white and blue poker chips and pennies and toothpicks.

Mrs. Pascal was the lunchroom dietician. I recall we had an abundance of turnip greens and corn bread, which was fine, but the black-eyed peas I could pass on. My parents did not like to serve beans. It reminded them too much of the Great Depression when meat was scarce. My mom cooked thin vermicelli spaghetti with sauce on top. I did not care for the thick noodles at school mixed with the sauce. We were expected to eat every bite so we could be in the Clean Plate Club. The teachers kept charts on the wall with daily check marks. This was long before the day of pizza, tacos, burritos, or chicken nuggets, but we ate what was put before us including a good bit of mac n cheese and rice with occasional thin, dry as a bone hamburgers or hot dogs.

The school family Thanksgiving dinner was very good. One little boy said his favorite part was "the bread that the turkey ate." I still have Mrs. Pascal's delicious punch recipe with the magic secret ingredient, almond flavoring. Once in a rare while when I was older, I took a sack lunch just for fun, secretly. I packed a sandwich with apple and cookie and bought milk. My parents believed in hot school lunch religiously. I had to drop the sack outside my bedroom window and pick it up on the way to school.

The only bad thing about schools was morning roll call. We lived in a small WASP town of homes, schools and protestant churches and one Catholic church. Everyone had names like Green, Thompson, Turner, McKinney and so forth. Papa was born an Austrian Jew, so our last name, Dattelbaum, (which was later changed to Datry) was long and strange sounding to the children. Whenever my name was called, many of the children roared with laughter and pointed their fingers at me and made fun of me. I had always been a very talkative, spontaneous child and mostly the center of attention in our family. This was the beginning of many years of shyness and low self-esteem.

Daddy told me to tell the students that my great grandfather had been born in a royal castle in Austria. That was probably not true or perhaps he worked in a castle, but it helped my feelings because I believed it and convinced the classmates that it was true. I would later learn that being persecuted or being a martyr is not the end of the world. Sometime it even leads to sainthood. Boy, I have a long way to go! The Good Book says when we share in the Lord's suffering we are molded into His image.

Papa's father, Grandpa Friedrich, had stopped going to the synagogue because he objected to the temple tax. He said poorer people should be allowed to worship God without having to pay money. Therefore, Papa never had a bar mitzva. His mother, Gramma Fannie told him that she believed the Bible because she knew it was a good book. My family still says her German bedtime prayer that is the equivalent of 'Now I lay me down to sleep.'

All children suffer from some kind of bullying or hang-ups sometime during childhood or youth. There may be a lack of money or feeling unattractive or having very embarrassing parents. Some children struggle with the academics and feel inferior. That is life. We learn to survive from these setbacks and disappointments. Character is built when we overcome difficulties and climb over hurdles and scale steep mountains. Daddy used to say, "They will tell you your nose is too big or your body is too skinny or your arms are too short or something. If they knock you down in the mud, get up and hose off and keep walking. You are a Datry. We survive! We conquer!"

I loved to write in my first-grade tablet and practiced penmanship to perfection with great pride. To this day, people see my handwriting and ask me if I am a teacher. Technically, I have an alternator brain and am ambidextrous, but prefer writing with the left hand. When drawing or painting or any other task I can use either one.

When I was bullied, Daddy told me: You are just as good as any of the other children. In fact, you show them that you are even better. Do the best school work you can. By high school the bullying was more sophisticated since the kids understood about ethnic and religious differences and had prejudice and racism down pat! Some teens spelled my name Jew-lie and wrote that on my notebook. Daddy said: Well Darlin', look what they did to the finest man who ever lived. They beat him to a pulp, dragged him outside Jerusalem and hung him on a cross. And you think that you deserve better? That was very profound for me and made a lasting impression. I chose to not be a whiny bird and to put on my big-girl britches and get over my little sweet self!

That January my baby brother, Eric, was born. It was a bit unsettling. It might remind you of Goths and Visigoths issues! Copernicus called and said that I was no longer the center of the universe! I had heard so many people tell pregnant women, "I know you are hoping for a boy." This made me feel uneasy. Were my parents still going to love me as much as they always had? I even said to Mumsie, "Now my Daddy is not going to love me anymore!" She assured me otherwise.

Eric was deathly allergic to milk and drank soy milk formula. In those days it was very thick with a funny smell and cappuccino brown color. 180 Midway Road was 'Little House without Dairy' by Laura Ingalls Milder. I did not like it any more than I liked that baby brother. Today, he is very good to me and one of my best friends and calls me every week. At age three the little imp seemed to live in my jewelry box. Like a parakeet or crow, he loved shiny objects. Daddy was very understanding of my distress, and he went to the hardware store and bought me a combination padlock. He installed a latch on my bedroom door for the lock. Then it was goodbye to bratty brother! However, one evening when Mumsie was babysitting, he was running down the hall with Mama's sewing scissors. When I tried to take them away from him, they cut my finger, and I bled all over the hall carpet. Thankfully it was a dark green and burgundy color geometric pattern, and no stains were left after it was cleaned.

My second-grade teacher was the very nice Mrs. Blaisedale. She was a kind grey-headed, older woman who really loved children and teaching. Her number one safety rule was: Never walk between parked cars. I think the transmissions and brakes were lacking in reliability. I always finished my work very early, so she sent me to the library to read since there were no gifted classes in those days. I typically gravitated to the Biography shelf and loved to read about women like Dolly Madison, Abigail Adams, Marie Curie, Annie Oakley and so forth. Mumsie found that we are related to Buffalo Bill on our Cody Quaker side. Bill was supposedly related to Annie Oakley. So, there you go, a claim to fame. That and $.75 will get you a doughnut!

We had a cloak room for jackets and the recess sports equipment. I wore a dark green hooded rubber raincoat and brown rubber galoshes when it rained. The coat had faint white geometric designs on it. Often Mama gave me a boiled egg to take to school for snack. I kept it in the raincoat pocket. I remember how the warm rubber smelled when there was a warm egg in it. It was also a very effective hand warmer when walking to school through avalanche snow drifts and glaciers, right?

There was a sweet housekeeper named Edna that came several times a week. She always got down on her knees when she scrubbed the floor. She was a devout Christian woman. I recall that she sang the hymn, 'Love Lifted Me' while she scrubbed in time to her song. She could not quite pronounce "lifted", so she said, "lilfted." Next our helper was Katie who did not last long. Mumsie caught her bringing her boyfriend, and that simply would not do in any case.

Finally, we found wonderful, loyal, lovable Lula. She was our housekeeper and nanny for seventeen years and the backbone of our family. She was a saint, patient and skilled and dependable and very intelligent. She read the Atlanta Constitution every day. She also had a truckload of horse sense. If Mama got upset or flustered, Lula would always say: Now, Miss Lynn, you just gotta' put the Lawd in front and the devil behind! Our house was shiny and spotless, and heavenly smells wafted around the house when she was cooking dinner. No one made more delicious fried chicken or biscuit than Lula. I loved the smell of damp clean white linens being ironed. Lula kept an open Bible in her room. She was a middle child in a family of twelve and grew up out in the country on a farm.

I am so thankful that when I was a teen, I found a full-length mink coat at Goodwill. The price was very reasonable, and I happily grabbed it up for Lula for Christmas. I put it in a large box and wrapped it beautifully all fancy-dancy like for a Mrs. Got Rocks. Lula was an angel who deserved to be dressed like a queen! I can still hear her saying, "Lordy, Lordy, Julie, I gonna' be buried in this coat for sure I will be." Oh, dear Lord, please let me live next door to her when I move to the sky!

Seven years old meant old enough for swimming lessons at McCoy Pool. I took to the water like a little fish in my red and white striped bathing suit with a red rubber swim cap. One slight problem was that I was too fearless in the pool and climbed up on the high board and did a royal belly flop that knocked the wind out of me. There must have been a good number of angels watching over me that day. It could have turned out badly!

Our friends, the Crane family, who owned the Decatur News, had a backyard swimming pool. We had an open invitation. I could walk there. We got plenty of practice. Their daughter Sheila taught me diving, back stroke, butterfly stroke and water ballet. I was afraid of getting water in my nose and wore a silly flesh-colored nose clip for years. If I spent the night with Sheila and we got in the pool after dark, small bats swooped down, and we had to go underwater to protect our hair and heads. We liked to sleep by the pool and watch for shooting stars.

Papa and Grandmother's house was immaculate. My only complaint was that they had an aluminum Christmas tree with royal blue glass ball ornaments. It seemed rather cold and sterile. Grandmother scrubbed bathrooms, dusted and vacuumed every day like her Dutch mother before her. They got a television before we did. It was the black and white cabinet kind with the screen on top and the works on the bottom. Not sure why, but I believed that the people on TV were tiny and lived in the TV. That meant that when the 'Woody Willow' puppet show came on, I chose to crawl down on my knees through the den to the kitchen. That way I was sure that the witch puppet could not see me and bother me or put me in a black cauldron.

I adored Papa's desk with the typewriter and all the office supplies. He collected mint blocks of postage stamps in small wax paper envelopes. A boy named Phil who sat next to me at school had a stamp collection. I took him several blocks. Later Papa patiently explained to me about his collection. He gently told me to not do that anymore. Also, there was a quart size glass jar in his bottom desk drawer. On the Howdy Doody TV show, Buffalo Bob allowed children to reach in a jar of quarters and grab as many as their little hand could hold. I naturally assumed that was the purpose of Papa's quarter jar. O contraire! My parents found the quarters in my little overnight bag and made me return them to Papa. Of course, he gave me some.

Aunt Sara finished Scarritt Methodist Theology College in Nashville, Tennessee that year. She was planning to be a foreign missionary but was not able to go into the mission field due to a heart murmur. Mumsie and I took my first plane ride to the graduation on an Eastern Airlines propeller plane. I wore a pink nylon dress with a black velvet ribbon belt to the ceremony. There were students from around the world. I met Juan and Maria from Cuba, and they taught me some Spanish. The Japanese students gave me a little kimono and some wooden sandals. The Chinese students had tea for me in teapots from their country. It was a wonderful introduction to loving, enjoying and understanding people from different cultures and ethnic groups. All sides of our family celebrate diversity.

My seventh birthday party was at home with parents, grandparents, aunts and uncles. This was the year I had my first lesson in diplomacy and "put a sock in it!" Aunt Judy and Aunt Kitti both gave me pairs of dark navy, chocolate brown and hunter green socks. This was a practical gift and very appropriate colors to match my fall dresses, and we need multiple pairs of socks in the drawer. The problem was that I opened Aunt Kitti's package first and thanked her profusely. When I opened Aunt Judy's package I said, "Oh, Aunt Kitti already gave me socks this color." My parents privately and gently made me to understand that I had been a tiny bit rude and had probably hurt my aunts' feelings. I was so embarrassed! It was one of those moments when I needed a glass of water to wash down my foot! I also needed a degree from The University of Shut Up & Say Thank You!

From that moment on I almost forever found it tedious to express my real true feelings. That was normal in those days. Children were often stifled for telling it like it is. I call it "misplaced moodifiers" when you are not encouraged to tell the news. There were still many holdovers from the Victorian Era. Some children's books had the "Goody Two Shoes" didactic approach to command children to be perfect miniature adults. The older generations in our family had been taught that Jesus died for their sins, but voila, they had not sinned. Therefore, the War Between the States was unfair, and they had been misunderstood. If you got an ulcer trying to defend yourself, it was worth it!

When my children came along, I had studied a lot of child development and psychology and would have said to them, "Oh, how wonderful to have so many pairs of socks. Now Mommy will not have to run the washer as often." Then after the party I would have given them a lesson in tactfulness without any guilt trip. We baby boomers were still subject to the Victorian rules of shame-based guilt trip childrearing under which our parents and grandparents had been rigidly raised in the south. When I was grown, I emphatically told Mama, "You have sent me on so many manners guilt trips, I have enough frequent flyer points to go all the way to hell!" But my parents were extremely proud of me in general and thought I was an exceptionally good and accomplished child.

Second grade meant that I could join the Brownie Scouts and wear that funny little homely brown button-up uniform dress with the brown felt beanie and brown socks. All scout equipment was purchased at Belk Gallant Department Store. Our leader was Miss Jinky. Her daughter Susie and I always played school after school, and I was the designated teacher. So, Miss Jinky had great confidence in my academic skills. Whenever we did a play at Brownies, she asked me to write the play. There was another choice to be a Blue Bird, the beginner level of the Camp Fire Girls. I did not know about Blue Birds right away. Later I noticed that they had really sharp navy-blue skirts and red vests and white blouses with a little red tie. Those uniforms were far chicer than our drab brown which was suitable for a char woman in the time of David Copperfield. Also, for fundraising, the Blue Birds sold chocolate peppermint patties in a long thin box. Now that was uptown and yummy! We sold boring Girl Scout cookies. In those days there were only the chocolate and vanilla sandwich cookies, so pitiful with no Thin Mints or S'mores! I loved my Girl Scout Handbook and aggressively tried to earn as many badges as I could to go on my sash.

Age seven was the year that I experienced modesty for the very first time. I wore a little ruffly red, Scotch plaid skirt up to Anne's house without a blouse. While there I suddenly felt uncomfortable and undressed. I wrapped the cloth sash belt around my chest and went home and got a shirt. From that day on, no one ever saw me topless or bottomless or any kind of no clothes arrangement! Plus, we grew up with so much female body-shaming. Girls often took their mom's measuring tape to see if they had a twenty-one-inch or smaller waist. It must have been a holdover from the days when women wore tight corsets that nearly choked the breath out of them. Why do you think they literally had a piece of furniture called a fainting bench? Skinny Scarlett O'Hara in 'Gone with the Wind' with her eighteen-inch waist did not help either!

Grandmother and Papa's closest friends were Ethel and Dick. They had a beautiful, tall, blond daughter named Nancy. Nancy got engaged to Bobby, and I was asked to be their flower girl. Nancy wanted me to have a dress precisely like the six bridesmaids. It was made of taffeta with gathered net in the shape of a fan at the bodice. The color was what I call ashes of roses. Mama asked a friend to help her make a pattern and sew the dress. They did a perfect job, and I was truly a miniature twin to the big girls. The bridesmaids carried large bouquets of purple violets in a nosegay with rose pink net and satin ribbon. The wedding was at an old stone Episcopal church downtown at Peachtree and Spring Streets. This time around, I knew how to be a five-star flower girl with no malingering along the aisle. Yes, this led to more playing wedding at home. By this time, I read the entire wedding ceremony out of the back of the old dark green Methodist Hymnal. My pronunciations were less than perfect. Mama corrected me when I said: And with all my worldly goods I "theeindough". She taught me that it was 'I thee endow."

At age seven I was allowed to walk across the road to the park. Shoal's creek ran through our bottomland went under Midway Road. It was a wonderful creek for children. DeKalb County kept all the brush cut away from the banks and maintained everything. There were swings that seated three of us and a grill for cooking hamburgers and hot dogs. There was one problem. Halfway down the park the creek sloped downward forty-five degrees on a massive natural slab of gray rock that spanned the width of the creek. Of course, lots of moss grew on the rock and it was very slippery. It was actually called "Slippery Rock." I did not know that and was crossing it and fell flat on my head! Another instance of guardian angels working overtime, wouldn't you say? I think my angels asked God to be unionized for better perks, pay, vacations and Christmas bonuses.

In those days children roamed freely through woods and fields all alone with no predator danger. Whether or not you are Catholic or like the Pope, his absolutes made for a more cohesive society. Unlike the media social manipulators of today who have very few morals, we knew the difference between right and wrong. We never had any kidnappings or assaults. I cannot remember hearing of a burglary either. It was a heavenly time to grow up secure and free from fear and paranoia. We explored everything in nature from bird nests to the roly-poly bugs under the rocks. We drank nectar from honeysuckle blooms. We knew all about lizards and crayfish and frogs and minnows. We watched ants crawl and dug up worms for fishing. Mothers were home watching their children and neighbors' children.

I had wonderful playmates around Midway Road. Pat lived between Mumsie and Granddaddy and Scotta and Don. They were across the street from Anne. Down from them was Donny. Around the corner I had Mel and Nancy. Up from them was Johnny, our pediatrician's son. Around another corner was Greer who lived next to Judy. Greer was the cute niece of Mama's close friend Frances. They were all in DeKalb County. Going up the other end of Midway in the City of Decatur were John and his cousins Cade and Steven. Linda lived on the corner. On South Candler Street there was Johnny next door to Heather and Jeanne. We were harmonious, basically well-adjusted kids, and I do not remember fighting and bullying. Of course, no one ever knows everything that happens behind those walls surrounded by the white picket fences, right?

I read an advertisement in a magazine to order packets of flower seeds to sell. Being an independent little professor type, I said nothing to my parents and ordered the secret seeds. I went to the mailbox every day until they came. I started going door to door with my little white wicker basket selling them all over the neighborhood. I think they were around $.15 per pack. I sold all of them and was delighted to have a nice little stash of cash in my desk. Somehow, I really did not understand that I was supposed to send back some of the money. Eventually my parents got a letter from some midwestern law firm demanding the money. Surprise! Surprise! They were blown away! Mama and Daddy were definitely realizing that they were raising a very strong-willed, clever, resourceful child, slippery as a little eel! This was only the beginning of this bringing up Cagey Child.

One day Mama had a dental appointment downtown at Dr. Silver's office in the Strickler Building. I was not ready on time, so Mama had to leave me home, or so she thought. I got out the telephone book and called myself a cab from the Decatur Cab Company. When we got to the dentist's building, the cab driver told me that I owed him three dollars and some change. I had never been in a cab and did not know that they charged money. No problem! I told the driver that my daddy had a store on the square in Decatur called "David's", and he could go collect the cab fare from Daddy which he did. Daddy was a bit bewildered and in disbelief. He and Mama had a child that thought she was an adult. I went in the elevator and asked the lady to take me to the fifth floor. Back then elevators had uniformed lady attendants in khaki shirts and brown skirts. Imagine Mama's shocked surprise when she saw me in Dr. Silver's office. She almost dropped the teeth that he had been filling! You'll wonder where your kid went, when you brush your teeth with Pepsodent!

In those days we had one pair of school shoes, one pair of Sunday shoes and Keds and white sandals for summer. There were no flip flops. I was thrilled to pieces when Mama said I was old enough to have black suede loafers with a shiny dime on top just like the older girls. Keds tennis shoes came in navy blue, red and white. I liked navy. We bought our shoes at Newsome's on Clairmont across from the bakery. They x-rayed your feet to see if you had outgrown your shoes. Yikes! Who knew? That store sold Buster Brown brand shoes and Poll Parrot shoes. There was a cage in the store with a large green and yellow parrot. It was constantly spitting out the sunflower seed shells, and they flopped onto the floor.

Anyway, for some reason I wanted to wear my shiny, Sunday black patent leather shoes to school. This was forbidden but possible for me, Sneaky Sue. It was just a matter of loosening the bolt on the screen of my bedroom window and tossing the shoes under the large gardenia bush under the window. I changed my shoes and left the school shoes in the woods under a specific tree, but there was a problem. I was very athletic on the playground at recess. I played kickball and softball with great skill and force. Therefore, the Sunday shoes were a bit scuffed. There was no way to explain that away. Mama figured it out pronto presto and gave me quite a scolding. It was not easy or very successful polishing patent leather, so I had to suffer through that year with imperfect shoes. That was real punishment for a girl who had her clothes arranged in the closet by color and type. Consequences of behavior was good discipline for me at this time. Who knew "Daisy Ducks in a Row" would grow up and get a master's degree from Emory Library School? And yes, the spices in my kitchen cabinet are in alphabetical order.

I liked to get up with the chickens, so I set my clock radio alarm for 5:30 am on school days. The night before I listened to WSB News and some radio soap operas like 'Stella Dallas' and 'One Man's Family' and 'Dragnet' with Sergeant Friday. At the crack of dawn, I listened to the Georgia Farm and Home Hour and could quote the price of pigs, eggs, corn and cows. I polished shoes at bedtime, but ironing took place in the cold, damp, dark basement early morning. We had no steam irons, so clothes were sprinkled with water from a Coke bottle with a cork that had an aluminum top with holes. Most of our clothes were cotton or linen or wool and had to be ironed. Lula would have done it for me, but I was fiercely independent. At the age of two, Mama and Daddy had heard, "By Meself," hundreds of times. I could do a pretty good job, but occasionally I dropped the iron. Once I had bare feet and there was some water spilled on the floor. Yes, I got a bit of a shock and learned a good science lesson from that without even reading anything about Benjamin Franklin or Edison or Tesla!

That Christmas I asked Santa for a cowgirl suit, a new radio and a bride doll. We all watched the Roy Rogers and Dale Evans show on Sunday nights. We liked another cowboy program with the Cisco Kid and his sidekick, Poncho. Once he came to the Belvedere Shopping Center and kissed me on the cheek. I spent a lot of time in my brown fringed cowgirl skirt and vest galloping on my pretend pony all over our three acres of land.

Those were happy days when children spent a lot of time outside doing creative play and using our imaginations. I made a playhouse on top of Daddy's flat-roofed tool shed and pretended that I was some kind of indigenous person. It was easy to climb up since Daddy stacked his chopped firewood on the side. He also built us a sturdy tree house up in the woods above the orchard. Mumsie allowed me to roll up her burgundy-colored wool living room rug and put all kinds of dishes and things on the hardwood floor and pretend I was living outside on the ground or in some forest or jungle. We had long attention spans and could amuse ourselves all day. I read that today's children have a shorter attention span than a goldfish!

Mama strung multi-colored bubble lights on the Christmas tree. They were filled with a fluid that bubbled when they got warm from the lights. They were so pretty; I should look on Amazon for a string of them. She also spent hours placing hundreds of wispy thin aluminum foil icicles on the tree one by one. On Christmas night when we were sound asleep in our beds, Mama rubbed fireplace soot on our cheek. Then Christmas morn, she told us to look in the mirror, because Santa Claus had kissed us and gotten soot on us.

I loved the smell of peppermint candy canes mixed with Christmas tree spruce and balsam aroma. It is such a vivid memory and a definite aromatherapy. Santa brought apples, oranges, kumquats and giant cluster raisins in a long flat box. Of course, hard-working Daddy picked up the tab for all of these festivities. He was so generous and enjoyed every minute of our delight on all holidays. Usually, Aunt Judy sent us ski pajamas from New Jersey. I did not like the tight cuffs around the sleeves and legs and really preferred night gowns and robes since they were loose and roomy. Other relatives gave doll clothes, boxes of Lifesavers candy and books and money. I did not like chocolate or hard candy, but caramels were good. Too bad white chocolate was yet to be invented. That's the ticket for me!

You know that familiar song, 'Sleigh Ride Together.' If I did not understand song words as a child, I just made up some gibberish that rhymed. With that song I sang: Giddy up, giddy up, giddy up, ontay, oh semi oh say, oh semi oh say. Also, there was a round roll of wire left over from the temporary electrical pole when we built our house. It was hanging up on a tree. Not knowing what it really was, I decided to call it a "patha." My parents had not one Sherlock Holmes clue what I was talking about, and it was a mystery miniseries. One day, Uncle Truman took me out to the driveway. We stood there for a long time until I was able to tell him what the patha looked like. He located it and triumphantly went back in the house and told everyone the answer to the riddle.

Daddy was still in sales on the road with Papa, but he was renting half of a Mrs. Barton's store in Decatur on Clairmont Avenue. She sold little girls Ruth Originals dresses and kept us stocked with the most beautiful little outfits imaginable. She was kind enough to sell Daddy's ladies dresses so he could earn enough traveling to open his own store eventually. Grandmother had a store on McDonough Street called Hazel's Gift Shop. It had gas space heaters for the winter. One day Papa took me there and told me I could pick anything I wanted. I pointed to a very life-like baby doll in a blue cardboard box up on a high shelf, and he reached up and got it and put the doll in my arms. We were standing next to a heater and I remember the cozy warmth of that heat and the cozy warmth of having a loving grandfather who adored me and would do anything for me within reason.

Back in those old days, though we had no Amazon or such, delivery trucks brought all kinds of treats and staples to our homes. It was probably because most families had one car which the dad took to work. Moms were often home without transportation. I remember the Highland Bakery bread man. Sometimes Mama bought raisin cinnamon bread with gooey sweet white sugar frosting. The Mathis Dairy milkman brought milk, cheddar and cottage cheese, butter, buttermilk, orange juice. It was my job to put the milk bottles out in the shiny aluminum insulated box on the front steps the night before delivery. I could hear milk bottles all over the neighborhood clanking as they were put in the Mathis boxes.

Later we discovered goat's milk. Every other week we drove to Mr. Bunn's goat farm down in Lithonia to buy goats milk for $.90 a quart which was very expensive compared to the $.20 a quart cow's milk. Shame on me! I told my brother and sister that the goat's milk tasted like goats smell. Watson's Pharmacy delivered prescriptions and such. It was two doors down from Mr. Ellington's grocery store on College Avenue next to Agnes Scott College. Ellington's delivered also. The best truck of all was the Charlie Chips truck. They brought chips and cookies in large metal cans. I still have one of those tins. I keep silica gel powder in it for flower preserving.

There were many fun things about Mumsie and Granddaddy's house. Mumsie taught me to plant purple petunias and radishes. I learned to weave multi-colored potholders on a small, red, square metal loom. I sold those for $.25 each. She made meringue cookies in the oven that were called "kisses". They had chopped pecans in them and were heavenly. One day we filled out a little order form on the Planters Peanut can and mailed it with $.25 to the company. Soon a little, aluminum nut grinder arrived. It screwed on to the top of a small glass maraschino cherry jar. I still have that nut grinder and jar. They had a tall, walk-in attic that was fascinating. It had plenty of old antiques from the Covington ancestors. There were pictures and lamps and quilts and ostrich feathers and no telling what else. It was a fun place to explore endlessly. I especially liked the old mahogany chifforobe with drawers and a mirror.

I found a jingle contest on the package of the Blue Bonnet margarine. It said that you were supposed to be eighteen years or older to fill it out and mail it in. Did that stop busy little Juliana? Of course not! I remember exactly what I wrote: I like Blue Bonnet because it is thrifty in the kitchen. Didn't win anything but was learning to be a competitive little go getter. I liked the taste of winning even more than Blue Bonnet margarine!

Granddaddy had a wonderful vegetable garden. I loved to watch him and help him pull weeds. Sometime he would pretend that he was Farmer McGregor, and I was Peter Rabbit. He would chase me around the garden, and I would laugh and squeal with joy. Granddaddy loved to drink coffee, but he had an ulcer. He chased his coffee with super strong tea so that the tannic acid would toughen up the ulcer or some such cure. As a boy, living in Haysville, North Carolina, he had learned a lot about Native American medicine from his grandfather. I know how to go out in the woods and dig up wild ginger roots for tummy tea, and I can make bread with acorn flour.

Granddaddy's grandfather learned from an old Cherokee chief that was hiding in their cellar. My great-great grandfather was protecting the chief from the dreadful Trail of Tears. That is one reason I was raised without any racism or prejudice. My parents said we were blessed for having Quakers in Mumsie's family. They believed in kindness and compassion for all peoples. Papa was very good to his travel chauffeurs who helped him lift heavy bags of dresses when he was too old. He bought them fine quality suits and made sure they had the best food and lodging that was available.

Baby sister Kim was born the summer I turned eight. She had the face of an angel and slept in a pretty little white wicker basinet with fluffy white nylon skirt and ruffles. Mama was very sensitive to the fact that I had been bumped out of my sibling spot three times now. She fixed me a blue plastic Even Flo baby bottle filled with cow's milk and told me I could keep it hidden behind the beige tobacco cloth curtains on the big picture window in the dining room.

She said it would be our little secret so that no one would tease me for drinking from a baby bottle. It was again soy milk for the lactose intolerant new sister.

Mama really had a complete meltdown when Kim was born. It was overwhelming to have four children with one profoundly disabled and two stairstep babies that were frail and sickly and allergic to wheat, eggs, milk, orange juice, peanut butter and so forth. Can you imagine growing up in an American household without peanut butter? Plus, I was a super busy child with so many self-generated activities. People have described me as a whirlwind lady who gives seminars for Energizer Bunnies to learn how to be optimally energized. One day I heard Mama sobbing inconsolably, and Daddy called Mumsie to come up to the house. Mumsie told Daddy that Mama was exhausted and burned out and needed a vacation. Daddy took Mama on a month long drive up the east coast all the way to Quebec, Canada. They should have taken new baby Kim with them so that she could bond with Mama. Unfortunately, that did not happen because in general, people did not understand the importance of that back then. Mumsie and Sara stayed with us.

My eight-year-old birthday party was a grownup lady luncheon in the dining room with Mama's Chantilly Royal Doulton china and Gorham Chantilly sterling silver and Chantilly crystal goblets. I set the table with a white embroidered linen tablecloth and cloth napkins and white candles. I invited nine girlfriends. Usually, one spent about $1.00 for birthday party gifts with friends. Often, they gave dollar bills. That was much desired. That year Mama and Daddy gave me the three-inch thick 'Amy Vanderbilt's Complete Book of Etiquette.' It thoroughly covered every possible manners situation that a proper young woman would ever face in a thousand years. Naturally, I was expected to read it and know it. I thought it was fun to read about place settings, table serving and wedding invitations. It explained all about being a hostess or attending social events from christenings to coffins and everything in between. It had lots of black and white drawings to clarify all the instructions.

Chapter 5
Eight and Nine,
Everything's Almost Fine!

Third grade was a milestone. I was old enough to walk to school. That meant going up the hill to the woods to cut through to Mimosa Drive. Some mornings I could not wait to get to school, so I skipped half the way. Other mornings I stopped by to pick up friends to walk with me. There was Cheryl, Doug, Eddie, Bobby, Dennis mostly. I loved to stop at Eddie's house. His big sister, Judy, was in seventh grade. She was a patrol, and I thought she was so pretty. She had pleated skirts that she herself sewed in bright colors like orange and lime green.

My teacher was pretty, slender, red-headed Mrs. Butler, probably in her forties. She often wore a lovely navy-blue dress with white polka dots and a large, starched white collar. In those days women taught until they married and stayed home until their children went to high school. I sat next to a little girl named Susan. Her mother died suddenly that year. I remember taking off my gold bracelet and giving it to her. Sadly, she was too grief stricken to accept it which was perfectly natural for child in bereavement. That was the day my generosity hit a bump in the road. I should not have been so easily discouraged, but I became a reluctant gift giver. Being a sensitive child, I did not handle rejection very well, and my spirit was wounded. I could have used a lesson in facing disappointment. Decades later at a class reunion, Susan told me how sorry she was for spurning my loving gift. I must say, that freed up something in my soul that had been wrapped in tangled barbed wire lo these many years. That is why with my own children during bedtime prayers I always asked them, "Is there anything you need to tell Mommy? Is something hurting your heart? Do you need to clear your conscience?"

Mama noticed that I usually came home with little panties that had been a tiny bit wet. She was genuinely concerned that I had some kind of emotional issue that should be dealt with. She went to Mrs. Butler and told her about this. The next day Mrs. Butler took me out in the hall and gently and reassuringly asked me about this. She wanted to know if anything was upsetting me at school or at home. I immediately responded without any thought. I told her I usually needed to go to the girls' room during math, but I loved arithmetic so much, and it was so much fun, I just could not leave my desk until my arithmetic problems were done. That led to a little leakage. I guess the adults were relieved that I relieved myself when the school work was done! Of course, there were times when I had to walk twist-legged to get to the "toidey" without an accident.

Daddy had a surefire way for me to get to school with my quarter for lunch money, as we paid by the day. He used Scotch tape to secure the quarter to my arm, and I pretended it was a watch. If he drove me to school, I insisted that he drop me off at a corner near the school. He drove a little blue English classic MG sportscar, and I was embarrassed. No one else's parents had a strange, funny little foreign car like that. I was fearful that the children would laugh at me. Later he traded for a white MG and finally had a burgundy colored one. By then the kids thought my dad's cars were awesome and sporty.

The Red Cross gave us small cardboard boxes to fill to give to children overseas in disaster areas and war zones. We filled them with a comb, small tissue packages, toothbrush and paste, pencils, crayons and so forth. On Halloween we took small milk carton type containers to collect coins for UNICEF. (United Nations International Children's Emergency Fund.) Americans enjoyed being big brothers and sisters to the world. They were proud to share with the less fortunate. When Daddy said the blessing at mealtime, he prayed for "those who are less fortunate than we are."

Did we have a lot of vaccines for children back then? Flat no! Oh, chicken pox! Oh, measles! I had really bad cases. My parents wrapped my hands thoroughly in gauze and adhesive tape so that I could not scratch those chicken pox and leave scars on my face and body. They itched like blue blazes, and all we had was calamine lotion, not even any antihistamines or cortisone! Ouch! I lay in bed in a darkened room to protect my eyes from the measles. Daddy did not know to not give milk to a child with fever so he brought me a great big Carnation chocolate malted milk. Well, I was really hungry, and it was nice and cold, but soon really looked awful on my pretty bed spread and sheets. Does anything smell much worse than sour, regurgitated milk?

In third grade the Girl Scouts went roller skating once a year at a rink downtown. I had skated a lot at home on the driveway and was even brave enough to skate down the steep driveway hill. We had those old metal skates that were tightened to your shoes with a "skate key", as it was called. I was very athletic and active. Later in life genetic testing informed me that I have the long twitch muscles of an athlete. I was quite the tomboy/ballerina in those days. I was either climbing trees, doing gymnastics or standing at the barre', pretending to be the ballerina in the film 'The Red Shoes.' Aunt Sara had taken me to see that movie. Truthfully, tap dancing was much more fun and engaging.

Daddy took me to the old black and white film, 'Moulin Rouge.' I fell in love with cancan dancers, so Mama hung Degas and Toulouse-Lautrek prints of dancers around my dressing table and room. In the 1950's, women wore fluffy petticoats and crinolines under their full skirts. The dress manufacturers in New York sent dresses with cheap, horsehair, starched petticoats in black and white for display purposes. When a customer bought a dress, they left the petticoat at the store, and it was discarded. I asked Daddy's manager, Mrs. Addie Peek, to save me thirty black ones. I took them home and made myself a fantastic cancan costume for Halloween. It was cold that year, and Mama sent me trick or treating in a thick, warm, gray wool coat. Children went alone in those days in the dark to their friends' houses. While walking through the woods to meet my friends, I ditched that coat one good time on the pine straw and went right on without even feeling the cold. I was determined, by gosh and by golly, that everyone in the neighborhood plus their parents was going to see my costume, or life would hardly be worth living! I would die of disappointment and win an Academy Award for my death scene. There are plenty of books about strong-willed children. I may have been a poster child for that.

In Girl Scouts we went on excursions such as the fire station or Mathis Dairy to milk the cow named Rosebud. School field trips were scarce since we had no school buses, but buses were rented to take us to hear The Atlanta Symphony. It played in the old concrete floor Atlanta Auditorium on Ivy Street where the Barnum and Bailey Circus also performed. Henry Sopkin was the director of the symphony. This was a joyful outing for me that inspired me to play piano. This was in the days before the DeKalb County Schools built the amazing Fernbank Science Center over near Coventry Road.

Age eight had one very dark, gray cloud hanging over it. Mama took me to Dr. Taylor, the pediatrician. He lived around the corner from us and had an office in Decatur. I had never minded or been afraid of checkups or shots, but this time, Dr. Taylor told Mama I was a little bit pudgy. It felt like I was at an Idiot's Anonymous meeting and needed to stand up and say, My name is Juliana, and I am an idiot! Being such an active child, it had to be some genetics from having mostly Nordic ancestors. My little sister, Kim, was as bony as a toothpick no matter how much she ate. Nonetheless, Mama was instructed to go to Watson's Pharmacy and purchase a box of Melozet Wafers. They looked and tasted like graham crackers, but they contained methyl cellulose which expanded in my stomach and made me feel full. This was the beginning of body shaming that would plague me for most of my life. I usually wanted to wear a sweater or loose-fitting clothing to cover and hide my unacceptable body. I hope that parents and doctors have learned better by now. In graduate school I read a study about women and their body shapes. The cross-cultural findings are that plumper women are more nurturing. I observed on my own that they carry larger purses that contain lollypops, band-aids, tissues, aspirins, safety pins, needles and thread, wet wipes and on and on. It was a wonderful day when I learned to sew long-waisted flapper style dresses, no waistbands. At last, I could camouflage anything about my figure that felt unacceptable!

My Aunt Judy whom I adored, was married to my Uncle Ted who worked for the 3M company that manufactures Scotch Tape. If Judy were home from New York for Christmas and wrapping presents, she kept me busy by putting about twelve pieces of tape on each of my arms. She told me I was her tape manager, and that made me feel very important. Uncle Ted knew how much I loved and used Scotch Tape. He mailed me a box of a dozen rolls. It was heaven on earth for me. He enclosed a note which I have to this day that said, "Please do not put tape on your cocker spaniel, Bonnie."

So, what was in our toyboxes? Most toys were made of wood or metal. Plastic had not dominated yet. Small children played with blocks, often made by their dads from scraps of 2x4's, sanded smooth on the edges. Girls had dolls and tea sets. Ginny and Ginger dolls were popular, and there was Betsy Wetsy with diapers. We had storebought paper dolls with clothes, and we could make our own clothes for them or cut out paper doll chains. Some girls had Chatty

Cathy talking dolls or Raggedy Ann dolls. Papa's sisters sent me a giant rag doll dressed like a Dutch girl in a light blue dress with Dutch cap. It was my height and had elastic on the feet to attach to my feet so that we could dance around the room. I named her Hilda after Papa's oldest sister. Girls played Old Maid cards. My favorite was the character named "Lotta Noise" who played the cello. We had board games like Monopoly and Parchesi. We sat on the cold, hard floor for hours. Girls liked Pick Up Sticks, and Jackstones also. Mumsie had dozens of View master slide disks about travel. I had seen the better part of the world sitting in her den on the sofa.

Boys played with Tonka Trucks, sling shots and marbles. Girls had cat eye marbles because they were pretty. I was the Chinese Checkers champion, and to this day, only one person ever beat me in that game. I loved my Scrabble game. We had no Pez toy candy dispensers. I had seen them in New Jersey, so considered them Yankee candy. We all had fun with our yo-yo. Mr. Potato Head was okay. Wooly Willy was iron filings enclosed in hard plastic covered man's face. The idea was to drag the filings across to make hair, mustaches and beards. Pogo sticks were wonderful! Wooden stilts were fun but challenging. Our cap guns made a bang sound and smelled funny when the miniscule amount of gunpowder went off.

Gyroscopes, kaleidoscopes, wooden Tinker toys and Slinkys were loved by boys and girls. We all enjoyed our backyard sand boxes and swing sets. We covered our bare feet with damp sand, pulled the feet out gently, and called that little cave of sand a frog house. We swinged so high the poles came out of the ground a bit. Boys had metal Erector sets for building structures. Mumsie taught me to play Rock School on the steps. You start at the bottom seated. One child has a pebble in one hand. If you guess which hand you get to move up a step until a winner gets to the top step and "graduates." Stretchy, pink, rubbery Silly Putty came in a plastic egg and was interesting. When you pressed it on newsprint words or comics, ink was transferred precisely to the putty. Sadly, everything was gender stereotyped. Girls pretended to be nurses, and boys were doctors. When I wanted to be a nurse, I wore Daddy's white undershirt. He took a folded tissue, drew a red cross on the top, and Mama secured it to my hair with a bobby pin on each side.

Children preferred the outdoors when the weather was pleasant. Honeysuckle covered our backyard fence. We picked the blooms by the hundreds to drink the sweet nectar. I had a habit of picking pine bark off the pine trees. I called the pieces of bark, pickled peppers and recited the nursery rhyme about Peter Piper and the pickled peppers. Go figure! Where do kids get their ideas? If we found a bird nest, we never disturbed the eggs or the baby birds. The laws of Moses call that "an abomination" along with eating shrimp and pork.

Coloring books were not encouraged at our house. Aunt Sara, the artist was opposed to them. She thought children should create their own original pictures to color or paint. Still, it had to be good for a child's fine motor skills to color in the lines of a preprinted book. We played with clay, but it was the old-fashioned oily kind until Play-Doh was invented. It had a salty taste, perhaps to discourage eating. We had no Elmer's Glue, so moms made paste out of flour and water and cornstarch. We had Le Pages mucilage glue made from horses' hooves. There were no felt-tip markers or acrylic paints.

Mama discovered Harry Belafonte and bought wonderful 33 1/3 records of all kinds of Calypso and Reggae Music. I memorized the 'Banana Boat Song' about "Come Mr. Tallyman, tally me banana, Daylight Come and I want to go home." We loved the song about 'The Harlem Man' who "lived on the isle of San Sebastian a long, long while." This was yet another instance of my parents teaching me to love and enjoy so many different cultures and their customs, clothing and music. We knew that cornetti were Italian rolls but looked and tasted precisely like croissant. That meant we did not always fit in with the Decatur, Georgia society. It was like we butchered a pig, but no one wanted bacon so to speak. So that's a fly in the cornbread, right?

Sadly, Aunt Kitti and family moved away to Birmingham that year, then to New Orleans and finally settled in Jacksonville, Florida until they retired. Even with three little ones Alan, Lori and Glenn in tow, she found time to make me such thoughtful gifts. I adored the white, tall chef's hat and embroidered apron to match. I know she spent a lot of time on that and neglected herself. Growing up with loving aunts is truly a special blessing. It adds so many layers of happy memories to the family story. It gives you the secure feeling that you belong to something that has deep roots and sustains you. That makes it easier to develop wings later when you need them. Psychologists' studies prove these kinds of roots laced with family history and stories help prevent anxiety, drug abuse and self-harm in children and teens.

Nine was a pretty smooth year with lots of new horizons. My fourth-grade teacher was Mrs. Hutchison. She had just graduated from college, and her husband was attending Columbia Presbyterian Theological Seminary next to our neighborhood. She was a good teacher, but there were some really mischievous boys in the class. Looking back, I am guessing they had attention deficit disorder and hyperactivity. They could not sit still nor be quiet nor do their work or follow rules. Educators did not know as much then about children with special needs. There was only one guidance counselor for the entire Decatur School System, Mrs. Honiker. One day, my teacher became so distraught that she started hyperventilating and crying. The teacher next door came in quickly and got her to breathe into a paper bag until she was calmed down. I'm guessing the next year she probably decided to start a family and leave teaching far behind.

I read the girl classics like 'The Secret Garden,' 'Little Women,' and most of the Nancy Drew mysteries, but I tended to prefer adult non-fiction books. Mama and Daddy had a huge, tall built-in bookcase in the den. I read 'Lust for Life' about Vincent van Gogh, 'The Agony and the Ecstasy' about Michaelangelo and 'The Magnificent Obsession' for starters. I got Mama's kitchen stool and climbed to the top shelf right at the ceiling. I brought down all the Dr.'s Gesell and Ilg child development books and a three-inch-thick black book called 'The Human Mind', by Dr. Karl Menninger. I secretly read those books from cover to cover. One day I was giggling incessantly. Mama asked me, "Julie, why on earth have you been so silly all day?" I answered, "I just read the chapter about nine-year olds, and it says they giggle a lot."

The Menninger book had many case studies of aberrant behavior of seriously mentally ill adults. It was a textbook Daddy had at Emory when he was in premed studying psychology. I can tell you that children should not read such scary books. Later when the staff artist at Atlanta Public Library, we actually experienced a case just like I had read, so I was well informed. It was a man who nailed a receptacle to the telephone pole outside the library and had a long electrical cord around his body and "plugged" himself in. He said he would die if anyone unplugged him. God bless them all!

I loved to go to my friend, Margo's house. Her parents had a large house full of Victorian antiques. Her dad taught at the Columbia Seminary. She was taking piano lessons and taught me some of her beginner pieces. I went home and begged for lessons. Thankfully there was a very fine teacher, Mrs. Barfield, right around the corner in walking distance. I had one thirty-minute private lesson per week and one group lesson to learn music theory and to write music symbols and notes on the treble and bass clefs. We bought a piano, and I learned rapidly and loved every minute. The only problem was that I really wanted to play by ear. Mama had classical music on 33 1/3 records, so I listened to pieces and played them. That is why I am not as good a sight reader as I should be!

Each household had one black, rotary dial phone usually centrally located in a hallway. Our number was Crescent or CR-8764. Mumsie and Granddaddy had Dearborn or DE-3112. There were party lines so you could listen to other people's conversations. We were told that was rude, and we did not do it. It did not require the US Government to have Congress pass a privacy law. It was just common decency and respect which was predominant and plentiful. Character qualities were taught at home, school and Sunday School.

The fantastic thing about age nine was that I was allowed to ride my bike to Decatur to visit Daddy or do shopping. My parents had wanted me to get a classy black English bike with gears, but I loved the shiny royal blue one with a basket and a bell. When my little brother knocked it over and scratched the back, his life was in danger! Downtown Decatur on the square had many fun shops that I loved. Woolworths five and dime store was my place to buy hair care items like rollers, doughnut shaped chignon bun bases, barrettes and bobby pins. They had a candy counter, and since I did not like chocolate the little sugar-coated orange slices or the marshmallowy circus peanuts were my pick. The lady gave me $.05 worth in a tiny white paper bag.

At Haynes jewelry store I could put a Gorham Chantilly teaspoon on layaway for Mama's Christmas gift and pay $.25 per week until the $3.00 was paid off. For Daddy I bought cufflinks and handkerchiefs the same way at Levy's and Ray's menswear stores. Watson's Drugs had Double Bubble gum for $.01. Each piece had an Archie and Veronica comic inside the wrapper.

Age nine was the year that Mama taught me to sew. I wanted to make clothes for my bride doll. She showed me how to make gathered and pleated skirts with snaps or elastic, but for blouses I needed a pattern. We went to the fabric store and bought a square pink sewing basket covered in quilted plastic. I still have some of those accessories like scissors, the seam ripper, measuring tape and six-inch hem measuring tool. I did the sewing by hand until I wanted to make skirts for myself and learned to use her Singer sewing machine. My first skirt was royal blue with one-inch pleats and snaps at the waist. I mastered button holes and buttons, but to this good day I would rather be horsewhipped than put in a zipper. That was my frustration threshold. Later in high school I enjoyed designing and making high-waisted dresses like Josephine wore in the Napoleonic Era. Of course, it was counter-productive for me to sew since Daddy sold ready-to-wear. Oh well!

My parents spent a lot of time taking us places to get things we needed for school or hobbies or fun. Daddy often drove our family on Saturday evenings downtown to the Varsity drive-in restaurant. I was not much for hotdogs and French fries, but the burgers, frosted orange drinks and onion rings were delicious. Chocolate milk with crushed ice was called a PC which stood for plain chocolate. They had real dishes with no paper cups or plates. Each server had a cardboard number on their cap to identify them. Whenever he was available, we had a server named Flossie Mae. He came to the car on roller skates and wore funny, outrageously decorated hats with feathers and ribbons and so forth. He sang the menu to us and was very animated and funny.

After the Varsity we stopped at a tiny shop on Ponce de Leon Avenue near Peachtree Street to buy a new tropical fish for our aquarium. We had neon tetras, black Mollies, sword fish and zebra fish mostly with a black snail to eat algae on the tank to keep it clean. The last stop was always Krispy Kreme for doughnuts. They had a few simple choices but nothing like the sprinkles and frostings of today.

It was not unusual for Daddy to drive all the way to Watson's Pharmacy to get us a couple of pieces of bubble gum. Our hands on parents were totally focused on our needs. They did not play golf or tennis or bridge. Their free time was for the children. Mama spent hours at Miller's Book Store watching me select art supplies. I had to touch each paint brush extensively to make sure it felt right in my hands and had just the right bristles. I am very ambidextrous for artwork but prefer the left hand for writing. I insisted on filling my fountain pen with peacock blue Parker ink from Miller's. Schaeffer's Black or blue from the drug store simply would not do! In reality my blue eyes are more of a teal blue color. Perhaps there is some genetic cellular knowledge involved there.

Mumsie started Belvedere Methodist Church in her living room. They moved to the DeKalb County Hooper Alexander Elementary School. Eventually they built a beautiful sanctuary on Midway Road at Columbia Drive. I remember the Sunday when they set in the Cornerstone. We were members there until in sixth grade I really needed to be in Decatur Methodist with my school friends. Belvedere had the most wonderful fish fry dinners downtown at Grant Park every summer. My favorite food there was the hushpuppies. After the fish fry, we could go to the zoo. There was also the Cyclorama, a huge circular diorama of the Battle of Atlanta. It had oil paintings of buildings for the background with life-size figures of soldiers, wagons and cannons and such.

Papa and Grandmother loved to take the whole family to Daytona Beach for vacations. Aunt Judy and Uncle Ted drove down from Hillsdale, New Jersey with their three little stairstep boys, Chrissy and Johnny and Mikey. After the vacation I always rode back to New Jersey in the red, Ford station wagon. We stopped halfway and spent a night at a Howard Johnson's motor inn which we did not have in the south. The restaurant was fun. They had a kid's menu with storybook meals. There was the Little Miss Muffet plate, the Tommy Tucker plate, a Little Boy Blue plate and a Mistress Mary plate and so forth. They had large, bright green frozen peas which I had never seen. No self-respecting southern woman served anything other than tiny, canned LeSuer peas. I called the big peas Yankee peas. The same held true for Velveeta cheese. We ate only yellow mild cheddar, so Velveeta was Yankee cheese in my culinary opinion. Papa always bought us corned beef and Swiss cheese from the delicatessen, so we were not familiar with salami and Polish sausages or prosciutto.

New Jersey summers were great fun for many years until I was fifteen. The children in Judy's neighborhood came to the door to ask me to talk so they could hear my beautiful southern accent. I should have said, "Hold my magnolia while I butter my cornbread." I am surprised they did not ask, "Don't you have a cousin you should be dating?" Or, "And please say hello to Opie and Aunt Bea on your way to Appalacheechopee." There was Karen, Gail, Lionel and Zuzzie.

They all had different pastel color houses. I loved to practice tap dancing on the avocado-colored Spanish tile in Judy's entry hall. My taps sounded so good and loud. Her house was a light blue color siding. The living room was a loft. Below was the dining room, kitchen, bedrooms and baths. Downstairs was a family room with Uncle Ted's bar and his accordion. I stuck my finger in each bottle and smacked a lick of spirits. I decided alcohol was the grossest thing I had ever tasted. Below there was the finished basement with laundry facilities and double garage.

I walked dogs for neighbors to earn spending money. The cutest dog was a little black dachshund at the Hadley's house next door. However, I found mashing up dark brown bananas for their mynah bird to be kind of gross. I walked Judy's boxer, Jinxy and ironed the little cousins' clothes. They had matching outfits with T-shirts and seersucker shorts in red, royal blue, gold and green. I watched them in the yard to prevent bug eating and stick fights. There were shiny, iridescent Japanese beetles which had not yet found their way to Georgia. I bathed the wee cousins and played with them. Occasionally there were very windy days from hurricanes. We went to Jones Beach in New York on weekends. Ted's kind parents lived near there. They spoke mostly Polish, and the food was delicious.

Judy blended egg in our orange juice every day. We ate bologna, tuna casserole and grilled cheese sandwiches I slept in the hall guest room. There was a huge Catholic Bible with Apocrypha in the middle with a book called Judith. I actually thought it was about my Aunt Judy, and was very proud that she made it into the Bible! Even more reason to emulate her behavior and have her as a role model, right? She really did have a cream-colored plastic Jesus on her dashboard like that song 'Plastic Jesus' that was in the Paul Newman movie 'Cool Hand Luke.' I was envious that my little cousins wore St. Christopher medals on a chain around their neck.

Due to some reason, my parents did not approve of my wearing Levi's jeans. They thought khaki shorts, black watch plaid shirt and red knee socks were more appropriate for the little preppy girl that was a fashion plate to advertise for her parents' ready-to-wear store. Well, that was no obstacle for our nanny, Lula Mae. She had a nephew named Hayward Lewis who was a couple of years older than me. Lula brought me jeans when he outgrew them. I wore them out to Margo's farm in Lithonia when we went to ride horses.

Lula was a saint when you consider how much trouble we could be. When she had enough of our mischief or messes, she chased us with her broom and shouted, "I'm gonna' whoop your butt." But that never happened as she was really very gentle and forbearing with a tender heart. Hayward Lewis fought in the Vietnam War, and he is buried right next to Lula on Jordan Lane in Decatur.

Lula taught me to make biscuit and to iron on Mama's large mangle ironer. I did the pillow cases, napkins and handkerchiefs for her. Eventually I knew how to do Daddy's shirts and our skirts. We had no perma-press fabrics in those days. Only nylon lingerie or stockings could drip dry without ironing. Energetic Julie loved to help Lula sweep. I did the front porch with fourteen steps down to the driveway and the driveway which was about a tenth of a mile.

One day I asked Daddy, "Daddy, why am I pink, and Lula is brown?" He told me there was absolutely no difference between Lula and me other than the fact that God had left her in the oven longer. Mama had a lot of Quaker ancestors in the Mobley family who originally came over from England on the ship with William Penn. Penn's niece, Phoebe Lovejoy was approximately my tenth great-grandmother. Our parents and grandparents raised us to never look down on any human beings. I can promise you if I had been unkind or sassy to Lula, I would have been in big trouble and forever regretted it even though my parents did not spank me.

Of course, Lula did believe in "haints." (Probably derived from the word haunt) That is what we would call ghosts. Daddy had to put pieces of new pine wood across the threshold of the sliding glass doors. Lula's pastor had told her that would keep the "haints" away. She also kept a glass of water on the dresser in her bedroom. That was because she said haints came in because they were thirsty. I told her about evaporation making the glass less full. She said, "I don't know nothing about "vapolration", but the haints, they done drunk the water."

When weather permitted, we were roaming all over the neighborhood playing outside games with our friends. There was a lot of hide-and-seek, kick the can, kickball and catching fireflies in the dark. We played Hopscotch and Red Rover. Daddy bought us an archery set for out bottom land acre by the creek. I became quite a good shot and loved my bow and arrow. It all went well until Eric shot an apple off of a bucket on a kid's head. Then my parents put the dangerous weapons away for good, and I prayed to God to not strangle my naughty brother, the Southeastern Distributor of Naughty!

Papa and Grandmother were on a country road driving back from Florida, and a speeding car sideswiped them in the days before seat belts. Grandmother was spared injury. Papa was thrown from the car against a barbed wire fence and had cuts and bruises on his face. Even though he was extremely sore, he did not protest when I climbed in his lap and covered his bald head with kisses. They brought us a box of Lifesavers as promised in a letter, but I was expecting white life rings like lifeguards threw to drowning people.

It was fun at their house on Coventry Road. On Sunday nights we sat out on the enclosed porch and watched shows like Lawrence Welk and Kate Smith. We enjoyed the comedians Bob Hope, Jerry Lewis and Jimmy Durante. I especially loved the Art Linkletter show when he interviewed children. He wrote a book about it called 'Kids Say the Darndest Things!' Grandmother always gave me an apple and a paring knife to eat while I sat between them. They lived near a railroad track where we learned to put pennies to smash them flat. They had sweet peach and plum trees in the back yard.

The neighbors across the street had homing pigeons. The neighbors behind them were from Greece and had yummy cookies topped with poppy seeds. I played at Papa's desk for hours, typing on the typewriter to send letters to his family in Cleveland, Ohio and Aunt Judy in New Jersey. They had a floor furnace. It was cozy warm to stand next to it on wintery days. Being a curious child who wanted to try out everything, I found a little bottle of Phillips Tablets in their medicine cabinet. Since they were peppermint flavor, that said candy to me. I chewed up quite a few and had the worst trots imaginable! They also had strange Smith Brothers black cough drops.

Our kitchen was outfitted with simple, non-electric gadgets. Mama did have a Sunbeam Mixmaster for cakes and cookies. There was no blender or coffee maker or electric can opener. Coffee was made on the stove in an aluminum coffee pot called a percolator. We had no instant coffee or grits or oatmeal and such. We ate Jell-O gelatin and pudding. Cheese was shredded by hand with a cheese grater. Black cast-iron skillets were fairly common, and you made your best cornbread in a skillet in the oven. Non-stick pans had not been invented, so all utensils were metal instead of plastic. We had aluminum foil and waxed paper but no plastic wrap to cover foods.

Mama regularly served broiled lamb chops with mint jelly, but Daddy forbade mac 'n cheese, tuna casseroles and kidney beans. He said he had had enough of those during The Great Depression and World War II to sink the Queen Mary! I was the rare child that loved liver and onions fried in a skillet. Mashed potatoes were rare. We preferred baked sweet potatoes with butter and a sprinkle of cinnamon. Southerners liked thick green pole beans. Dinner always had a yellow vegetable and a green vegetable plus meat, chicken or fish and very little bread or rolls unless Lula baked biscuit. Lula made the tastiest yellow squash souffle' casserole ever with plenty of onion, cheese and buttered bread crumbs. Cooked carrots were buttered and served with some Sioux Bee brand clover honey. Mama made pickled Harvard beets. Sometime there were fish sticks with catsup. I did not like sugary cereals at all. Wheat Chex, Rice Crispies, Raisin Bran and Shredded Wheat suited my taste. I thought Tony the Tiger was Grrrross! Don't depose me for an explanation, but I took raw spaghetti noodles and covered them with Crisco vegetable shortening and ate them. Lula ate the laundry corn starch and called it "white dirt."

Chapter 6
Ten and Eleven,
Not Quite Heaven!

I had the most wonderful fifth grade teacher in the world! Her name was Mrs. Elrod, and she was a gem in every way. She was a friend of my grandmother, Mumsie, so I came highly recommended. She was a slender woman around fifty years old with black hair and a beaming smile. She was calm and patient with a soothing voice. I was actually in a Fourth-Fifth grade combination class with well-behaved students. Every morning we said the pledge to the flag, and Mrs. Elrod read to us from the Bible. She read the entire Eggemeyers Bible Story Book for Children. Then we memorized quite a few of the Psalms from the King James version of the Bible. That is why I had no problem understanding Shakespeare. We had learned Elizabethan English that way by default.

After lunch Mrs. Elrod read fiction books to us while we put our heads on our desks and closed our eyes. She read all the Dr. Doolittle books and all the Mary Poppins books. Then we would have art time before afternoon recess. I loved to draw caladium leaves and dachshund dogs and some horses mostly. I was good at copying art such as corporate logos. Mama bought me a snazzy long, flat box of Prang twenty-four crayons. It had a gold and a silver and a copper crayon. Crayola could not compete with that! I took it to school and a classmate named Bob borrowed the copper crayon and broke it. I went home very upset. Mama understood I couldn't handle broken things, so she bought me another box. It had something to do with the heartache from having a "broken" sister, Davilyn.

Aunt Sara lived up the street with Mumsie and Granddaddy. She turned their basement into an art studio. She painted beautiful portraits and did some sculpting with metal or clay. She had studied art at High Museum in Atlanta.

Grandmother Mobley objected to art school for decent young women, but Mumsie and Granddaddy encouraged her. Sara taught art to the neighborhood children every Saturday morning, and it was loads of fun. Can you believe that she let children melt paraffin on a hot plate to make candles? Then we poured melted wax into a bowl and beat it fluffy with an egg beater and spread it like frosting on paraffin blocks with candle wicks in the center. Totally true, there were not many lawsuits in those days if any.

Children were patient with long attention spans and better impulse control back then. Sara painted a black spot on the wall. If you were having your portrait done, you sat there for endless hours staring at the spot. It was not boring because she had such a fun personality and we laughed and talked about family stories and overcoming obstacles.

Since religious themes had not yet been banned from the public schools, Sara painted Christmas nativity scenes with tempera paint on the school windows where she taught. They were there for the entire month of December and into January just past Epiphany. We had school-wide programs in the auditorium with children acting out the Christmas story with angels and shepherds and wise men. Whole classes recited the favorite Psalms of David from the scriptures.

On rare occasions an art teacher named Mr. Calder came to our class. I hated that some boys made fun of him for not having the muscular physique of a football player. They mistakenly thought art was for sissies. Their loss! We had crayons, pastels, colored pencils and tempera paint. Usually, we drew or painted on newsprint paper, but on special occasions we had nice, thick 11x17 inch white paper. Colored construction paper was available for holidays. We cut out white snowflakes and made red and green paper chains and girls made paper dolls. We probably could have done more art if we had not been busy eating the paste. I don't know why children did that! It was non-toxic, of course. We sculpted animals and such with newspaper strips dipped in paper Mache' paste. A project assignment for Geography or book reports might now and then be a shoebox diorama or a large poster.

Once in a blue moon the one and only city music teacher, Mrs. Moore came to the school auditorium. We had songbooks and sang Americana songs like 'O, Susanna', O My Darlin' Clementine', and all of the patriotic songs like 'America the Beautiful', 'My Country 'Tis of Thee,' and so forth. On rainy days when there was no playing outside for recess, our teachers taught us some square dancing and the Bunny Hop and The Hokey Pokey dances. We played games all in a large circle: Drop the Handkerchief, Button Button whose got the button?

Granddaddy died that December. My parents did not take me to the funeral home or to the funeral, thinking they were protecting me from trauma and bereavement. It was as if he had just vanished and left a huge Granddaddy size hole in my heart. I missed climbing up on his lap when he rocked in his rocker. Sometime when I kissed him on the cheek, he had a stubble of white whiskers that was a tiny bit scratchy. He usually sat by a gas floor furnace, and it was warm and cozy in his chair. He was kind of quiet and frail from Chron's Disease, but I was always happy to walk up the street to see him. It was just comforting sitting with him, watching him drink his coffee. He beamed when I entered the room but rarely said anything. He had hardening of the arteries and died with uremic poisoning from his kidneys.

One of Mama's best friends was the sweet Margaret. She had four children and lived on a lake behind Briarcliff Road. Margaret was a beautician and had her salon in the basement of their home. I loved to spend the night there with her older daughters Sandra and Brenda. We spent a lot of time in the salon after hours shampooing and curling each other's hair. It was fun to sit under the dryer and pretend we were grown up ladies. Later Margaret had a shop on Clairmont Road in Chamblee. She was a woman of great faith and used her salon as a ministry to women. You could always take assorted Bible tracts from her tables.

Margaret told Mama about the famous Jack Eppley dance school downtown on Ivy Street near Georgia State University. Mama signed me up for tap and ballet. I took lessons there for three years and loved tap dancing most. Mama drove all that way every week, and that was our special time together. After the lessons she gave me a nickel to get a Coca Cola out of the machine. Cokes were in small light green six-ounce glass bottles then. Ballet, though a bit slow and boring, was okay until I graduated to toe shoes. I found toe dancing painful even with half a box of lamb's wool in the toes. Also, ballet was not jazzy and jivey enough for me. Recitals were so much fun at the Roxy Theatre. I loved the costumes and the lights and the crowd. The first year our costumes were red, black and green designed like harlequin court jesters. The second year we did a Mexican hat dance and had orange costumes with black ball fringe and black sombreros. The third year our costumes were black and fuchsia. The ballet teacher, Shirley Webb, did a solo at the recital and wore a red tutu. To me she was the most beautiful dancer in the world. She was slender with shiny black curls and a face like Vivien Leigh in 'Gone with the Wind.'

Chief Peek, the Fire Chief in Decatur, was the husband of Daddy's head sales lady, Mrs. Peek. Chief and I had the same birthday. He liked to take me to lunch on our birthday, and you guessed it, we drove in a fire truck with siren blaring. Neither citizens nor police minded a bit. They thought it was fun.

There were so many adults to look up to in Decatur. I adored Daddy's saleswomen, Madge, Beth, Anne, Dot, Connie. They worked for Daddy for decades. He was such a wonderful patriarch and was so good to them and appreciated them. Mama gave them nice gifts. Mama from time to time did beautiful and interesting displays in the window. I remember the one that looked like a barnyard. She made chickens out of chicken wire and feathers. There was a log with an ax on it.

All the merchants were admirable. Daddy took me to Moody's and Siegel's jewelry stores. He bought me my first watch for $8.00. It was fun to have lunch with Daddy at the drug store or at Tom's diner. I met and got to know attorneys, judges, merchants like Mr. Levy and Mr. Canglin who sold menswear. We were taught to respect and look up to accomplished adults who served the community. My parents had wonderful character qualities and set a good example as model citizens. Whenever we went on a trip, Daddy said a prayer as soon as he started the engine. They wanted to keep our feet on the path to Heaven and teach us to reverence and serve God's kingdom.

We bought groceries on Clairmont Avenue at the Colonial Store called C & S. Their logo was the C & S rooster. Mr. Johnson worked in the produce department. He had all the time in the world to pick my mom's fruits and vegetables and put them in little brown bags. He was a slender man with thinning brown hair who wore a white shirt, khaki pants and a white apron. It was nothing like the huge supermarkets of today, but it was what we had.

Across the street was the Decatur Cake Box Bakery where all of our birthday cakes were made and custom decorated. I can still smell the aroma of fresh baked bread, cookies and doughnuts. There was also the Locker Plant where Mama rented a freezer space so she could buy chicken, fish and meat on sale in bulk and keep it there to use as needed. We loved and respected all the gentlemen in blue (police and firemen) and the service station and hardware store owners.

Mama and Daddy's good friends, Buck and Ev, owned a fine furniture store with the best quality pieces of Sprague and Carlton furniture. My parents gave me a Governor Winthrop canopy bed for my tenth birthday. It had the serpentine top. It came with bedside tables, a large dresser and a dressing table. It was made of the finest hard rock blonde maple. They put glass tops on the furniture so that I would not scratch it. That was very prudent, but one night when my little sister, Kim, was in my bed, we were laughing and singing silly songs we made up. She fell off the bed onto a corner of the glass on the bedside table and got a cut on her ear that required stitches. I felt so bad for making her laugh that hard and get so wound up at bedtime. Mama sewed me a blue chintz bedspread with tiny pink flowers and made a white ruffled canopy out of sheer organdy fabric.

We had a black and white TV. My favorite program was the Mickey Mouse Club every afternoon after school. I idolized the cute Mouseketeers on that show. Papa had a cousin named Archie Dattelbaum who was a cartoonist for Walt Disney in California. I had seen Archie's name at the theater on some classics like Snow White. That led to one conclusion. I could definitely be a Mouseketeer. I announced to Papa that cousin Archie would surely make me a Mouseketeer because I could sing, dance, tumble, play piano and twirl a baton. So much for that crushed dream. I never did become an Annette Funicello. Rotten luck and so sad and disappointing! But as long as there is breath in my body, there is hope!

Some day one of my 17 original entertainment characters WILL be discovered. I can see it now: t-shirts, caps, lunch boxes, posters and talk shows. Call me fruitcake/blonde but never accuse me of NOT being a dreamer! Tyler Perry and Madea, here I come. The Grandma Moses of comediennes is right behind the curtains until Kismet bangs the gong.

Decatur, Georgia does not have snow very often at all. If it did snow, Mama collected a pan of snow and made snow ice cream. She added cream, vanilla and sugar. That was a delightful treat. We could also make ice cream or sherbet in the freezer in ice trays with an added powder called "Junket." As soon as it froze, you took it out and beat it to make it fluffier. Then it went back in the freezer until firm. On Sunday evenings in the winter, we often had soup in a large, white oval soup terrine. We sat by the fire and cooked grilled cheese sandwiches. We roasted potatoes and apples wrapped in tin foil and placed in the hot coals. There was also a wire mesh basket with a very long wooden handle for popping popcorn. There was not much cocoa since Eric and Kim were allergic. However, we had that fakey Russian tea made with Tang and some ground McCormick cinnamon and cloves.

Mama and Daddy decided to remodel our kitchen. Yes, you guessed it! They chose bright turquoise GE frig, double ovens, electric cooktop and dishwasher that matched Mama's turquoise and white Ford station wagon. The manufacturers called it "sea frock green." Sadly, we had a small kitchen fire around that time, but Mr. Bush, the cabinet man, came and fixed everything to perfection.

Mama was a gourmet cook, preparing dishes like duck l'orange and giant flounders stuffed with crabmeat and such. Lula did the daily cooking, but Mama enjoyed doing the culinary pizazz. I loved her salad with green grapes frosted with sweet cream cheese and served on a real grape leaf. On holidays we ate broiled grapefruit topped with brown sugar and a red maraschino cherry. She could garnish even a hotdog to look like it came from the dining room of the Dinkler Plaza Hotel. Of course, she made plenty of simple, old-fashioned foods like popcorn balls and boiled custard. She taught me how to use a candy thermometer to get sugar syrup to the hard-crack temperature to make lollypops or the soft-crack stage to make taffy. Daddy liked steak broiled in the oven or on the grill.

Mrs. Pace was our sixth-grade teacher. She was an attractive middle-aged lady with one grown, married son and a grandchild. She lived on Pinecrest Drive in the Glenwood School neighborhood about three miles from us. She was newly widowed and still suffered from a lot of grief and sadness that you could see on her face, but she was a wonderful teacher, and I continued to love school and make excellent report cards. We received a small weekly publication called 'Read Magazine.' They had a page with jokes sent in by sixth grade students. I was the gutsy kid that wanted some fame and notoriety, so I sent one in. That was my first officially published anything. Of course, they misspelled my long, complicated name. It read from Julie "Dottelbaum" with an o.

Our school schedules were so flexible and laid back. Our teachers were teaching us to think and do creative problem solving. They wanted us to love learning and become life-long learners. There was none of this state and federally ordered "43 minutes of math, 52 minutes of language arts" and so forth. They believed in those "teachable moments." If there was an interesting butterfly on a bush outside the window, we needed to stop our lessons and see that and talk about it and look it up in the encyclopedia. In today's education a frenetic frenzy of madness prevails, and test scores ain't all that good. Our country spends more education money annually per child than any country in the world, and gets the poorest result. Maybe someday when we are not so much a baby culture of the world, we will take some hints from the older societies.

That year Mama and Daddy were having some marital problems that they hid very well from us. Above their closet were four locked cabinets where they kept Christmas and birthday presents and such. Mischievous child that I was, I figured out how to climb precariously up on Mama's tall kitchen stool, take a screwdriver and totally remove the hinges and the doors to see what was in there. Wednesday evenings Mama and Daddy went out to eat, and we stayed home with Lula, our nanny, and ate spaghetti and tried to make noodles (no sauce on them) stick to the kitchen ceiling. When Lula was getting the children ready for bed, I had my golden opportunity to do my snooping. Sadly, I found some divorce papers and read them and clearly understood what it was all about.

The next night I ran away from home after dark and walked all the way to Mrs. Pace's house, across the railroad tracks and through several neighborhoods. God gave my guardian angels A+++ that time. He should also have given them $100.00 gift cards to the Heavenly Halo Shop! Mrs. Pace let me in and tried to comfort me, and, naturally, she called my mom to come and get me. The next day I had a session with the Decatur Schools one and only counselor, and I told her why I ran away. After that, Mama and Daddy put forth their best efforts and stayed together. But it was never spoken of at all, not one word. Our parents were from such a repressed generation. I believe that if I had told Daddy that there was a feeling in the living room, he would have said, "Oh No! Quick! Stomp it and kill it before it gets loose in the rest of the house!"

Piano lessons and practicing were still so fun. Every year at the National Auditions I made between 96 and 100. If Mrs. Barfield assigned a recital piece that was not my favorite, I pretended to be flustered and nervous and played the one I liked best. Oh, Lord, what to do with strong-willed children? I began to take baton twirling lessons and could practice in our large living room. The huge plate glass window was shatter proof, and my twirling was fairly accurate. There was only sturdy furniture and no lamps or other breakable nick-nacks. My teacher was a nice teen girl named Kay several streets away. I could walk there once a week. I think she charged $.50 per lesson.

Recess was enjoyable and laid back at Winnona Park School. The teachers sat on benches up on the hill by the building and chit chatted. We completely managed our own sports with boys and girls separately. It varied from monkey bars and swinging to kickball or softball mostly. I could kick home runs and hit that softball hard and usually got chosen for a team third after Peggy and Kathy. Of course, we wore dresses and skirts, no pants allowed. Our shoes were hard sole loafers or saddle oxfords. There were days when we were allowed to sit on the bank, smell the sweet purple kudzu blooms and make clover chains. That was a nice time to socialize and get to know the girls. Jumping rope was very popular. Daddy went to the hardware store and bought me a very long, sturdy, thick rope. My friends were quite happy about that.

We lived very close to the Methodist Children's Home on Columbia Drive. My family had always supported the home and had a lot of interest in helping orphans and buying them bicycles. For a while Mama and Daddy took in a teenage girl named Johnny Sue. Her mother had been the mistress of a very prominent citizen in a small Georgia town. Due to some reason which we could probably guess, the father had killed the mother. Johnny Sue had a younger brother named Wade. Their baby sister had been adopted, and they had no clue where she was. I was very envious of her $2.50 per week allowance. I got only $1.25. Daddy outfitted her in beautiful, stylish clothes from his store.

Johnny Sue eventually went back to the orphanage. Perhaps she had a hard time fitting in at Decatur High with students who were from upper middle-class families and not from broken homes. Years later Johnny Sue came to visit us with her husband, John. They had met at Young Harris College in north Georgia. She had two children, Johnny and Susie and a very successful life with the happiness and security she so deserved.

Sixth graders typically started taking ballroom dancing at Miss Rena Grisell's house in the neighborhood. Ms. Grisell had added a spacious dance hall onto her house. She had a green light by the steps up to her front door and was called, "The Green Light Lady." I chose to not take the dance lessons that year, but when I saw my friends long, beautiful net dresses with hoop skirts that they wore to the end of year dance, I signed up for the seventh-grade year.

Susie had a beautiful royal blue dress with silver trim and a dozen yards of net for the skirt. Her mother had it custom made by a local seamstress.

Mama and Daddy's very close friend, Buck Talman, was my Sunday School teacher in sixth grade. Buck had been a pilot in World War II and got shot down but escaped. He was full of enthusiasm, charisma and gave dynamic lessons each week. The classroom was jampacked with eager students who hung on his every word. He was the person who taught me about tithing. I pledged $.50 per week and put two quarters in a little white offering envelope at church every week. My allowance was only $1.25, so this caused a budget crisis crunch for me. My pennies, nickels and dimes just could not stretch far enough. One Sunday I put a small note in my offering envelope that said: Due to circumstances beyond my control I must now reduce my pledge to $.25 per week. Working in Daddy's store had taught me to be very precise and businesslike. Don't you know the gentlemen who counted the offering got a big chuckle out of that note?

We started taking vacations at St. Simons Island. My parents rented a spacious white cottage with screened porch right on the beach. Lula went with us. She loved to fish. It was great fun setting out crab traps. When you set a trap down in the water, the sides collapsed and the crabs went for the chicken thigh secured to the middle of the bottom with a string. Mama boiled the crabs in a huge pot on the stove. She put the cooked crabs on newspaper, and we picked the meat off and ate it. Our parents did not know back then that sunburns were bad, so we were encouraged to get "brown as little berries." They thought that looked healthy. Oh, well! Can you spell m-e-l-a-n-o-m-a?

One summer we were sitting at the edge of the water as the tide came in and the foamy, salty water lapped against our legs. Davilyn let out a shrill cry and began to sob. She had sat on a Portuguese man o war sea creature. It was oval round like a light bulb with ridges and was a milky white color. We had to rush her to the hospital. She had second degree burns on her little legs and bottom. When we got back to Decatur, Dr. Watson at the pharmacy compounded a jar of Furicin burn ointment that was thick as Vaseline and dark yellow and smelled funny like Sulphur. I still have that small, white glass jar with black plastic top and the green and white Watson label on it and with some remaining ointment inside.

My youngest sister, Kim, had some traumatic injuries. Once she got in the tub to bathe, but was so modest she did not remove her swimsuit. Somehow her suit strap got stuck on the faucet and scalding hot water was pouring on her legs. Lula rescued her quickly, but she still required medical treatment. Another time, she and Eric were rolling down the steep grassy hill behind our house. Thankfully they always rolled sideways. Someone had carelessly thrown a broken Coca Cola bottle near the bottom. She rolled across it and cut a deep gash on her ankle that required quite a few stitches. Thank the Lord it was not on her pretty little face! We hardly ever drank Cokes or ginger ale other than on special occasions or if we had an upset stomach, so it is likely the bottle was dropped by some delivery man. The oil for our heating was delivered there next to the hill down the back steps to the basement furnace.

Daddy's store backed up to an alley behind the Decatur News owned by the Crane family. Their daughter Sheila and I loved to play in the production room. We could type on giant typewriters that printed the articles on bars of lead which went into the printing press and were later melted down to start over for the next Wednesday paper. Parents did not worry about liability in those times when people were not focused on suing each other. My parents did not have to sign any safety waiver. It was a live and let live world that worked very well. People behaved properly and legally in small towns. Sociologists call it "social control." No one wants to be ostracized in a society where everyone knows what everyone is doing. People believed in working for a living and not looking for freebee handouts.

I could bike to Decatur and take my shoes to Bailey's Shoe Shop for new heels or half soles. Mr. Bailey's elderly father sat by the window every day hunched over his sewing machine repairing leather things. I bought shoe polish and shoestrings there. When your dad is an ex-marine, shoe care is a significant daily activity and a matter of pride. I liked to go to the old white marble post office on Trinity Place.

There was a solid, secure steadiness about Decatur. People worked at the same jobs and lived in the same houses for decades. It is a very homogenous world when you live, work, shop and go to school and church with the same people. Everyone understands each other and why they are the way they are. People make allowances for each other's shortcomings. Let me tell you, it really cuts down on things like road rage and Hatfield and McCoy feuds! In my entire childhood and teen years, I never heard of even one shooting or robbery. There were even a couple of harmless mentally cheese off the cracker people who wandered here and there on the streets or in shops or at church.

People just accepted that and treated them with deference and kindness. The only facility for such was the state hospital in Milledgeville, and no one wanted to send their loved ones there unless it was absolutely necessary.

Mumsie preferred Compton's Encyclopedias to World Book. I used them a lot for school work assignments and also loved to read them and look at the black and white pictures for hours just for fun. When Lula's little girl, Nita (Albonita) was old enough, Mama bought her a set of Compton's. She was a very bright child, and my parents wanted to encourage her. She later graduated from DeKalb College and was a bookkeeper at Egleston, Emory's children's hospital. At school I liked the large fancy Encyclopedia Britannica.

We lived walking distance from the women's Presbyterian school, Agnes Scott College on Candler Street at College Avenue. It had a planetarium open to the neighborhood and wonderful professors that were always available to advise us on projects and assignments on most any topic. Robert Frost came there almost annually to read poetry, and he stayed with the high school English teacher, Mrs. Dieckmann and her husband. I think they knew one another from their college years. Many of our teachers were the wives of Agnes Scott, Emory and Columbia Seminary professors, so our Decatur schools were top notch intellectually. There was a climate of academia that was hard to rival in the average small town. We were admired for being diligent students and not thought of as being nerdy or dorky.

Mumsie's family strongly believed in higher education for their girls. Grandmother Mobley had graduated from the first chartered women's college in America, Lucy Cobb Institute on Milledge Avenue in Athens, Georgia. A historic marker was being put there by the curb, and she was asked to come and unveil that marker. Mumsie and I drove to Covington and picked her up to drive to Athens. I remember she was so precise that she took some red, white and blue curly ribbons to tie back the cloth cover on the marker when it was being unveiled. She was a strong, alert take-charge woman. My family had bold matriarchs whose husbands had died leaving them with children to raise, businesses to run and land and sharecroppers to manage. In Mumsie's case, she had to be strong as steel when Granddaddy became disabled and there were four children to feed. She sewed dresses from flour sacks and knew how to squeeze nickels until the buffaloes said very bad words!

My parents sometimes needed custom built cabinets or shelves for our home or display racks for the store. A pleasant, jovial plump Mr. Bush had a cabinet shop on College Avenue right near Watson's Pharmacy. I remember his bright smile, light blue Scottish eyes and very fair skin with rosy cheeks and plump sturdy physique. I loved to go there with Mama or Daddy and watch him work. The smell of fresh cut wood and the buzz of his saws and drills was pleasant to me. Of course, the floor was always covered in sawdust and wood curls from the drill. Being such a neatnik, I truly wanted to take a broom and sweep the floor for him.

Mama and Daddy took Davilyn to the Brown School for special needs children. It was in Texas and almost as costly as sending a kid to Harvard. My parents wanted to do everything for Dede that could possibly be done. After six months, the school told them that they had not been able to help her. It was really hard on them having Dede sleep near them. She was up and down all night. There were no good medicines invented yet, and they did not like the idea of keeping her doped up most of the time. They felt that they were often sacrificing three healthy children for a profoundly disabled child. The solution was to take her to live in Augusta, Georgia at the Gracewood facility. DeKalb and Fulton County had absolutely no group homes or special needs schools or state hospitals at all. It was a gut-wrenching decision, but Dede lived in the Magnolia Cottage with the dearest, most loving housemother named Mrs. Maddox, who met all of her needs. Mrs. Maddox had a record player, and Dede loved music. She had the Augusta Hospital and doctors for every possible medical issue.

We drove to visit Dede whenever possible on weekends. It made a pleasant family outing even though we missed Dede at home and were forever sad about the situation. One day Daddy stopped the car at a fence in the country so we could see the cows up close. Being a city girl, when a cow mooed, I proclaimed that I had always thought the moo came out of the horns. My whole family roared with laughter. My siblings will never let me off the hook from that day. They will tease me about my gross ignorance forever!

I remember once when Daddy was holding Dede in the Crane's swimming pool, and tears were streaming down his face. It was often hard having a special needs sibling. Some children were very cruel and made fun of her with that hateful "R" word. I missed brushing her hair and singing to her and rocking her. Mama had always dressed her so cute in the beautiful little Ruth Original dresses. She took her to Margaret's hair salon for cuts and permanents. There was definitely a Dede-sized hole in our hearts when she moved away. In reality she got more and better attention at Gracewood. The social workers told us that she was content and very well adapted to her life and environment.

Chapter 7
Grades 7, 8:
And She's Off, Out the Gate!

Our amazing seventh grade teacher was Miss Crawford. Everything she did was so engaging and interesting. Our wooden desks were arranged around three sides of the large rectangular class room. The desks had arms and a book storage space under the seat. I was fortunate to be able to get a left-handed desk. In the center of the room were tables with six chairs each. These were for science activities and group projects and so forth. Our teacher brought a tape recorder, and that was the first time I had ever heard my own voice. My exact words were: In my father's travels he brings back interesting candies to us. (Those would have been from China Town and Little Italy in Greenwich Village in New York.)

Miss Crawford's desk was up front in front of the blackboard, and yes, it was black. We wrote with white chalk. There were no such thing as white boards with colored markers. My desk was halfway back, fortunately for Clara Closetphobia on the window side. I was having difficulty reading things on the board and was writing assignments down incorrectly. Mama took me to the local optometrist, Dr. Reagan, and I got some pearly pink glasses for simple myopia, or near-sightedness. I wore them only in class.

Also, I was not adjusting well to having a developing figure. Growing up seemed like a pain and an inconvenience. I wanted no part of womanhood yet! Mama bought me my first bra, and guess what genius idea I designed? If you turn the bra inside-out and take a one-inch tuck in the cup, it rather flattens you a bit and hides the teenage top blossoms. Before long I embraced the new era of my life and unstitched those bras. We had only the most awful razors then, and I went through plenty of small Band-Aids while grooming my legs. Thank heaven for Venus, our current goddess of razors! And don't forget the tiny cordless battery-operated Braun bodyscapers.

One of the joys of a big seventh grader was being a safety patrol with the white belt and shiny silver badge. Our belts had to be washed regularly and folded a certain way when not in use. The patrol captain inspected them weekly. My post was on the front steps of the school where fourth, fifth, sixth and seventh graders lined up by grade before school. Mary Tolbert and I had to keep the lines straight and the children quiet and orderly. We stood at the top of three steps. School started at 8:30 am sharp. My job was to ring the very old, large, brass bell with a wooden handle. You could practically hear it all over the neighborhood. It seemed as old as the Liberty Bell. I felt very important and authoritative.

One day the bell handle loosened from the bell and it pinched the fire out of hand and made a small wound that bled a sum total of about three drops of blood. Our principal, Mrs. Burgess had the custodian put a reinforcement screw on the side, and that did not happen again. No, my parents did not sue anyone. We were raised to be tough and brave and suck it up. Accidents happen. Get over it!

The school and the teachers were highly revered and honored and respected at all times. Most students behaved at school other than a few rowdy boys who probably had an extra Y chromosome and were genetic risk takers. Who knew? No one, so they constantly had to stay after school and write hundreds of sentences: I will behave in class. I will not be a clown in class. I will use my inside voice. I will not throw spit balls.

Schools had a monthly paper sale to raise money for the PTA (Parent Teacher Association). Families subscribed to the Atlanta Constitution or the Atlanta Journal newspaper. That was just a given. It was fun to take a little red wagon up and down the street with your friends and collect papers from neighbors, even in freezing cold weather. On the day of the sale there were cardboard signs on wooden stakes for each class grades one through seven. We had no public Kindergarten then and no middle schools. Your parents drove you to school with the papers, and you set them out by your class sign. Then a PTA mom measured the stacks with a yardstick. There was a first, second and third place prize for the largest pile of paper. We had no pizza then for ourselves or our pet dinosaurs, and I do not remember what the prizes were. Might have been Krispy Kreme donuts. The PTA used the sale money to buy books for the library, have a Halloween carnival in the fall and Field Day in the spring.

Our principal's daughter, Barbara Ann Burgess, had the heart problem called being a "blue baby." It had something to do with her blood being Rh negative. There was a very fine surgeon in Washington, DC who had developed the first open heart surgery for this problem. Mr. and Mrs. Burgess took Babs to Washington when she was eighteen years old. The surgery was not successful, and sadly she died. I remember the day of the surgery when Miss Crawford told us that Babs did not make it. We all sat in our desks and cried for a long time. Beautiful Babs had been written up in the Sunday Magazine section of the 'Atlanta Journal' that year regarding her high school graduation formal dress. Girls wore long, white fancy dresses with hoop skirts to graduation. It was made by a lady in the neighborhood named Mrs. Wells. It had one hundred yards of white net and was a fluffy, ethereal creation that was out of this world, created for some fairy tale princess.

I was still often that tomboy ballerina at heart, loving the woods and the creek and tree climbing. One day far back in the woods, I discovered a very tall, red clay mud cliff. Someone had dug out a roomy little cave on the side about half way up. There was a ledge which made it easy to ascend and go in the cave. I went home so excited at this find. When Daddy got home, I told him all about it. The next day he came home from work early. We made sack lunches with cheese and mayo sandwiches and apples and hiked to the cave and had a memorable picnic. Daddy figured out how to attach a rope to a sturdy tree the next time we went so that we could swing across the little canyon. What a fun adventure! I will cherish that memory of my hands-on Daddy forever. He was never too busy or too tired to do the dad things. I believe he truly enjoyed being our daddy. He knew how to delegate authority at his stores so that he could have plenty of leisure time. And Mama equaled him in the "We Love Our Mommy Club."

My parents frequently took us to Avondale Lake in the Avondale part of Decatur. Downtown Avondale is built in the English Tudor style with white stucco half-timbered buildings. We made wooden toy boats and sailed them on that lake. One day when it was particularly windy, a beautiful little boat turned over and sank out in the deep middle. After that, we had thick strings on our boats to make them retrievable. The grass was often tall by the lake, and one day Eric found a perfect, fancy, black Parker fountain pen with a shiny, silver cap. Four-year-old little brother had no use for it nor any idea of its value, so I bought it from him for $.25. I still have that pen, and it writes after lo these many decades.

There was a large, open field in Avondale where we sailed kites and watched eclipses with Mama and Daddy. For eclipses Daddy gave us a piece of smoked glass or a photo negative to protect our eyes. Some kites were homemade, and some were store bought. It was great fun, and we were never rushed or in a hurry. Later, that field became the site of Avondale High School. Life was laid back and leisurely. Schedules were flexible and stress free. Families had time for quality time together making memories. Studies show that involved dads are very necessary for teen boys and girls. They encourage various behaviors and negate the negative ones.

Saturday mornings often included a trip to the kiddie movie at the Decatur Theatre. At home we had a very few children's shows like 'The Little Rascals' and black and white cartoons. The movie cost $.25 and candy was a nickel, and popcorn was $.10 per box with no extra luxury fake chemical butter bath. Since I did not care for chocolate, my favorite candy was the Good and Plenty licorice and the Black Cow caramel sucker. I hated the smell of Reese's cups. There was no peanut butter at our house since Eric and Kim were allergic. We watched cartoons. Some were in color, and some were black and white like 'Mighty Mouse', 'Popeye' and 'Tom and Jerry'. The newsreels were black and white. Daddy liked to pay for a $.50 adult ticket and sit in the theatre when he was tired and take a nap.

One afternoon I went to the movies alone and sat half way down on the far-left side. It was summer, and I had on shorts. A man came and sat beside me. That Pillsbury Dough Boy Son of a Biscuit put his hand on my leg! No adult in the family or at school had ever mentioned the stranger danger of predators to us. We knew to not take candy from strangers or get in a car with a stranger, but that was it. No one spoke about molestation. It was as if no such thing existed in Decatur, Georgia. Anyway, it gave me a creepy feeling that something was very wrong, so I got up and moved to the far-right side. I did not know that I should go to a trustworthy cinema employee and report the man. But he did not follow me, so it ended alright. I don't even remember telling my parents about it. I was the proud, brave girl that could tell Little Miss Muffet she better tough it!

Early Saturday morning I went to Junior Choir practice in the choir room at the church. It was girls grades seven through twelve. The director was Mr. Herbert. He was a middle-aged man with sparse amount of white hair and the physique of a baritone opera singer. He was kind and patient and I stayed in the choir for years. Jean, Elizabeth, Susan, Pat, Jane, Anne and I plus some others sang from the choir loft on Sunday evenings and then went down and sat in the pews for the remainder of the service. I loved our pastor, Reverend Crawley. Somehow, he made the Bible and the Gospel so real to me. He was highly revered in our community. (And after Sunday night church he toked on ciggies with Daddy and the other civic leaders under the streetlight on the Barry Street side of the church.)

Mama and Daddy were the recreation counselors for seventh graders after Sunday night church. We played games and had refreshments. Daddy went to the library and checked out a book about games. The most embarrassing one was called "If you love me, please smile." A girl or boy would go up to a boy or girl, get down on one knee and ask the question: If you love me, please smile. If the kid did not smile, whoever was it had to go to another kid of the opposite sex and ask the question. If they smiled, then they were it. Thankfully the entire City of Decatur adored my parents and thought they could do no wrong. Otherwise, I might have died of embarrassment. Sometime the preteens came to our house, and Daddy or Mama did a slide show with our projector. They showed our family vacations and birthday parties and holidays and such family events.

I had started doing the ballroom dance classes. I was scheduled to attend a dance at Glenwood School with Bobby who was in my piano class. He was called a sissy for playing piano, but he was very smart and later became a fine physician with a wife and children. A mean girl with a broomstick and flying monkeys commented that I should not go to a dance with a "girl". I ignored her! Mean girls could not get to me anymore.

Mama attempted to make me a beautiful, long formal dress for the dance. She bought yards and yards of peacock blue silk organza and taffeta. She chose a chain of small rhinestones for the belt. There was something about the fit and style of that dress that just did not suit me from hell to breakfast. I really felt guilty, but I detested that dress. She even asked the neighborhood seamstress, Mrs. Cogbill, to finish it. It never got finished. Yes, you guessed it. I felt fat in that dress. She purchased one for me that was comfortable, flattering to my satisfaction and fit correctly, and that was the end of that! Or rather that was the beginning of my missing the heavenly peacock blue chiffon and taffeta fabric and feeling guilty for wasting the money. Nonetheless, Mama probably gave it to one of Lula's nieces who finished it and loved lit to pieces!

In the spring the seventh-grade patrols went on a train trip to Washington, DC and then on to New York. It was fun and exciting. The only downside was the dorky uniforms the girls wore. We purchased them at the Belk Gallant store on North McDonough. The skirt was a smoke gray twill fabric in an A line style. The blouse was a short-sleeve lighter gray with buttons. We wore our patrol belts and badges. If I could imagine how reform school uniforms look, I would say those patrol outfits were carbon copies more than likely! Nonetheless, the trip was completely successful and enjoyable. The parent chaperones said we were very well behaved and cooperative.

I actually like to do household chores and cooking. One job was defrosting the refrigerator for Mama. I was careful enough to safely put a pot of boiling water in the freezer to melt the buildup of ice. We had to make our own ice cubes in aluminum ice trays with dividers that yielded individual cubes. I learned to bake cakes and make pie crust from scratch. It was fun to separate eggs and make fluffy, sweet meringue in Mama's Sunbeam Mixmaster. We put this on top of the lemon meringue pie that Daddy adored. I liked making sugar cookie dough and cutting out the Christmas cookies.

Moms had funny-looking kitchen tables covered with Formica like our counter tops. The aluminum chairs had plastic padded seats. I hear that style is called "Early Beauty Parlor." Mumsie and Grandmother always made fruitcake, and I actually liked it! Grandmother soaked her fruitcake in Manischewitz blackberry wine, but Mumsie was a teetotaler who never went near any alcohol unless it was isopropyl rubbing variety for wounds. However, when she was in her eighties her doctor said, "Now Miss Lucie, when you have bronchitis, you need one tablespoon of scotch every two hours." I had to buy it for her at the Toco Hills liquor store, because she would not have been caught dead in such a sinful place!

Mary Tolbert lived next to Ginny on Mimosa Drive through the woods from me. We were fast friends, good students and very well-behaved young ladies that never got a U for unsatisfactory in conduct. We called Mary Tolbert "Tollie". One afternoon we were sitting on Tollie's tall front steps while her mom was at the store, and I got a wild idea. I guess it's a teen and preteen thing to have thoughts that perhaps should not have been thought or done. Nonetheless, I asked Tollie to bring me some paper drinking straws, some Kleenex tissues and some matches. Straws were plain white paper spiraled into a straw and coated in paraffin to make them waterproof. Somehow, I took miniscule shreds of tissue and used a toothpick to stuff them into a straw. When the straw was jam-packed full, I lit one end, and we tried to smoke it. This obviously did not work or last long. We had the good sense to realize that it was a bad idea though an interesting concept. I wonder why the paraffin did not flame up and burn us! Weary guardian angels were standing by as per usual! Once a DeKalb County Extension agent told me: Teenagers will smoke peanut butter if you tell them they will get high from it!

Seventh graders always gave a class gift to the school at the end of the year. To fund this project, we sold taffy for $.10 for a seven-inch roll which was wrapped in wax paper. It came in four flavors: Chocolate, vanilla, strawberry and lemon. I remember eating quite a bit on the walk home from school. Perhaps that is why my brain was "stuck together with taffy", and I have no earthly memory as to what gift my class gave the school! Thankfully I inherited my dad's very strong healthy teeth.

At the beginning of eighth grade, Mama took me to a Merle Normal makeup studio to learn to care for my skin properly and get some cosmetics. I was fortunate to have clear skin with only a rare blemish. We removed makeup with sticky, pleasant smelling pink cold cream, and wiped it off with tissues. Then there was the peach-colored facial mask that smelled horrid like industrial chemicals and burned my skin somewhat. It had to dry and stay on for about twenty minutes. At home our shampoo had egg in it for the protein. If your hair was a bit dirty and there was no time for washing it, you rubbed corn meal all on your hair and scalp to absorb the oil. Then you brushed and shook it all out.

Mama took me to a hairstylist named Jerry at Clairmont and North Decatur Road. He cut my hair in the ducktail style with the entire back brushed up. My hair was soft and fine and naturally curly, so he sold Mama a heat lamp for me to sit under. It encouraged the curls. My haircut was also called a lamp cut. Girls with longer hair rolled a lock around their finger and secured it with a bobby pin. This was called pin curls. We had metal rollers that were like a spring covered in plastic mesh.

Mama took me to select some perfume. Many teens wore Evening in Paris cologne. Together we decided that it would be Tigress cologne by Faberge'. That was very appropriate. Though I looked like the most innocent little angelic miss, there was definitely a little tiger inside that was full of feistiness and perseverance. I started wearing stockings and gloves and hats to church. Mama bought me beautiful kid gloves in black and navy. We had no panty hose, so our nylon stockings were held up with very uncomfortable, binding garter belts. If you damaged your stocking and got a "run," you could stop the run by putting a little clear nail polish on either end of the run. For Valentine's Day one year Daddy gave Mama a pair of stockings with Chantilly lace at the top.

In high school, girls were old enough to wear straight skirts with the zipper and button in the back. There was a pleat called a kick pleat so that one could take larger steps. Shirt waist dresses were very popular, and I had them in all the pastel colors for spring and summer. We bought dime store brand white tennis shoes and dyed them colors to match our shorts outfits. We wore nylon head scarves in the winter. In December we had Christmas corsages for our coat lapels. They had tiny pine cones, red or silver ribbon and plastic holly. Our wool slipover sweaters had round necks. We purchased lacey white collars that snapped on.

The veterans sold little, red, crepe paper lapel poppies for $.10 to raise money for the VFW, Veterans of Foreign Wars. Daddy sold tons of friendships rings, circle pins along with bathing suits, sportswear, dresses, costume jewelry, lingerie and sleepwear. Accessories sold for about $1,00. If someone wanted a fur coat or evening dress, Daddy's New York buying office, Steinberg-Katz, sent exactly what the customer wanted in their size and color. I was a terribly spoiled princess. If I saw a cute outfit in 'Seventeen Magazine,' it could be in my closet in about two weeks. Of course, that was Madison Avenue type advertising and was superb for our business.

Mama was good about taking us on fun, educational outings. She was influenced by Granddaddy who took his children on mountain hikes to learn the names of all the vegetation, animals, rocks and birds. She took us with Lula to the Catawba River. There were Catawba trees on the banks loaded with Catawba worms. Lula gathered worms and used them for fishing bait. I thought it was kind of creepy when the plump green worms fell down on us! We saw kids rafting down the river on innertubes. We also went to Soapstone Ridge south of Atlanta, a twenty-five square mile area rich with a mineral called metapyroxenite which is similar to soapstone which can be carved. It is in the talc family.

One year we had Granddaddy's younger sisters as house guests. Aunt Dettie (Odessa) was the first female attorney to practice law in the Supreme Court of Georgia. Her specialty was real estate law. Her deceased husband, Uncle Steve Hilsman, had been a diamond merchant in Africa. She wore black opera type sparkly dresses all the time and had diamond bracelets on both arms up to her elbows and diamond rings on every finger except the thumbs. To call her eccentric was an understatement. She and her brother, Edgar, owned motels in Jacksonville, Florida. They called them the Hilsmoore Motels. Aunt Dettie was so much fun and generously gave us lots of dollar bills.

Aunt Lila was a famous water-color artist who painted flowers. She was called "The Camellia Lady." How did she become so well-known? They had a cousin named Claire Merritt Hodgson Ruth. She was from Athens, Georgia where her staunchly Methodist father, Dr. James Merritt, taught law at the University of Georgia. Claire married an old, well to do gentleman, had a daughter and was widowed young. She went to New York. Long story short, she was Babe Ruth's second wife. That was when her father disowned her. He said, "Babe Ruth is a Yankee and a Catholic and he drinks whiskey!" When Aunt Lila visited Claire and Babe, he was very impressed with her art and got her a showing at Madison Square Garden. I saw two of her magnolias prints in the lady's room at the London Hilton in 1967.

Papa's sisters Hilda, Mildred, Helen and Ellie came from Cleveland, Ohio also. Hilda worked for Western Union. Mildred was a legal secretary, Helen worked at Halle's department store, and Ellie was a dental hygienist. Mama was very good to them, but there was so much culture shock. She did not understand Yankees altogether, and they did not understand the south that well. Their parents had been Jewish, and Gramma Fannie kept a kosher kitchen. Still, Papa's sisters had a hotplate in the cellar. They cooked bacon by an open window, and their mother never knew! They spoiled us a lot with nice gifts and were warmly affectionate and fun loving. They were all hard workers, and family ties meant the world to them.

The summer before eighth grade, my parents signed me up for summer school typing class. This was not optional! They believed every girl must know how to type and go to college to get a teaching certificate. This was just in case her husband died, and she had to support little ones. It really was not so bad since my dear friend Ginny was in my typing class. The daily session lasted a couple of hours in the morning, and then we could go to the pool or the movie or the drug store for lunch. Only boys were allowed at Tatum's drug store lunch counter on East Court Square. For some reason, if a girl went in there, she was labeled as a tramp. So, we stayed far away from there. Woolworth's ten cent store had a lunch counter, and so did the Jacob's drug store on East Ponce de Leon.

My eighth-grade teacher for English and Science was Mrs. Juanita Goforth who was new to Decatur High. We realized we were in a class with the gifted students even though it was not called that. Mrs. Goforth read in my file that I was wonderful at creative writing. I had written a book in seventh grade. She appointed me to write the script for the fall Stunt Night program. I had never been to a Stunt Night like the students with older siblings, so I was clueless. It was supposed to be a musical with a dilemma and a moral to the story at the end. I wrote something about television news clips. I was the NBC peacock. I made the tail from wire coat hangers stuffed with rainbow-colored crepe paper, and it could actually open and close like the peacock on TV. Our principal Mr. Purcell's daughter, Claudia was dressed like a Native American. She was supposedly putting out a pretend campfire and accidently poured a bucket of water on the footlights. Stunt Night was halted until the custodians could replace the bulbs. I felt humiliated that our stunt was so wrong, but my classmates did not seem to notice and praised me for my creativity and thought of me as intelligent and a leader.

The next two years Peggy and Mary and Billie and I got the clues and wrote wonderful scripts, and I designed fabulous costumes, sets and props. Ninth-grade was a skit about business letters and love letters and so forth locked in a post office because of a villain named Black Mail. To the tune of Pat Boone's song, 'Love Letters in the Sand,' I wrote "Love Letters Stranded Here". Tenth-grade we were the inside of a sick horse. The villains were the bacteria and viruses. The classic line I wrote was, "At ease, disease. These are fungus among us!"

Mr. Phillips taught us Math and Georgia History in the afternoons. He had been my dad's math teacher twenty-one years previously. I loved Algebra! History, take it or leave it other than biographies. When Mr. Phillips stood at the blackboard writing equations, if he heard one peep behind him, he turned around like a bolt of lightning and threw his chalk eraser like a bat out of hell right square at that kid's head. We mostly knew we better behave in that class, but we loved him dearly and really learned a lot from him. Surprise! No parents sued him for abuse or tried to have him fired. They wanted their teens to behave in school, accept authority and focus on learning.

I hated P.E. because of the ugly, royal blue, one-piece jumpsuit uniform with a metal clasp to hold the belt together. To me, the locker room was the pit of hell because of my modesty. Thankfully, I had no more P.E. after joining the band!

Wanting to be a majorette for ninth-grade the next year, I had to be in the marching band. They were out of small, feminine girl-type instruments like clarinets and flutes, so I happily took the last instrument available which was a huge baritone horn. Mama and Daddy would have bought me an instrument, but the gargantuan horn suited me just fine. I liked the way it sounded. Of course, it was a little bit gross when you had to empty the spit valve. I was the only girl in the brass section. The boys played tuba, trumpet, trombone and French horn. Due to some crazy reason, I tried out for drill team that spring instead of majorettes. The judges said my routine was wonderful, but I did not smile. That was my signal to go back to the baton. Our band director was Mr. Miller. He was quietly eased on down the road for dating a senior girl who played in the band. They later married and had a long, happy life together.

The Christmas dance was called the Snowball, and a nice young man invited me. Daddy ordered me an emerald green long dress to die for. The long-waisted strapless bodice was satin folds, and the skirt was endless layers and yards of net. I wore what was called a Claxton Hoop underneath. It was a collapsible, three tier, white, plastic structure that reminded me of the safety gates we put on the doors when my siblings were small. You can only imagine how difficult it was to get into and sit in a car with such contraptions! I will not even mention trips to the lady's room which could challenge an aeronautical engineer! The Saturday morning of the dance, several girls and I rode the bus down to the Dale Striebel beauty school on Ponce de Leon Avenue. We had our hair done free. The piece de resistance was the thick layer of bright green glitter on my bangs. It was stuck there with stinky hair lacquer.

When the young man's brother drove him to pick me up, my seven-year-old brother ran like the wind to answer the door and shouted loud enough for God and all the angels to hear, "Oh, so you are the boy Julie says she is going to marry!" I had said no such thing whatsoever. I was ready to have Mama and Daddy lock him up in a reform school in Outer Mongolia and throw away the key!

Susan and I did a science fair project together that involved a little white mouse. Unfortunately, the mouse got loose in the school and was missing for several days. When the custodian found it, it was filthy dirty and looked more like a gray mouse. I don't remember what the project was, but we obviously did not win any prize ribbons!

The high school was a block down the hill from Daddy's store on McDonough Street, so he drove me to school in the mornings. After school, all the teens walked home together, carrying our heavy stack of textbooks. Can you believe no one had thought of backpacks yet? We stopped at Watson's Drugs for snacks. We ate grilled cheese sandwiches and drank cherry cokes and my favorite, fresh limeade with cherry syrup. There were chocolate and vanilla milkshakes which I did not like. My parents had a charge account at Watson's so I could purchase lipstick or shampoo or bobby pins and barrettes for hair and such.

On Saturday nights many eighth graders went to the Decatur Recreation Center next to the library. Parents took turns being chaperones. They played music for us, and we danced and socialized. We knew the Stroll and were learning to do the Twist. It lasted for about two hours from 7pm to 9pm. Surprisingly, I don't remember any refreshments being served. No one could get away with that in today's world! Young people today expect chips and dips, cookies, ice cream, pizza, chicken nuggets and so forth. Amusements were few and far between. We could go to Stone Mountain for picnics and climbing the mountain or swimming in the quarry. Once a year the county fair came, but my parents were not real big on honky-tonk situations with cheap thrills and "Made in Japan" prizes and trinkets.

We had winter snow probably at least once a year or so for a day or two at the most. There was obviously no school on those days, though we could have walked to school. The Decatur System was small with houses close to the schools, so there were no school buses. The DeKalb County School System was spread out more and was still more rural with lots of farms, so they needed buses. They even still had a few small schools with pot-bellied stoves for heat. The very best hill in town for sledding was West Ponce de Leon Avenue near Trinity Place at the beginning of the Druid Hills area. It was plenty steep for a great sled ride on a card board box or metal trash can lid. A few kids had real sleds. We walked in the snow all the way from home to downtown Decatur to sled with dozens of teens. There was no ice skating since there were never any frozen ponds. To ice skate, one had to go downtown to the ice rink. No one ever got hurt, and I do not even remember feeling cold even though we didn't really have snow boots, and our socks were pretty wet. Nearby moms were always happy to provide bathrooms and cookies and hot chocolate. Our version of Door Dash was simply dash to the nearest door!

Chapter 8
Grades Nine & Ten: Succeed & Win

Ninth-grade was fairly uneventful altogether. Things went smoothly, and I had made some good friends. I had more tenth-grade friends than ninth, but Ginny from elementary school was still my bestie. My church friends were nice, and I was elected president of the MYF, Methodist Youth Fellowship for two years in a row. We met on Sunday evenings before church. It began with a picnic-type supper on white paper plates in the fellowship hall. That typically consisted of a sandwich, potato chips and a cookie. Then we had a devotional type program with some kind of topic that was relevant for teens. Pat and I took turns playing the hymns on the piano. She was much better at that than I was. I was too fearful of hitting a wrong note and getting embarrassed. Our pastor, Reverend Frank Crawley, was a true man of God who was down to earth and so relatable. I loved to hear him preach.

I liked the girls in the youth choir, and some were upper classmen. The alto soloist, Dianne, worked part-time in Daddy's store as a junior saleslady. I thought I was something else when I got to eat lunch with her at Tom's café next door to David's. In those days no one had heard of "vegan", so we ate things that had parents. She was probably bored to tears with an underclassman my age. Tom always gave me one piece of Double Bubble bubble gum. Tom was from Greece, and his daughter, Tilly, worked there as a server. There was a lunch counter, but I loved the booths that had juke boxes. We put in a nickel and selected the song of our choice from printed lists on the box. There was one song that Daddy hated with a passion: Maybelline by Chuck Berry. I went to Clark's Music Store on Sycamore Street and bought that record for $1.00 and played it at home to tease him. Oddly, the record kind of disappeared into thin air for good. We also had pocket-size transistor radios. Mine was a tiny one the size of a deck of cards, silver color, and Mama had my name engraved on it in case I lost it.

Clarks gave us a fun pastime. Their son, Harry, sang in the Methodist choir, and was kind of a hero to me. Mr. & Mrs. Clark had listening booths. We were allowed to try out 45 records before purchasing. Mama bought a couple of 33 1/3 records there per month. She selected classical, Gilbert and Sullivan operettas, Broadway musicals like 'My Fair Lady' and 'South Pacific'. She bought popular albums of showtunes and movie soundtracks from artists like Ferrante and Teicher. I liked to play my favorites by ear like 'The Apartment' and 'Exodus.' Mama made sure that we were exposed to the whole gamut of musical works to go along with our home library of intellectual periodicals like 'American Heritage' and 'Horizon.' Clarks was also the place to buy batons and fire batons. I purchased many and still have several and especially like to twirl the fire baton on New Year's Eve.

Hula hoops came out that year. They were fun for everyone, but I can tell you for certain that high school girls played with them to trim their waistlines. Kathleen and I spent hours having a contest to see who could do the most hula hoop circles without the hoop falling to the ground. That was around the time when pop beads were invented. They were plastic beads of many colors that could be fitted together in any sequence of colors that one desired. Truthfully, I thought they were tacky and did not desire them at all!

I was the stereotyped bright, A type personality young woman who developed IBS and reflux. I say, "IBS" stands for I've Been Sliced. (Twice by a surgeon to repair the strange genetic relationship twist between stomach and esophagus.) My sisters have the same. Women with this disorder can get what I call "cornstillpated" if you catch my drift. My stomach promised me the moon, but gave me the outhouse with a moon-shaped window on the door.

This was the year when my friend, Jimbo, went away to Baylor Military School in Chattanooga, Tennessee. He invited me to several formal dances. Mama drove me there. I had a pretty long pink formal with sparkly beads on the bodice and a long white dress decorated with tiny pearls. The semi-formal was fuchsia satin with thin straps. The bottom had three tiers with petal shaped layers.

I mentioned to my friends about a plan to redecorate my bedroom. Herb, a strapping young football star, offered to help me. He lived walking distance away and went places with Kathleen, Linda, Ginny, Frank and me. We chose a white and purple decor. Herb painted my walls white. By then we thankfully had acrylic water-based paint for easy clean-ups. I wanted bright purple carpet, so Mama ordered some from St. Clair Carpet on Church Street. I had lots of plastic purple violets in little white, porcelain vases that looked like miniature, antique bowl and pitcher sets. Mama made a white, organdy bedspread with two layers of gathered ruffles on the side skirt. I kept the organdy canopy from the previous ensemble.

Daddy continued to take me on an Eastern Airlines plane to New York every summer so that he could drop me off at Aunt Judy's. We saw the sights like the Statue of Liberty, Empire State Building, Rockefeller Center, the Rockettes at Radio City Music Hall and so forth. We ate at the automat which was a very fun, new experience. You found the food you wanted, put money in a slot, and the glass door for that item opened. Papa's cousin, Fauncie and her husband, owned a restaurant on Broadway called Headquarters. It served international fare including some dishes inspired by their Austro-Hungarian ancestry. That was where Broadway stars had late dinners after the shows. Fauncie's husband had been a chef for General Dwight Eisenhower during World War II. Eisenhower gave him a huge bonus that enabled them to open the very nice restaurant. One day when Daddy and I were there for lunch it was quite hot and humid in the days before air-condition units. Free-spirted Fauncie said a small apology and then unhooked her brassiere and pulled it off through her short-sleeved blouse. So, who needed an HVAC?

There was a nice, Italian boy up the street from Judy named Frederico. We watched a lot of black and white TV together at Judy's. She popped in every few minutes to chaperone. In those days the favorite shows were 'I Love Lucy', 'My Little Margie,' 'Topper' and 'The Loretta Young Show.' At Fred's house, his dad taught me how to play pool which was loads of fun even though I was borderline not so hot. It was quite an event when Fred's family took me to an authentic Italian restaurant. I wore a cotton sateen, mint-green dress with pleated skirt, Irish lace trim and leg o mutton sleeves. Thankfully no pasta sauce spilled on my princess dress. That was my first time to try spumoni. That is Italian ice cream with small bits of fruit in it. It was wonderfully tasty!

I helped out a lot with the little cousins. Now we had baby Kelly David. Sweet, precious Kathy had not been born yet. The bathtub was a fun splash blast. I can promise you that Cousin Jon, the famous East Coast sculptor, started young trying to "sculpt" in the bathtub. But older brother, Chris, who later raced sailboats to Hawaii, would say, "Julie, Shonny (Jon) made a boat!" Incidentally, little Jon was totally convinced that I was the Disney child star Hayley Mills, and he told his friends that. Mikey was my little shadow and sat outside the bathroom door waiting for me. Chris was well-behaved.

Tenth grade was a mixed bag, for sure! I was on top of the world being a majorette and marching in parades around Decatur and doing the dance/twirl routines at football half-time. We filled quart-sized glass jars with gasoline from Mr. Parker's Texaco station on Church Street. This was for our fire batons. We had drum major type hats and wore white leather boots. The uniform was long-sleeved, and the skirt was mid-thigh length. I don't recall feeling cold at October and November games.

I had many fine friends and we were basically good kids. I really loved studying Latin. Our teacher was Mrs. Brown. She made it engaging. In December we had a Roman Saturnalia festival and wore togas made from white, cotton bedsheets. I was very diligent with Algebra II and all of the other subjects. Science was very interesting. I loved working in the lab, but dissecting a worm and a frog, maybe not! The problem was the nauseating smell of formaldehyde. English was easy, and literature was fun.

Somewhere in the Maud Burrus Decatur Library, I had read about the beginning of life on earth. There was an article about how electrical charges from lightning had probably struck inorganic chemical elements and turned them into organic chemicals. Then one-celled animals like amoeba, paramecium evolved. Sea creatures, birds, mammals, insects and so forth came on the scene after millions of years. This article had a drawing of a glass lab apparatus used by a scientist to supposedly prove his theory. I was so fascinated that I showed the article to my parents. Mama picked up on my excitement and made it her mission to help me bring this project to completion even though it was way too advanced for a teen. I was precocious, but Mama believed I was related to Sir Isaac Newton or Einstein. All I knew about Euripides was that if you "rip a deese" pants, you have to mend them with a needle and thread!

Mama contacted the lab glass blower at Georgia Tech, Mr. Don Lilly. He agreed to make that complex glass form and mount it on a 3 foot by 4-foot piece of plywood. We went to the Chemistry Department at Emory University with some football bladders. A chemistry professor filled one bladder with oxygen, one with nitrogen and one with probably hydrogen. Long story short,

I never was able to complete the experiment using the electricity, but I made a solid A++ in science that year. We kept the glass structure in the basement until it later got broken somehow.

Kathleen and I had our wisdom teeth removed that Thanksgiving week by the oral surgeon, Dr. Allsup, who was the best in town. We were overnight at Piedmont Hospital in the same room. I got scared the night before the procedure and got in Kathleen's bed for comfort. A nurse reported me missing, but they found me pretty quickly. The surgery went well, but my mouth got seriously infected and was very painful. Being the brave oldest child, I never liked to complain. My body and brain were desperately poisoned, and I had amnesia for six weeks in a hospital/rest home.

It was very interesting and inspiring that the thing that reminded me who I was, was my sheet music of Chopin's Prelude in C. The doctor sat me on a piano bench in front of my music, and all of a sudden, I was back which was a great blessing. It was hard to go back to school. My friends and teachers were very patient and supportive and understanding, but I felt like a strange and different person from another planet. It was a hard adjustment. The other downside was that I was still a little disoriented. It was harder to find my way around the three school buildings, and I had a fear of getting lost wherever I went for a long time.

The scriptures tell us in the eighth chapter of the Book of Romans that all things work together for good to them that love God and are called according to His purpose. I learned all about art, music and dance therapy in that rest home. This was invaluable when teaching special needs children later in life in the DeKalb School System. Also, it enabled me to be very effective going to war-torn Bosnia after the five-year siege to work with traumatized children and teens. I love the last chapter of the Book of Genesis when Joseph tells his brothers: Evil meant what you did to me for evil, but God has used it for good. The dear Lord can prevent things, but when He allows them, there is always a purpose that we would not have guessed. His ways and thoughts really are way above what our finite minds can think or dream.

All of the teachers liked me, because I studied hard and had outstanding conduct and knew how to smooze them like a pro. I probably would have been a Class A great snake oil salesperson! The lady teachers bought much of their clothing from Daddy, and I must say, what could be more humiliating than having to fit your English teacher for a girdle! It made me feel very shy and embarrassed. Yes, women teachers were expected to be ladylike and wear girdles under their skirts. Flopping behinds and cleavage showing were considered lewd and totally unacceptable in our polite society. We wore slips and half-slips under our dresses. Slips and bra straps were not supposed to show. If your slip showed, a dutiful friend said, "It's snowing down south." That meant go pull your slip up. Very few offspring dared to bring dishonor on their parents' names. I believe it was a good thing, though one will always find a few hypocrites or judgmental, critical citizens who are "holier than thou." Girls from nice families were told that you could never marry a nice boy if you were not a good girl. We had a lot of fear in that department and guarded our reputations.

Tenth grade was the landmark year to learn to drive. Mama had a little baby blue Thunderbird, and she was the primary instructor. No telling how many times we went to the church parking lot to practice turns and parallel parking and everything. She was very patient and calm and made it easy to learn and have lots of self-confidence. She was never in a hurry, so the lessons were really relaxed. Daddy had the little burgundy-colored MG. He taught me to drive a stick shift and was also an excellent teacher. We bought our gas for $.20 a gallon at Johnny Newsome or Mr. Parker's Texaco stations. They filled the tank, checked the oil and washed the windshield. What a deal! Streets had only two lanes, and traffic was light, so driving was not so challenging like today.

At Decatur High, the standard way to make money for your class dances and projects was to sell boxes of Krispy Kreme doughnuts on street corners on Saturday morning in groups. It is hard to believe, but a dozen doughnuts sold for $.50 total. I probably sold hundreds of boxes over the years. When you are a teenager and your metabolism is like a Pittsburgh steel factory fiery furnace, you can put away quite a few doughnuts with zero weight gain. But I tried to be disciplined since Mama always said, "You are what you eat." She made up a little story about Puggies. They were the round, naughty nutrition squad that lived in doughnut holes and ate only cookies, candy, cake and ice cream. I would think, "I can have three cookies or jelly beans: One for the Father, the Son and the Holy Ghost." Problem was you want to eat one also for Matthew, Mark, Luke and John, right?

My majorette friend Jeannie's parents were separated. Her dad lived down in Cocoa Beach, Florida at Cape Canaveral, later named Cape Kennedy. We rode a Greyhound bus down there to see the very famous launching of John Glenn into space for his record-breaking three-day orbit around the earth. It was ultra-exciting, and something I could never forget. We enjoyed the beach and did some shopping. Jeannie bought a red bathing suit with red fringe from top to bottom. She looked like a cute Vegas showgirl for sure. I knew better than to show up back at home in such a grown-up suit. My parents would have had a flying fit or sent me to the circus to be a trapeze artist! I imagine Jeannie hid her suit from her mom. I don't know if she ever wore it in Decatur at the neighborhood pools.

We had city pools called Glen Lake and McCoy. It cost about a quarter to get in. Venetian was a private pool club that cost a whopping fifty cents and was very fancy. That was where we had majorette camp in the summer before football season. No one knew about the dangers of sunburn, so we lathered ourselves with baby oil infused with iodine and got lobster red on more than one occasion. My dermatologist makes a lot of money from me at the annual checkup zapping pre-cancerous spots on my forehead with liquid nitrogen.

Kathleen's grandparents lived nearby at Pine Lake. They had a wonderful swimming pool with dressing rooms and so forth. Dr. Threadgill had originally owned Watson's Pharmacy before he retired. One Saturday we went to visit them. We had the bright idea that we should use some Sun-In on our hair for blonde highlights. That was innocent enough, but when I jumped in the pool, my hair turned a lovely shade of light green. Oops! It was going to be a hot time in the old town when I got home! Anyway, Mama took it pretty well and cheerfully drove me up to Elizabeth's salon on College Avenue. She skillfully turned me back into my real self, and I learned some valuable chemistry lessons, or? Lucky Kathleen had brown hair that cooperatively stayed brown.

Mumsie was on a limited school teacher budget, but gave us unlimited quality time all through the years. She was always available when we needed her. Papa and Grandmother liked to take the family to fancy restaurants. We loved Chinese, but the all-time favorite was the Polynesian restaurant in Buckhead called The Luau. It was decorated to look like Hawaii or tropical Tahiti, and the food was different and delicious and had a lot of pineapple, mango and papaya. They always took me to the Merchandise Market on Sundays when Papa had a dress show. I adored the booth across from Papa's. It was Mr. Kreschner who sold the sparkly, glamourous, gorgeous Emma Dome formals. I worked in Papa's booth sharpening pencils, hanging up dresses and getting Cokes and corned beef sandwiches for people. He paid me $1.00 per day, and I had a prime rib dinner with his salesman friends and their wives afterward. I grew up knowing the same salesmen for years.

My older friends Linda and Kathleen had driver's licenses. They could take us on Saturday nights down to the famous Varsity drive-in restaurant on North Avenue next to Georgia Tech. Nice girls did not go inside the Varsity, but eating in the car was completely decent and socially acceptable. The only problem was that one night I had the brilliant idea to stop on the way home at the Maud Baker flower shop at the corner of Ponce de Leon and Briarcliff. I knew from a friend who drove a florist delivery truck that there were tons of flowers in the back trash cans on Saturday nights that would not have made it to Monday. We went behind the shop and loaded Kathleen's trunk with "rosies and posies" and ferns of every description. We quietly put them on the front lawns of various friends. They waked up on Sunday morning to a colorful, botanical surprise.

Our choices of eateries were totally slim pickings! There was the Zesto Fat Boy hamburger joint on North Decatur at Clairmont. They served foot-long chili dogs and fries and so forth. Finally, we had our first pizza parlor, Pizza by Candlelight across the street from Agnes Scott College. Soon there followed the first McDonalds. Most items on the menu were around $.15. The menu was very limited to burgers, fries, drinks, shakes and apple pies. There was a Krystal somewhere, but we did not really like those hamburgers very well. Families often went to the cafeteria on Clairmont after church.

I enjoyed staying in Covington with my godmother, Mabel Dennis, who owned the 'Covington News'. Papa Dennis had died of cancer. We missed going to dinner with him at the Atlanta Athletic Club where he had played golf with Bobby Jones. Mother Dennis lived in an old, authentic, large, antebellum colonial house with tall white columns. It had a secret compartment behind the fireplace for hiding soldiers. Sherman did not burn Covington because he had a close friend at West Point Academy who was from Covington.

Mother Dennis told me a deep dark secret that no one else knew. She said Papa Dennis was found on the front steps of the home of the prominent Dennis family in North Carolina when he was a newborn. A note in the basket revealed that he was the out of wedlock child of a young Jewess. He was adopted by the Dennis family and raised Christian. The Atlanta Athletic Club never admitted any Jews whatsoever under any circumstance, but Papa Dennis belonged to that club. They would have pooped a brick if anyone had found out!

The Dennis's had gone to the premier of 'Gone with the Wind' in 1939. Papa Dennis bought the convertible that Vivian Leigh rode in in the parade on Peachtree Street. He also bought Mother Dennis the real, green velvet dress that Scarlett O'Hara wore in the movie. She had her portrait painted in that dress. She told me that it would belong to me when I turned twenty-one, but she went into a nursing facility and her sister Mary gave it to the Atlanta Historical Society. I was heartbroken, but that really was the appropriate thing to do. Besides, I can sew well enough to make a dress like that someday if life cannot go on without it! Mama and Daddy loved to drive to Miami, Florida to stay on the Dennis's yacht at Bay Front Marina.

Mama had a younger second cousin who came from out of town to stay with us. He was twenty-two years old and had a Playboy Club key. Atlanta had a Playboy Club downtown near the Roxy Theater. Being very curious about all of this, I begged the cousin to take me and devised a scheme to pull it off. He was skeptical, but he was dealing with a little cousin that was so gutsy, she had never been waiting for a spine donor! I dressed up in a black, long-sleeve dress with black shoes and stockings and gloves. I put a black veil over my head, and went disguised as a widow. I had a white hanky and wore Grandmother's Toujour Moi perfume that was heavy and screamed "Mature woman in her J.P. Allen black." I truly did love costumes and playing roles. It has always been something deeply rooted in my soul. I guess I won an Academy Award, because they let me in, no questions asked! I was not a drinker, but that $1.50 steak was delicious. Everything was a buck and a half there.

Chapter 9
Grades Eleven and Twelve & Not Much Rhymes with Twelve

When I was sixteen Mama and Daddy started buying real estate investments to ensure that we would have college educations and go to colleges and graduate schools of our choice. How blessed we were! First, they bought the Feld Avenue Apartments off of College Avenue. Next, they purchased the Windsor Apartments in Avondale on Covington Highway. Finally, they bought a building with six units on Clairmont called the Chateau Apartments. It was biking distance from Emory, so I lived there for a while when in graduate school. Mumsie lived there also.

This was around the time when Daddy opened his second store at North Decatur Plaza on Clairmont at North Decatur. He was a cracker jack good business man and knew how to manage anything. For this reason, he was elected president of the Decatur Merchants Association for many years in a row. Emory girls shopped at this store and jolly well paid for my education and loved my parents. Daddy often helped merchants that were struggling to stay in the black. He analyzed their cash flow, business practices, books and inventory and told them how to turn things around. He was highly revered and so loved in that town. I remember when he bought a sewing machine for an African American widow so she could support her children by doing alterations.

One Sunday night after church I was taking some kids home in Mama's baby blue T-bird, and we decided to drive down a short gravel road to the left of the high school on South McDonough Street. Some resident of that street had replaced their commode, and the old one was sitting out on the curb for trash pickup. I stopped and got out of the car and said to my friends, "Do you realize how awesome that would look on the top step of the library?" They all agreed, and it was sparkling clean, so Wesley, the son of the assistant fire chief picked it up and put it in my trunk. In the pitch-black dark, we drove to the library, and the boys put it on the steps, front and center. I have no clue what happened to it the next morning or what the library staff thought or said, but we were just lucky ducks that the Decatur police did not catch us. It would have been so embarrassing! They would have given us a warning and probably thought it was funny. All the officers already knew us and our parents. There were not any really juvenile delinquent kids in Decatur High. There were some boys that smoked under the bleachers and drank a bit of beer, but we had never heard about marijuana or hard drugs or gangs.

Police Chief Spinks was the uncle of my majorette friend Lynne. She was two years younger and could not drive yet. After the Homecoming parade, Chief Spinks turned over a Chevy convertible to me to drive for the rest of the afternoon. It belonged to Southern Chevrolet on West Ponce, but somehow it was all acceptable and not a problem. The awesome thing was that it had a bull horn in it. We went all over town and all the way out South Candler to South DeKalb and said silly things with that loudspeaker bull horn. I was a careful driver and we did not frighten anyone. Chief was a good friend of my parents, and he knew I would not technically misbehave or have an accident.

My friend, Herb, found a dingy, shabby store way out Memorial Drive that sold the old forty-five records that came out of jukeboxes. This old store looked like a rustic cabin out in Tombstone, Arizona or something. It had unpainted wooden walls, unstained rough wooden floors, a patched roof that looked leaky and dirty windows. The wooden tables were covered with the records scattered on top of each other in no particular order. The vinyl disks were in good condition and not scratched. They cost only $.25 each. For rock n roll teenagers, this was like finding a hidden treasure with a chest of Spanish gold! I was able to find most of my favorite songs that we listened to on the radio at home or in the car. I found tunes from Ricky Nelson, Buddy Holly, the Everly Brothers, The Big Bopper, Chubby Checkers and on and on. Cassette tapes had not been invented yet, and definitely not eight track tapes.

There was one other naughty thing that teens did in the dark of night. Before the days of battery-powered yellow warning lights for construction sites, the Department of Roads and Drainage had red, kerosine lanterns sitting on top of sawhorses. If someone was mad at a girl or just wanting to tease them, they might set a red lantern on her front porch. We knew it meant something kind of bad, but honestly, I don't think we comprehended the concept of "ladies of the night" who lived-in red-light districts. I suppose some might say it bordered on bullying, but I never heard of anyone getting upset about it. Of course, it was very wrong to leave a hole in the road without a lantern, but teen brain frontal lobes do not consistently think things through with adult reasoning. Plainly stated, they make questionable choices without realizing the full gamut of the consequences. Impulsiveness reigns supreme!

I had some older friends who took me to a night club. They were positive that I would not be able to get in, but I had a plan. When the server asked for my ID, I spoke to her with a German accent and said, "My driver's license is in German. You will not be able to read it." She swallowed it, and I was in. Of course, think about it. The numbers on a German license are identical to the numbers on an American license, but she did not think it all the way through to say, "This kid is full of beans and baloney and quite the con artist!" Some will say I crossed the line, but, hey, isn't that where most of the fun is? Let's hear it for ingenuity kid. I'll see that "wow" and raise you a "zowie!"

When walking home after school I liked to stop at Ginny's house. She had a quick, simple recipe for making a cinnamon roll. We made some regular pie crust dough with flour, salt, water and oil. It was rolled out flat and sprinkled with cinnamon and sugar dotted with margarine chunks. We baked it until brown, and then took it into her living room to watch American Bandstand. This teenage dance show was popular all over America for years. The star was Dick Clark. Our rock and roll music back then sounded fantastic. The words had a lot of meaning, and the music was melodic. I still enjoy Music Choice channel 931 which is the Golden Oldies from the 1950's, 1960's and 1970's. I can dance to those songs for a full hour. We loved to dance along with the teens on the show. They pretty much had the same kids there every day, so you got to know them rather well.

Ginny's older sister, Lynn, was usually there. We thought she was especially wicked/cool because she taught us phrases like, "Poop fire and save the matches!" She taught us the intellectual way to sing 'Row, Row, Row Your Boat.' It goes, "Propel, propel, propel your craft, gently through the liquid solution. Ecstatically, ecstatically, ecstatically, ecstatically, life is but an allusion". There were also a few naughty songs we learned from her here and there about boys from Georgia Tech and girls from Agnes Scott.

My brother, Eric also took piano lessons which he hated. Mama bribed him to practice and do well on the national audition. She asked him what he really wanted for a prize if he scored 95 or above. Surprisingly, he said he wanted a little monkey. Mama kept her promise, and soon we had a big metal cage with a brown, squirrel monkey in his room. Eric named him Sammy. Lula had no use for Sammy and thought he was a stinky creature. One day when Lula was straightening Eric's room, she was not aware that Mama was in the next room. Lula scowled at Sammy and said, "Sammy, I may be browner than you are, but you are the ugliest!" We have laughed about that for five and a half decades. Sammy died of a sun stroke out on the patio. Eric did take guitar lessons from a guy in Decatur named Lefty, and he enjoyed that until Lefty was killed in a car crash.

I had Mrs. Hammett for chemistry and thoroughly loved it and found it fascinating. Most of us had watched a kid's TV show called 'Watch Mr. Wizard.' He did various science experiments and activities that were fun and safe. This show probably got many of us started liking science. Plus, he promoted nutrition and always told us to eat a good, balanced breakfast: fruit, cereal, milk, bread and butter. On my own, I thought it was interesting to try to make things like lotions or cosmetics or cleaning products. This still interests me. It taught me that $5.00 moisturizer is usually just as good as the $50.00 bottle! Madison Avenue, the home of advertising, just knows how to play on the female psyche. We Eutero-Americans are so sensitive about fine lines and wrinkles and skin spots. In reality, staying out of the sun, staying well hydrated, eating raw fruits and veggies and sleeping well are the best tricks.

Mrs. Davis was my geometry teacher, and I hated that subject. Due to some reason, I just did not get it and had trouble memorizing the theorems. It was so bad for me and several other students that Mama hired another teacher, Mrs. Keller, to tutor us. Finally, we made it through geometry by the hardest, but it made me understand that I would never, ever in my lifetime sign up for trigonometry or calculus. That would open up the window and let all the worry out!

Spanish was a different situation altogether. Our teacher was the wonderful Dr. Carreras from Havana, Cuba. He had been a biology professor at the University of Havana, but obviously fled with his family when the communist leader, Fidel Castro, came into power in Cuba. We were so fortunate to have a teacher who modeled the correct pronunciations for us. I loved Spanish! It came very naturally for me. Being so musical, I had good ears and could emulate Dr. C's sounds very well. I had two years of Latin, and that was also very helpful. Later when living in Europe it made French and Italian doable. Sadly, the curriculum called for translating the paragraphs in the textbook, and the class did not do conversations. One should always learn a new language naturally like a small child: hear, understand, speak, read, write.

I was still friends with the same teenage girls and boys. On weekends we often went as a large group to the drive-in theater on Scott Boulevard. There were times when a kid was put in the trunk to sneak in and save money. Being horribly claustrophobic, that was decidedly not for me in a million years.

The drive-in was next to Lawrenceville Highway. If you were going north and turned right on Jordon Drive and drove all the way to the end, there was a cemetery called Washington Memorial Gardens. Why teenagers like to walk around cemeteries at night I will never understand, but that was a reality for us. Probably since it borders on the scary/dangerous level, it appealed to our undeveloped brains' frontal lobes. We would never have disturbed any graves or headstones. Once Frank and Herb had made those tin can "telephones." They attached a very long forty-foot waxed string to one can on each end. They crept up under a house that was built on concrete blocks. Then they backed away forty feet and made eerie ghost sounds to startle the residents of the house. No one came out on the porch to look, so it obviously did not work. Our last trip to the cemetery was one night when we came upon a grave digger. Since it was hot summer, he probably dug at night to stay cool. Anyway, he was less than overjoyed to see us. He shouted enough to wake the dead and chased us with a shovel. Goodbye, graveyard forever! (Until we are the bottom side of the daisies)

When a new drive-in was built on the Northeast Expressway, Kathleen and I decided to sneak in for the fun of it. Very bad decision! That's where fun went to die that night! We had to shimmy across a creek on a rotted shaky log that could have given way. Then we climbed over large concrete boulders that were piled up there to keep intruders out. We arrived at Linda's car with scraped knees, and the movie was almost over. Live and learn! I decided that saving $.75 on a movie ticket was only for the parsimonious. Parsimony is stinginess to the tenth power!

By this age, girls had moved away from the cumbersome long dresses with the uncomfortable, impossible hoop skirts. We were wearing simple, short semi-formal attire to the dances. In eleventh grade for the Snowball, I had a black and white floral design, taffeta, sleeveless dress with a bell-shaped skirt. The coolest thing of all was that my corsage was one black orchid and one white orchid. Fairview Florist had sprayed a white orchid black. For the Junior Prom, my dress was white taffeta with a cascade of satin pink roses, stems and leaves coming down from the bodice to one third of the skirt. My shoes were moss green. For dances we bought cheap, white satin high heel shoes from Butler's Shoes and had Bailey's Shoe Shop dye them to match our dresses. My feet were narrow and the cheap shoes were medium width. Not to worry. We tossed our shoes over to the side anyway so we could dance fast jitterbug and twist.

At the end of that school year, I was out on the football field trying out for majorette captain, and the North Building was on fire. Kind of reminded me of Nero fiddling while Rome burned. The tryouts continued, but finally were stopped and had to be postponed. I'm not sure how the fire started, but it was rumored that it was a teen boy. I have no clue as to his identity or the accuracy of that report. The end result was that building had to be totally renovated. That meant that our daily schedule went to double sessions. The first session was eight-thirty to eleven-thirty. We went home for lunch and stayed home. The second session for the other half of the students was twelve o'clock until three. Somehow this met the academic standards for the State of Georgia.

In High School most everyone had a blue denim three-ring binder notebook. The left side had a strip of royal blue canvas that said Decatur High in gold or navy-blue letters. The fun thing about these notebooks was that you were supposed to write and autograph on the denim side with a ball point pen. That's right, we finally got away from fountain pens and bottles of ink, even though our ancient wooden desks had an inkwell hole on the top right side. The slanted top of the desk lifted up revealing a metal compartment for our books. Since school let out at 3:01 daily, everyone wrote on their notebook: Life begins at 3:01. We made our own protective covers for our textbooks out of brown grocery bags cut to fit and folded a certain way.

Magic Markers came on the market, and that was the end of tempera poster paint. I despised the smell of the markers, and they were permanent and would badly stain floors and fabrics and such. We made a lot of posters for school events and elections. When decorating the gym for dances, we typically used crepe paper cut in two-inch widths and twisted. Mostly they were the bright blue and gold Decatur Bulldog colors.

I was in a Young Life group. Our leader was an adult pastor and his wife. They were in their late twenties and a lot of fun. The guy swallowed a goldfish at one of the meetings. That was a stunt that teens did when my mom was young in the late 1930's. The summer before twelfth grade my Young Life group took a bus trip to a dude ranch in Colorado called Star Ranch. I was small enough to sleep up in the luggage rack above the seats. Can you believe that the bus driver and our leaders had no objection to that? It was loads of fun going to the old gold mines in Cripple Creek and sliding down the very tall hills called the sand slides. I had one small problem. I wore contact lenses, so I had to put them in my tube of lipstick to protect them from the scratchy sand. Then they were greasy and hard to clean. Our lenses were expensive and not disposable. I learned my lesson at the lake when I put them in a tiny paper cup of water one night, and Daddy drank them the next morning when he brushed his teeth!

Mr. and Mrs. Peabody from our church took a group of Boy Scouts and girls to their wonderful beach house on St. Simons Island for spring break. It was loads of fun and great fellowship. I remember when the clock struck twelve midnight on Easter morning. Two faithful Catholic girls shouted alleluia because their Lent fasting was over, and they could scarf down a small brown bag of chocolate bars. Also, Greer sweetly advised a distraught girl how to deal with some parental problems.

I had zero experiences with alcohol. My parents never had more than one drink on special occasions. I had sniffed the contents of bottles in my Uncle Ted's bar in the playroom and thought it smelled atrocious. One night Linda and I went to a party at Frank's house. In the dining room there was a large punch bowl that appeared to be filled with Welch's grape juice. It was summer, and I was thirsty. The problem was that the punch was a concoction commonly known as "purple passion." It was infused with vodka which I really could not taste. When we left the party, I felt woozy and was not walking all that straight. Linda took me home to get my jammys and toothbrush. I told Mama I was spending the night with Linda. When I got in her bed and closed my eyes, the room started spinning like a gyroscope or a Texas tumbleweed on the prairie. It was a miserable night. That cured me one good time! I never in my life got intoxicated again. To this good day, one glass of wine is my limit. It seems alcohol just makes me sleepy anyway, so why bother, right? I'll have a Shirley Temple and don't be chintzy with the Shirley!

Also, that summer Mama and Daddy signed me up for Camp Morehead by the Sea, a sailing camp in Morehead City, North Carolina. My parents were in a piloting and seamanship group at Lake Lanier, and that is how they heard about the camp. A lady on our dock at Lan-Mar Marina named Mrs. Douglas told them about it. Mr. and Mrs. Douglas actually owned a real Chinese Junk sailboat made of teak wood. I loved Camp Morehead and got my Skipper badge when I learned to manage twelve-foot sailfish boats and sunfish boats. We sailed to an island with a frying pan, oil, cornmeal, catsup and matches. We built a fire and cooked our fish. This was supposedly survival sailing or something of that category.

I met my friend, Alison, at camp. She was from Rome, Georgia and two years younger. We visited back and forth from Rome to Atlanta, and are still closest friends now and forever. Her Daddy started one of the first nursing homes in Georgia. He was described as the man who made a million dollars selling bed pans.

We had a blue and white fiberglass Boston Whaler boat for water-skiing and exploring the lake. It had a modest size motor and was very safe and could not sink. If my parents caught us without a life jacket, we were in big trouble and had to sit it out for the rest of the day. It was fun to find islands that had been hill-top orchards. We took apples to Mama, and she baked apple pie for us in the oven in the galley of our boat. First, we had a sailing sloop with a forward cabin and salon. Next my parents bought a Chris Craft cruiser with a forward cabin, head, galley, salon and aft doghouse cabin with a head. This wooden boat required a lot of maintenance. It had to be pulled out of the water and put in dry dock, as it was called at the boat repair shed. So, our family finally got a Lazy Days fiberglass houseboat built by Mr. Jack Beachem. It had a big Chrysler engine powerful enough to pull water skiers. Mr. Beachem asked my parents if they would like to take houseboats up and down the inland waterways to advertise his design, but they declined.

A man on our dock named Herb Wooley owned a Styrofoam company in Chamblee. Daddy designed an eight-sided Styrofoam and wood raft and anchored it out in a quiet cove beyond Brown's Bridge. Friends tied their boats up there on weekends, and we had the joys of fishing and swimming ashore to build campfires and so forth. We loved to wash our hair in the lake. The rainwater made it unbelievably soft even if you shampooed it with Dial soap. Our dachshund, Pepper had a bad habit of rolling in dead fish, so we had to bathe him with Head and Shoulders Shampoo to restore him to be presentable. Once someone stole the raft, so Daddy went up with a pilot in a small plane and located it, brought it back and had divers anchor it with much stronger cables.

Judge Hamilton from the recorder's court and Scott Candler, Jr.'s family often went boating with us. Judge Bill taught me to water ski. My parents bought me a catamaran slalom ski from Sears. It produced a whistling noise and a ten-foot tall "rooster tail" behind me that was awesome! My friends went crazy over that ski! Batchelor Bill lived in our Chateau apartments. Daddy rented to a First Methodist Church widow, Mrs. McKibben, two elderly sisters Pauline and Quilla and Mumsie. Can you imagine the uproar that was created the Christmas when Bill wrote "BAH HUMBUG" on his front window with shaving cream? Those little old ladies were horrified! I'm sure they thought the "Ghost of Christmas Jackass" would come for him.

Judge Hamilton had a Formula V race car, and Daddy liked to go to races with him to help with pit crew duties. Judge drove a Sunbeam car around town. Once Daddy and Scotty installed a fake receptacle on the telephone pole where Bill parked his car. They ran an extension cord from the car and plugged it into the receptacle. The police department did not bat an eye. The entire City of Decatur thought that was hilarious, but the piece de resistance was yet to come.

Scotty had connections at Emory having to do with Candlers and Coca Colas. He went to Yerkes Primate Center and borrowed a chimp. He and Daddy showed up at the Recorders Court at a time when Scotty's attorney calendar said no one would be having a case during that time slot. There would only be a bailiff and a clerk. Scotty pretended the chimp was his client, and Daddy was a witness for the defense. Now that is something no one will ever again see in a courtroom anywhere in the world! My, haven't things changed on our planet? I wonder what Judge Guess and Judge Hubert and Judge George thought about that? They were older gentlemen. Oops!

Eric and Kim liked to catch frogs near our dock and had the mischievous practice of putting them in the Coke machine on the shore. Coca Cola had an ad that was a song: Have a Coke and a Smile. I sang to my naughty siblings: Have a Coke and a Frog! We also loved to go up the road to Mathis Bait Shop. Mr. and Mrs. Mathis were a pleasant, friendly older couple. Mama and Daddy gave us money to buy drinks, candy and crickets and worms for fishing There were blackberries to pick along the way. The dirt country roads were safe for exploring. The crime rate was practically at the zero mark.

One thing was not safe at the lake. Our marina was in Forsyth County. That was a totally racist, bigoted county to the max! One Wednesday Mama took Lula to the lake to fish. Ten minutes later the nasty mouth sheriff of that God-forsaken County strutted down on the dock like a prestigious peacock and gave Mama a stern warning. He said that if Lula was not out of his county by sunset, she would be dealt with and finished. Mama was terrified and shaken to her core. Immediately she flattened out the back seats of her burgundy Chevy station wagon. Lula lay down in the back, and Mama covered her with quilts and rushed home.

That hurt me so deeply and made such a lasting impression on me that I became a peaceful civil rights worker in 1968 after Dr. King was killed. I could not bear the evil injustice that anyone would threaten my black Mama that way. It made me unpopular with a few older relatives, but I knew I was in the right. My mind and heart and spirit told me to persevere. I knew the words of Jesus, "Blessed are you when men revile you and persecute you and speak all manner of evil against you for my sake." When confronted I would say to the small handful of naysayers: You went to church where we learned the hymn, "In Christ there is no east or west, in Him no south or north. But one great fellowship of love throughout the whole wide earth." I told them I guess I was just the dummy that believed that!

Gainesville Methodist Church sent a pastor every Sunday to have a service on the lake at the Holiday Marina. Daddy drove us in our boat, we tied up at a dock and walked to shore. My brother liked to climb a tree and sit in it during the service, so I called it "The Zacchaeus Church." We took our dachshund, Pepper with us.

One Sunday we boated to a shore that had a restaurant with wonderful country cooking. Pepper and I were attacked by a wild dog that seemingly came out of nowhere. Daddy instantly became an adrenalin cowboy and jumped up in the air like a Ninja warrior and kicked that dog in the head. Pepper's stomach was slashed and bleeding, so we rushed back to our Lan Mar Marina dock. Our dentist friend, Dr. Griffin, grabbed his medical bag and stitched Pepper up, and he recovered splendidly.

I adored spending time with Mumsie and helping her. One of my jobs was to straighten her linen closet. This was right up my neatnik alley. I enjoyed folding the sheets and pillow cases just so and stacking them in orderly piles on the shelves. She asked me to drive her places. We drove down to West Point, Georgia to see her sister-in-law, Aunt Cordie Mobley. Nearby was the town Hogansville where Mumsie had spent a lot of her childhood until her dad died. Her dad owned a general store just like the Olson family on 'Little House on the Prairie.' He also owned a seed and feed store and a farm equipment store.

We went to the old home place, and I learned so much about the early 1900's, our family history and the family stories. She showed me the old springhouse with icy cold water where they kept butter, cheese, and milk. I was surprised to learn that my prim and proper ladylike Mumsie who probably had notarized certification papers from Queen Victoria had ridden horses bareback when a young girl.

The summer before twelfth grade, Mama drove us to Washington, D.C. We visited Cousin Ruthie and her husband Woody. Their first baby, David, was several months old. We saw all of the historic and government sites in downtown Washington. We toured George Washington's Mount Vernon estate and Thomas Jefferson's Monticello. We went to Williamsburg and ate at the King's Arms Tavern wearing bibs.

I was on my ear to get home to my friends and played a bad trick on Mama. The night before we were to drive home, I set Mama's alarm two hours early. That meant that when we got to a breakfast restaurant that opens at 7am, and it was not open, the jig was up. Mama was SOOO mad at me for depriving her of her sleep. I redeemed myself by driving the car all the way to Atlanta.

In twelfth grade it was a big deal being a senior, or so we thought. We really did not have any special privileges and had horribly over-inflated opinions of our selves. We had senior rings that were gold with a bright blue stone, and that was about it. They were ordered from the Balfour Company that printed our annuals. During lunch seniors sat on the long wall between the gym and the South Building. That was where so much socializing took place. It gave us a deep feeling of camaraderie. Seniors had a kid day each year and dressed like kindergarten age children. The girls had short pastel-colored dresses with puffy sleeves and white pinafores. Gingham check was the popular fabric type. Boys dressed similar to a Little Lord Fauntleroy suit. A problem always arose if a boy or two arrived at school in nothing more than a diaper and carrying a baby bottle!

My parents allowed me to have a giant spend the night party after Homecoming, I invited all of my friends plus the cheerleaders, majorettes and drill team. Our living room and dining floor was completely carpeted with sleeping bags and cosmetic cases loaded with makeup and hair rollers and large bonnet electric hair dryers in zippered plastic cases. Daddy stood in the backyard shooting his shotgun straight up in the air to scare away young men who were interested in bathrobes and pajamas. Right? One slippery baby-faced fellow named Skippy crashed the party wearing a girl's robe and curler cap. It was all in good fun and totally innocent teen mischief. Mama stood out on the patio for hours and hours grilling three hundred and twenty hamburgers. My folks were such good sports and loved young people.

My favorite teacher was Mrs. Cotton who taught English. She and her children lived with her mother. She had been a widow since expecting her second child. Her husband was killed in a plane crash. She lived in our neighborhood and loved to have visits from students. That was perfectly acceptable back then but would be totally frowned on and discouraged in today's world of education. These days teachers are terrified of false accusations and law suits if they don't hold their nose right. When I was a teacher, we were not even allowed to pat or hug a young child that was upset or injured.

It was time to start picking a college or university. That fall the week of Thanksgiving, Mama and Mumsie drove me up to Duke University in North Carolina to have a look see. We were actually driving around the campus after my interview when we heard on the radio that President Kennedy had been shot and killed. Mama stopped the car, and we all cried. It was unbelievable! It was tragic! It was earthshaking! The shock and sadness were overwhelming. It was like a very bad dream and yet all too real. The bereavement would last for a long time. I was not completely sold on Duke. It seemed awfully far from home and so large.

I took my SAT college entrance test in a rickety, trailer-type temporary building on Clifton Road at Emory University on a Saturday morning. I might have guessed they would not have a left-handed desk. I had to twist my body half way around to write on that right-handed desk. It was totally awkward, and I must have dropped the test booklet twenty-five times. To add insult to injury, right outside on the curb a man with a jackhammer was loudly busting up the sidewalk through the entire test.

Then a very fortunate thing happened. A girl named Anne who sang in the choir with me went by Daddy's store and told him how much she wished I would go to Emory at Oxford down by Covington. Her little sister was enrolling there, and we could room together. She invited me down for a social event, and I fell in love with that campus and the students. That settled it! Oxford was for me and not very far from Decatur. I was going to love the quiet, sleepy little town where I had relatives from Mumsie's family. In fact, back in 1836, my ancestors had helped encourage the founding of Oxford College which became Emory University in Atlanta.

I was a conscientious student and had permission from my parents to write myself a note, sign Daddy's name and get out of school every once and a while. I did not abuse this privilege. The only problem was that one day when I left school to walk up the hill and have lunch with Daddy at the drug store, there was Mr. Fisher, the assistant principal. You might think I got in really big trouble for skipping school, but au contraire, Mr. Fisher was one of Papa's good poker buddies from the Elks Club. Everything was cool, and no one got busted.

A lady named Elizabeth who went to Mumsie's church had a beauty salon on College Avenue next to Bush Cabinet Shop. That is where our entire family had our hair done. Mama got manicures there also, but I had an aversion to nail polish. I did not like the way it looked or smelled or felt on my nails. That holds true even today. I like my nails very short so I can dig in the dirt and do arts and crafts. I was fiercely independent. I let Elizabeth wash and cut my hair, but I liked to roll it myself and then go sit under the dryer. Elizabeth combed it out and sprayed Aqua Net hairspray on it. They thought my stubbornness was some kind of comical, and no one objected or chastised me for being a very different kind of little hair salon creature.

We attended sock hops in the gym after football home games. Basketball was played at the Decatur Recreation Center. Please do not ask me about the high school cafeteria or what they served. It was probably a lot of hamburgers, cheeseburgers mac and cheese, fish sticks and spaghetti or whatever. Underclassmen and Seniors pretty much sat outside during lunch. We talked and laughed and enjoyed our friends. Lunches cost $.50, so I accumulated a pretty good little stash of change over the years. That was where we were standing when we found out about the Cuban Missile Crisis. I heard some kids saying that everybody should run off and get married, because the world was going to end.

Our band and majorettes were invited to march in a parade in Washington, DC that spring at the annual Cherry Blossom Festival. We had to raise enough money to make the trip. Our band director decided that we would sell light bulbs. That was something that every family in town needed, so we easily raised enough cash to go on the train ride trip and stay in a hotel. It was exciting, but I must say my legs were cold when it snowed a bit on the cherry trees, and we twirlers were wearing very short skirts. Thankfully, our tops were long sleeve and high neck. We got very little sleep on the train coming and going. The girl's car was an endless sleepover party atmosphere.

This was the year when Villager skirts, blouses and sweaters hit the teen and college ready-to-wear market. This was the first time anyone had really cared about having certain prestigious labels on their clothes. Up until then, the idea was to look nice and ladylike in attractive clothing and be well-groomed. Daddy was not authorized to sell that brand. The company had given the franchise to Casual Corner store which was owned by Mr. Maas. He and Daddy were very close friends and even did some real estate deals together, so I had full access to the Villager clothes. We also started wearing the madras style shirts and blouses.

Next thing we knew, it was also the very coolest thing to have loafers made by the Weejun company. Mama went all out and bought them for me in navy blue, cordovan, hunter green and brown. I had no clue how spoiled I was, so I really did not act spoiled. There were a few girls and their moms who might have desired to scratch my eyeballs out from jealousy. There were rumors that there were girls who would have loved to be set loose in my closet that was twelve feet long. It was crammed full of clothing tighter than the wadding in a shot gun!

Anyway, I worked hard in the family stores posting books, printing charge account bills and addressing the envelopes by hand. Having pretty clothes was just the fruits of my labor. I painstakingly sewed the cardboard and string price tags on the clothes from the new shipments, made boxes for the layaway department and wrapped gift packages beautifully and made ribbon bows. I straightened the shelves and dress racks, and filed invoices. There were no VISA cards then. Those David's charge account cards had to be copied on a

Thermofax machine monthly to be mailed. Then it had to have postage stamped on the envelope with a Pitney Bowes postage machine from the post office. On Christmas eve when those husbands came in to pick up whatever Daddy had ordered or selected for their wives, I got a dollar tip for the giftwrap job. Now that was really high cotton!

One day I was walking home from school and almost to the woods where I cut through to our back yard. Two small boys approached me and started throwing handfuls of pebbles at me. I turned around and made a roaring sound and showed my teeth. They ran home and told their mother that I had attacked them. She walked through the woods huffing and puffing and intending to blow our house down like a big, bad wolverine. She rang our doorbell. Mama was not home, but Lula told me to go to the door. I explained to the lady that the little boys were the bellicose agitators. She deflated her anger balloon that was big enough to take Dorothy back to Auntie Em in Kansas! She apologized and slumped home.

Mama and I went driving one Sunday afternoon that fall and wound up on Briarcliff Road at Clairmont, five miles from Decatur. We found a new subdivision called Briarcliff Woods. We went in a beautiful, three-story old-brick, Dutch-colonial house and fell in love with it. We went home and told Daddy that it was time for our family to move. He drove to see the house and thoroughly agreed. The Naab family bought our Midway Road house. Zuher from Syria was a physician at Emory, and Nellie was from Switzerland. They had three little boys and lived in our house for at least two decades.

We were all moved in before Christmas and Mama began the arduous task of decorating the rooms. She hired a lady from Rich's Department Store named Mrs. Bush. She selected attractive furniture and lamps. Mama bought her rugs from Mr. Sharian in Decatur on West Ponce. His family was from Armenia. They started their rug cleaning business at their home. They bought a house by a creek and washed the rugs in the creek, letting them dry on a deck. That large family business is still there on West Ponce de Leon, and is very well-known around Georgia.

We had interesting new neighbors. The childless couple next-door raised Welsh Corgis dogs. A vice-president of Davison's Department Store from Macy's in New York lived three doors down. They had five children who went to St. Thomas More Catholic School. My brother and sister started to Sagamore Elementary. Down at the corner was the Herndon family with four children. Dr. Herndon was head of Endocrinology at Emory Hospital and later dean of the medical school. Dr. Laney and his wife lived on the side street across from us. He was dean of the Theology School at Emory and later the president of Emory and finally the Ambassador to South Korea. There were various neighbors who worked at the CDC as physicians or biologists in research. A retired botanist told us that his job during the Vietnam War was to produce a strain of papaya that was very low in vitamin C. This would obviously affect the health of the enemy. War can be so cruel.

Every day after school I came home exhausted, so that called for a nap in Daddy's Lazy Boy recliner in the family room. No matter how much noise Eric and Kim made in there with jabbering and laughter, or how loud they played the TV, I slept like a dead rock. I am such a lifelong deep sleeper that I probably need an easy chair from the "Hopeless Slack Butt" recliner company.

After graduation, Daddy took me down to Southern Chevrolet on Ponce de Leon Avenue and said, "You may pick any car other than a corvette." But there was a catch. He was going to drive it for three years. Then, when I was a senior in college, if I had saved $900.00, the car would be mine. That was the year that the Chevelle Malibu came out. I selected a yellow convertible SS Super Sport with black interior and top. It had the automatic transmission in the console. We did not order a huge engine like a teen boy would have wanted. I think mine was a 210 horsepower.

My first trip was to go to Rome, Georgia to visit Alison. It was crazy, but the dealer had forgotten to put fluid in the differential housing compartment, and I got stranded just outside Rome. Alison's dad came to get me and have the car towed to their Chevy dealer. No one wanted to take responsibility for the catastrophe, so Daddy called the president of General Motors and spoke with him personally. He ordered them to fix my car immediately!

Alison and I drove to Chattanooga to see Peter, Paul and Mary in concert. On the way home we had a narrow escape while passing a slow car on the highway. I learned a good lesson for sure about safe driving and yellow center lines on highways.

Alison and I were invited to a party. When we arrived, we saw that the parents were not home. The girls gave us a glass of beer, so when no one was looking, we poured the beer into a plant. An older guy in his twenties came. He had huge muscles, and said that he had been a Mr. Universe one year. He took his shirt off and started flexing his muscles and looking in a mirror. I got scared, ran up the stairs, climbed out a window and scooted down the gutter. I ran toward town and found a phone booth. I called Alison's dad to come and get us. Sometime you just have the wrong feeling about things. Listen to your gut level feelings! Let your sensitive spirit speak to you. It knows a lot. This crazy guy actually taught history at Avondale High School in Decatur.

I had seen a counselor from time to time to deal with problems and feelings. He was supposedly one of the finest and most competent in Atlanta and was well known and associated with Emory Medical School. Tragically he committed suicide, and I was really shaken up and deeply saddened about this. When you see a certified therapist who is certifiable, you lose your trust in the field of psychology. After that I decided that pastoral care ministers were a better choice for me. After all, we all have five parts of ourselves: body, mind, will, emotions and spirit. Why not treat your whole person? Why not talk to someone who has more hope to offer you?

Mama bought me a light blue and white Royal Safari portable typewriter for college. It was manual and came in a black metal case and was not very heavy. There is no telling how many term papers and reports and letters were written on that machine! It required little other than a new ribbon now and then. I used it for years after graduate school. My children typed on it for their school work. We kept it until we purchased our first computer with a printer.

Chapter 10
Emory at Oxford, Brace Yourself! Here Comes the Little Girl with Big Ideas.

Before college started, Mama took me to a downtown wholesale linen company. My roommate to be, Jean, told me to pick bedspreads and sheets and towels for us that I thought we would both like. I selected medium solid moss green cotton that would go with most any decorative items or posters. Mama made sure that I stocked up on comfortable dresses, blouses, skirts, sweaters and had plenty of lingerie. For my footlocker my brother gave me his metal army diving chest that he had taken to Athens Y Camp. I painted it white and antiqued it with golden yellow and painted my name on it in royal blue surrounded by flowers done in a tole painting design like Pennsylvania Dutch.

I packed my piano music books and took the horseback riding hat, boots and crop. We had a surprise roommate, Georgia from Augusta. She was very nice and extremely smart and scholarly. Our room was all the way up on the third floor of A section. Our leg muscles soon got very strong and firm, what you mean!

Once I left the dorm, and it started raining. I hollered up to Georgia to throw me my pea green umbrella. I caught it wrong and got cut on the hand but not seriously. We had radiators in our rooms for heat. That was a perfect place to cook simple things if they were left in a metal cookie tin for several hours. This was probably an early version of a crock pot. I have always been good at creative problem solving with that "out of the box" style of thinking. Jean had one of those metal coils that you plug in and put in a cup of water to boil to make tea. Dummy me! I put it in some oatmeal and it all burned and ruined the gizmo.

The junior college was in the sleepy tiny town of Oxford, Georgia right next to Covington where Mama and Mumsie and Grandmother Mobley grew up. It was about an hour drive from home on the Covington Highway. Interstate 20 was not yet completed. It had a tiny post office and a little general store, and that was just about the sum and substance of the whole town. Covington had a bank, courthouse, city hall and some churches, a drug store, a furniture store, hardware store and a Woolworth's five and dime store. There was a Dairy Queen and a gas station and not much more than a lot of very old, well-kept houses of ante-bellum and Victorian gingerbread styles.

We were fairly isolated, and that was the magic of it. One had to be creative and think up things to do for spare time and recreation. I dipped my drawing paper in strong tea and burned the edges to look like antique manuscripts. Then I wrote certificates for people or copied piano music onto the paper. I have Chopin's Prelude in A, opus 28 on our den wall even yet.

Oxford has some interesting history such as The Zora Fair House. Zora was a refugee from South Carolina living in Oxford. She was a spy for the Confederacy. She heard about a General Sherman plot. She disguised herself to look African American by staining her skin with black walnut juice. Then she went here and there warning people that the Yankees were coming. Some people say she was wounded. Anyway, she died not long after the war.

I had been to one dance at Oxford that spring, so I knew a few students. During rat week we had to wear rat hat Emory beanies. They were bright blue with a gold E on the front. I did not have to jump in the mud pit that the boys dug. The president of the sophomore class forbade the older students to even lay a hand on me. The hazing was honestly very mild and merciful. Jumping in the mud pit was called "playing the M & M Peanut game." After you got out of the mud, they drizzled syrup on your head and sprinkled it with lots of corn meal.

There were some annoying Freshman activities in Haywood, our girl's dorm. Sophomore girls got us up at two am and made us do a fashion show up and down the three flights of stairs. We were required to put on our Sunday best with hats, gloves, stockings garter belts or girdles and the whole nine yards! You had to describe your outfit as if you were a designer. Also, there was a game called "Submarine." The sophomore girls made you stand in a clean commode. When they yelled, "submerge" they flushed the commode. It could have been much worse. I'm not sure what happened behind closed doors in the boy's dorms. It certainly might have been head swirlies, if you know what I mean.

Our dean was Dean Eady, and he was a friend of Mumsie's family. Registration for classes turned out to be quite interesting. You had to sign up for a math, so I chose Logic with the teacher Miss Perry. We were also required to take a history course with Dr. Gregory, a literature course with Dr. Brittain and a Humanities class with Dr. Guillebeau. I was standing in the line to sign up for Spanish so I could exempt a bunch of semesters. There was a new German teacher, Dr. Austin. He had looked through all the Freshman applications and memorized the faces of any student with a German sir name. He charismatically came up to me and said, "Fraulein Dattelbaum, you are going to be in my German class." He obviously had the magnetism of the Pied Piper of Hamlin, because I followed him like a rat from good old Hamlin. That was one of the best decisions I ever made in my life. It was decidedly my destiny, and has taken me down some fascinating avenues all through the years. Learning that language has opened many doors for me and introduced me to some wonderful people and diplomats and countries.

In Physical Education I had Mrs. Lurie, and we played soccer. For girls our soccer was called Speed Ball. I was a tenacious little forward that could practically scoot under the other girls to make goals. The next semester I loved every minute of her interpretive dance class. It gave me truckloads of self-expression.

All of our professors lived very close to the campus, and we were often invited to their homes for cookouts and parties. On April Fool Day, I convinced Miss Perry to have a spaghetti supper. I put blue food coloring in the noodles, and that was really funny, memorable and a big hit. Our classes were small, so you got to know your instructors and felt very sheltered and shepherded at all times. If you missed class, they checked on you. They were always readily available to discuss grades or any concern you might have. I had seriously considered attending Duke University, but thank heaven I chose Emory at Oxford. They later changed the name to Oxford College of Emory University.

Mama's Aunt Sarah Mobley and great aunt Sallie Mae Sockwell lived in Covington. Aunt Sarah was a scholarly lady who was retired from teaching French. They often invited me over for dinner at their house on Floyd Street. It had belonged to their grandfather, J. W. Sockwell who was in Cobb's Regiment and married Julia Cook. I have his burgundy velvet rocking chair and her tiny sewing rocker with an underneath drawer for needles and thread. My aunts were very proud of me for being a good student and going to Emory.

German was a breeze for me, and I began to learn it quickly. Dr. Austin said I had inherited genetic cellular knowledge from Papa that worked between my brain and tongue and ears. He said my accent and pronunciations could pass for a German native. It was such a shame that Papa did not speak German to us. After World War II that was just not proper or acceptable. But he did sing a couple of children's songs to us when he bounced us on his knee. There was 'Du, du Liegst mir im Herzen,' and 'Hopp, hopp, hopp, Pferdchen lauft galopp.'

Dr. Austin had a wife and two preschoolers. He started a small brass choir. He was a wonderful musician who played the pipe organ at a church. Again, he had looked in the files and discovered I played the baritone horn in high school in the winter concert band. He borrowed a baritone for me from Covington High School. I was the only girl in this group. Rodney played trumpet. He later became a physician and started the Longstreet Clinic in Gainesville. Coy played trombone. He got ordained to be a Methodist pastor and many years later was the district superintendent for the Atlanta District. I am still in touch with those fellows, and Coy led my Daddy's memorial service when he died.

History was very hard for me, so I drew a visual time-line that helped me remember. Dr. Gregory thought it was clever and interesting and boosted my grade a little for putting forth extra effort. I did love biographies, though, and could remember all the facts of a famous person's life. It was the dates that were elusive for me. I found Humanities a bit tedious. Reading Plato and Aristotle and Socrates was somehow over my head and horribly boring, and I just did not see the point in studying about ideal chairs. The reclining Lazy Boy chair at home was ideal to me, and that was good enough! I thought philosophy was for the birds. Literature was fine. I especially loved Theater of the Absurd. Dr. Brittain and his wife Nancy and I became lifelong friends until they died. He was the head of our drama club.

Dr. Gregory's wife was our wonderful, nurturing nurse. She was available twenty-four hours a day. Once I left my contact lenses in way too long. In the middle of the night, I had sharp, shooting pains in both eyes. My roommates called for Mrs. Gregory, and thank Heaven she had some anesthetic eye drops. She knew the problem and warned me about that. Another time I went to her because I was having trouble sleeping. She told me to not worry. She said that if you are lying in your bed relaxed, your body was still getting good rest.

Since we were a Methodist college, we had required Chapel every Wednesday at the Allen Memorial Methodist Church on our campus. We were admonished to avoid the beastliness of bacchanalian excess regarding our flesh. You sat in the same pew and seat each week so that the head counter could know that everyone was in attendance. I never heard of any Jewish students complaining about this chapel service. People were more laid back in those days and were not staying up late at night to think of things to be offended about, for Pete's sake! We did not live in such an angry, bellicose society where people act like sore tailed cats in a room full of rocking chairs! People usually avoided fiddle faddle and clap trap.

Our cafeteria was quite plain and simple. I slept in my clothes on top of the spread under a blanket on the top bunk to be ready for the next day. I awoke early to be at breakfast at 7am on the dot. I had scrambled eggs, toast, orange juice and coffee every day. Cereal did not suit me. My roommates slept in and thought I was positively insane to be such a breakfast nerd. They drank a glass of Tang and got vitamin C and sugar and artificial food color. For lunch and dinner, we went through the line, and the servers gave everyone the same kind of simple, traditional American foods. There were positively no choices whatsoever. I don't remember much fresh fruit or salads.

Boys had a bad habit of throwing butter pats on the ceiling. The custodians took them down, but they left a greasy spot on the ceiling tiles. Those tiles were likely made from asbestos! When I eat at Oxford now, it is like a fancy commercial cafeteria from the planet "Pleasurize." It has the following bars: cereal, fruit, salad, soup, sandwich, Italian, pizza, traditional, Chinese, Mexican, cookie, desserts, and Eddy's ice cream dispensers! Well, our tuition and room and board were only $600 per quarter plus $50 or so for all of our books, so what did we expect? Today the tuition is over 50k per year.

Very few of us had cars, so we stayed pretty close to campus. Our housemother was Mrs. Gladys Shannon, a widow the age of Mumsie. She was very sweet and loved Mama's family. A girl on our floor named Lady poetically gave her a nickname. She called her "Happy Butt." It was a derivation of her name Gladys with the y removed and an s and an a inserted in just the right place. I often went to see her after dinner. We chatted and I took her little packages of saltine crackers. I called her "the duchess" and she loved that and beamed with pride.

Mrs. Shannon's mother, eighty-three-year-old Mrs. Mamie Osborne Odum, lived about a mile down the road on Emory Street. She had one of those huge, white Victorian houses with the fancy gingerbread trim. I enjoyed biking down there to visit her. She was the poet laureate of Newton County. Her book of poetry was called 'Blended Thoughts.' She remembered that my great grandmother had kept the Covington Library often as her volunteer lady's society job. I told her how much I loved to write poetry and took my notebook to let her read my poems. She said I definitely had a way with words and the talent to write melodic poetry. She spent time teaching me about writing. She told me to keep a notepad by my bed in case I woke up in the middle of the night and had some inspiration.

I walked in the woods behind the college down a red clay dirt road behind former professor Squire Carlton's house. I sat on a stump and wrote poetry. One day when it rained, and the road was muddy, I wrote a poem called 'Ode to the Chocolate Road.'

When December came, Mrs. Odum climbed on a twelve-foot ladder and hung long swags of Christmas garlands and ribbons and shiny red glass balls at the ceilings of her living room and dining room. I vowed to myself that I would be just that spunky and active and independent when I grew old. So far so good! Of course, now I must be slower and more cautious on ladders and stools, especially the ten- and twelve-foot ones needed to change the bulbs in our entry hall chandelier or den ceiling fan.

Mrs. Shannon was very famous for knowing everything that was happening in our dorm. She had a sixth sense and knew just when to appear in the evening if someone were smoking. Amazing since her apartment was in C section, and we lived in A section. The best trick up her sleeve was finding out about the boys proposed spring time panty raids. Sure enough, when it happened my first year, she was waiting right there at the door in the middle of the night with a big broom to chase the young men away.

I came up with an idea that has been written about in memoir books about Oxford. I went to the kitchen store room and got over one hundred feet of green butcher paper that was used to cover picnic tables. I cut out seven-foot-long foot prints. I took a white bedsheet and made a gigantic pair of white, ruffly bloomers. I made a poster that said, "Ho, ho, ho! You can't stop me!!! The Jolly Green Giant." I secretly gave everything to my friend, David. Not another living soul knew about it. In the middle of the night, David crept out of the boy's dorm and put the footprints on the driveway leading up to Mrs. Shannon's window. He quietly hung the poster and bloomers on her window. Obviously, I don't think we had a security guard in those days. We were not wild kids, and Oxford was a quiet, safe town. The next morning it was a very funny surprise for everyone. I got my money's worth in laughter. Mrs. Shannon never said anything to anyone. I don't know if she knew who did it or not. Anyway, it was an innocent enough harmless prank that lightened the mood after the disappointing foiled raid.

I was working on saving the $900 to buy my Chevelle convertible from Daddy. Since there were no babysitting jobs to be had, I started giving haircuts to boys and girls for $1.50. I had sat in Elizabeth's beauty salon for years and watched her cut hair in all kinds of styles. Honestly, at that time in history the girls mostly wanted long straight hair like California surfer girls. They straightened their hair by literally ironing it on an ironing board. Blunt cuts were not that hard. A girl named Mary Elizabeth wanted me to straighten her dark brown ringlet curls, so I started doing straightening also and charged $5.00 for that chemical procedure. Another girl in D section cut someone's hair one day and royally botched it up. The girls told the haircut recipient, Marilyn, to come to my room and have it done properly. I fixed the problem, and she was very grateful. Later that was also written up in a book by someone.

I rode the train to New Orleans that New Years with some friends. We went to the Sugar Bowl football game and toured down town New Orleans and the French Quarter. We enjoyed Bourbon Street and tasted the famous hurricane drink which came with a souvenir glass to take home. Once was enough of Nola for me, and I have never been back. Bar hopping is just not an enjoyable pastime for me. I hear that funeral marches there are memorable and surely worth seeing. Also, Mardi Gras is touted to be a blast, but noisy public events do not hold very much interest for me, and jazz music gets on my nerves. I find crowds too confusing and avoid them to protect my hyper sensitive ears that still test at 100% other than the loss of 2 high frequency sounds.

I joined the photography club, and there again was the only girl. It afforded me the opportunity to get to know a nice fellow from my German class named Lou. We had a wonderful platonic relationship. When I decided to enter my paintings in the 'Mademoiselle Magazine' college art competition, Lou kindly photographed my paintings and made them into slides to mail to New York.

They called me and asked me to mail four of the paintings so the judges could get a better look. I got an honorable mention only, but it was a good experience and boosted my confidence about painting. I still have the letter to me from that magazine. The still life painting 'Lunch at Jacques,' hangs on the wall of our dining room.

We had some funny pranks to play on girls on our floor. They were typical teenage craziness. There was no malice or bullying intended. If someone were in the shower, we could quietly push dressers in front of the door so that they could not get out of the bathroom. Another thing was to blow up a tremendous number of balloons and fill someone's room so that they could not get into their room. That could also be accomplished with "oodles and scoobootles" of wadded up newspapers. Anyway, it always afforded lots of laughs and no hard feelings.

Sophomore year I roomed with Dixie. I sewed olive green burlap bedspreads. Our accent color was sky blue. We were given a surprise roommate, Janice, and that was an asset. She was a lovely girl and wound up marrying my friend Lou. I am still in touch with them by email and phone. Gail and Emily had graduated and gone to big Emory. Knoxie transferred to fashion school in Atlanta, Marsha took a year off, but we still had Lady and Nona. I really loved a couple of the incoming freshmen, Peggy and Allie. We were in the drama club together and had a lot of things in common. Peggy loved to write and later went to Hollywood to write screenplays, but became the assistant producer of the Ralph Edwards game show called Cross Wits. Allie was a sociology professor at Appalachian State in Boone, North Carolina.

Allie loaned me her acrylic paints and brushes. I went to the flat roof of a building being renovated and collected some scraps of wood and started doing mostly flowers and still-life paintings on them. I went home for a visit, and Mama bought me an artist paint box and many tubes of oil paint, brushes, linseed oil and turpentine. I preferred painting on thin canvas oil painting pads instead of wood-framed canvases or canvas mounted on thick cardboard. I painted like a non-trained folk artist just right out of my spirit to my hands to the canvas. I went to Dr. Guillebeau and asked him if we could have a student art show outside on the quadrangle in the spring. He thought that was a marvelous idea, and it turned out wonderfully well. I ran clothes lines between trees (One of them was planted by my great-great grandfather in the 1880's) to hang the art work. Dr. Brittain's wife, Nancy, said that I painted in the style of the impressionist Marc Chagall. I painted a rustic fireplace scene for their cabin at Clairmont Springs in Alabama near Cheaha State Park.

That year I had survival swimming in January at 8am. This course was required to graduate. They tied your hands behind your back and tied your feet together and threw you in the deep end of the pool. You had to push hard with your feet to get back to the surface of the water, take a deep breath and let it out and sink again and keep doing that until the P.E. teacher, Coach Burnett, said you had survived. For ocean survival you must bob by taking a deep breath and holding it. Then you let it out and flapped your arms to rise up from the water and take another breath. Ocean survival also involved taking off your long pants or shirt, blowing them up and tying knots on them to make a float of sorts. I was very brave, and did not mind this course at all. I loved proving to Coach that I was as tough and gutsy as the boys. The only problem was that at 9am I had German. This meant going to class in the dead of winter with wet hair. That in itself was a kind of survival. Thankfully, I never got sick with colds or flu.

Even though I was not majoring in science, I dearly loved qualitative analysis chemistry. Quantitative analysis was tedious and boring and involved too much math. I asked Dr. Autry if he needed an assistant in the lab. He actually did, so I took that job. It paid the small fortune of $50.00 per semester. There were rumors that the iced tea in the cafeteria was spiked with sodium nitrite which you can look up on your own. I analyzed it, and sure enough Dr. Autry and I saw the green flame for sodium and something for the nitrite, and he laughed and laughed! The chemistry students who became doctors and dentists did not have problems with the lab work, but a couple of fellows who became attorneys have told me that they would not have passed lab if I had not helped them out on many occasions.

Allie had been to a girl's school in France the previous year. She declared to us that she knew how to make wine. None of us were really drinkers, but it just sounded like a fun challenge with just the amount of devil may care craziness that college students love. We assumed it was highly against the rules, so we concealed the fixings in my metal diving chest trunk. We took a gallon of Welch's grape juice in a glass jug. We added sugar and yeast. I brought a piece of rubber hosing from the lab and inserted it into a hole in the jug cap and sealed it with candle wax to keep the air out. We certainly did not want to make vinegar! I ran the tubing into a glass coke bottle of water so that gas could bubble off. That way nothing would explode or turn into champagne.

We kept everything very quiet so that no one else knew. It would not have been good to leak this info to our housemother, Mrs. Shannon. The funny thing was that when the wine was finished fermenting, we really were not gung-ho to drink it. We had a student friend from Hawaii. We told him and his roommate to climb up the fire escape to get the jug. We gave the boys some Hawaiian Punch. They accidently dropped the can, and it rattled all the way down the fire escape. Thankfully, they escaped back to the boy's dorm, and no one got caught even though Mrs. Shannon heard the rattle, rattle, bang, bang! When we made the second batch, I got smart and bought a huge $.25 balloon from Woolworth's and put that on top of the jug. The balloon would expand, and it was easy to let that air out gently.

We found a small brown abandoned puppy near the dorm and adopted it and fed it milk from a baby bottle. It was fun while it lasted. This was fine until Mrs. Shannon found out. She did not dislike dogs, but for practical reasons it was just not suitable for a college dormitory to have pets. Thankfully, one of the custodians took the little fellow and gave him a good home with children to run and play with him.

Boys did not have a curfew, but girls must be in the dorm by 10pm. The joke of that was that girls were only allowed to sign out during the week for the library or the snack bar. If I needed a bedtime snack, I went and bought a stack of small hamburger patties. They cost $.10 cents each. Everyone said I was the healthiest eater on our floor. Evenings after dinner if we walked to the little country store next to the post office, I often bought a bag of carrots or apples.

If you ran out of stamps, you could put a nickel on your letter secured with Scotch tape, put it in the school letter box and the postal workers would put a stamp on the letter for you. When I sent an airmail letter, I wrote on the flap, "Fly it, Dad!" The postman then wrote "OK, son!" I think airmail letters were $.07 or something.

Dr. Austin declared that I was his best German student in Georgia. He wanted me to spend my Junior year in Germany. My parents and I agreed and loved the idea. I would be the first Emory student ever to do that, kind of a guinea pig if you will. He did all of the necessary applications and paperwork. The study abroad program was called I.E.S. which stands for The Institute of

European Studies. They had programs in Paris, Vienna, Madrid, London and Freiburg, Germany where I would go.

Since there were four German marks to one U.S. dollar, our money went so far that it was quite a lot cheaper to study in Freiburg. That included spending money and warm clothing and train trips and everything. A whole cup of yogurt was only $.12.

Right off the bat my Papa became very frightened and worried. He did not like the idea of my living in Germany with a Jewish name only twenty years after World War II. There were only three survivors of his family that we knew about. A cousin and her mother escaped to Budapest, and she had a baby named Tomas there. Papa's cousin, Blume, from Cleveland, Ohio went back to Europe to marry the husband of her deceased sister and raise her five children. The family had heard rumors about the situation in Europe, and they begged her not to go. She said, "It is my duty according to Jewish law." So she went, and they all perished.

Years later Cousin Ruthie's family moved to Vienna for three years with their three young boys. Her husband Woody was working there for the Atomic Energy Commission. Ruthie went all over Eastern Europe looking for family survivors in Hungary and Czechoslovakia mostly. Since the caretakers for Jewish cemeteries were long dead and no one had keys, she often had to climb over brick and rock walls to get in to read headstones.

A most fortuitous event happened one night that was truly a Godwink! She was checking into a small hotel. She had been doing a lot of genealogy searching with microfilm from the Mormon Church files. As per usual she had a list of family names to show the clerk. The clerk's eyes got as big as saucers, and she proclaimed, "Oh, my God! You are related to Tomas." Ruthie was able to visit with him, and they spoke German.

Tomas told her about a widowed eighty-three-year-old cousin in Rastislavova Czechoslovakia named Reli. Ruthie visited Reli even though she was still under the communist regime. Reli had been a piano teacher, but the communists took her piano away from her. Ruthie asked her what our family could send her later. She said, "You could send soap or towels or fabric. Anything else they will take from me."

Julius Caesar said, "Veni, vidi, vici." I came, I saw I conquered. For me it goes like this: I came, I saw, I said, "God, you are kidding, right?" It's always best to ignore when facing prejudice, rejection and insulting bullying.

Nonetheless we think of all kinds of things we would like to say if we had the gut or the opportunity. My favorite would be: I'll flatten you so flat, you will have to roll down your white pants to eat crème Brulé, Napoleon!

The solution was for our family to go down to the Fulton County Courthouse with a petition and change our name in front of a judge. This had one stressful aspect to it. Our driver's licenses were blue cardboard handwritten in ink by ourselves after passing the driving test. I had made a tiny alteration to my birthdate by bleaching the ink with a Q-tip with Clorox bleach. I was really scared, but the judge did not ask to see my license at all. Whew! I know God forgave me for being the mischief girl. I mean really, I guess He thought the fear of going to jail and anxiety of embarrassing my parents were punishment enough!

Dattelbaum means "date tree." In Hebrew it is "Etz timarin" which means tree of tamarind. Papa had cousins in Los Angeles who had changed their name to the Americanized "Datry." So that is what we all did. It was short and sweet and was bound to keep me safe overseas. It was also bound to eliminate most of the antisemitism. We all attended the Methodist church with Papa, so why should we be labeled as something that people like to hate? And the blunt version of that is that they kick us when they say their bigot baloney.

That spring the Drama Club performed a Noel Coward play called 'Hay Fever.' I played the part of a naïve ingenue named Jackie Coryton. I was dressed in a rose-colored Roaring 20's type long waisted outfit with long white flapper girl beads and a headband with a feather. I had only one line, but at one point I brought the house down with one action. I was standing on the right side of the stage with a cup of tea. When one of the cast members said something that I found shocking, I dropped the saucer from under my teacup. This was not rehearsed and not in the playwriter's script. I was just so deeply into the character that I did it spontaneously.

So much for being a drama queen, right? I suppose it was the product of having an intensely focused personality and taking life seriously. It took me several decades to master Mary Englebreit's quote: Life's mysterious. Don't take it serious. Part of that is first-child, parent pleaser syndrome. In my next life I will be the baby of the family, right?

Daddy let me take the Chevelle to school for the last month of sophomore year. The morning of graduation, I drove myself to the river all alone at the crack of dawn and went skinny dipping. It was very deserted there, so I encountered no one. It may have been foolish, but I counted on my angels to be on duty with their halos straight and shiny while overtaxing their patience. Perhaps it was some unnamed right of passage fed by impulsiveness. Having Nordic ancestors, I have always had an overabundance of red blood cells. I get red-faced and overheated easily. Therefore, I wore a damp bathing suit under my graduation gown to keep cooler. Basic logic, wouldn't you say?

The Dean of the College evaluated my transcript and required me to take two extra courses that summer. That was in case studies in Germany did not fulfill enough academic requirements. It was kind of ridiculously redundant because one course was poetry and the other one was some kind of physical education exercise and fitness. This was totally new territory for the university back in those Dark Ages times, so the administration had to travel in covered wagons, so to speak. I was a pioneer exploring new avenues for students.

Daddy ordered me some nice, warm ski outfits for Germany. One was white with green and brown Swiss embroidered trim, and one was burgundy color with white and blue trim. I turned out to be a lousy skier and spent so much time with my rear end in the snow, I once got a cold in one of my kidneys! We decided that I would buy a very warm coat once in Germany. In reality Freiburg is in a protected valley and does not get very cold or have much snow. When you ride the train a short distance up into the steep mountains of Hinterzarten and Titisee, they can even have some snow in July at the very top. That's when you ski in Bermuda shorts and a shirt. Mama and I packed my same tole-painted metal trunk. I was rearing to go for this big adventure. It all seemed so exciting, and I had no trepidations or regrets.

Chapter 11
Germany, My New Beloved
Extra Homeland

In September of 1966, Mama and Daddy and I flew to New York and stayed in a hotel before my ship sailed. There were sixteen other American students there that would be in my I.E.S. program. They came from Minnesota, Alaska, Las Vegas, California, Pennsylvania and so forth. I needed to take the subway to Greenwich Village to get my international driver's license. Everything went smoothly until I was trying to return to the hotel and got lost. There was a truck stopped at a light. I asked the driver for directions. He told me to hop in, and they would take me there. They were Seymour and Miguel from Puerto Rico. They were very friendly and dropped me off right at the hotel. Afterward I did not tell my parents how I got home. I suddenly realized that hitchhiking in Manhattan was probably not one of my smarter ideas. I thanked the Good Lord for getting me back safely and bragged on my angels for being Johnny-on-the-spot alert and vigilant! For all I know, those guys may have been angels! The dear Lord works in mysterious ways, you know.

Our ship was the student ship the SS Seven Seas. This was its very last voyage. It is exciting to sail out of New York Harbor, but as my parents and the New York skyline got smaller and smaller in the distance of the horizon, some fears and anxieties got larger and larger. I pumped up my courage and decided to be brave. The realization came that age twenty was going to be a whole new different world. I had never been homesick a day in my life, but I was praying to be up to the new challenges with so many new experiences and heavy-duty academic responsibilities. This ship was also taking European students who had studied in the U.S. home. My cabinmate was a girl from Basel, Switzerland named Ute. I ate meals with seven other students that would be in Freiburg with me. The German waiter was kind of sweet on me. After dinner we walked on the deck, and I seriously practiced my German. Then there were activities such as writing and performing one act plays or mini-musicals and such. The voyage was to take seven days, but we hit a very bad storm in the Atlantic. The old ship was leaning a bit on her side. It should have been somewhat unnerving, but we were young and unafraid.

Finally, we arrived in Rotterdam, and the ailing ship was retired and became a youth hostel tied up at the dock. Our director, Herr Wronka and all of our tutors were there to meet us to take the bus trip south to Freiburg in the Black Forest. This region of Germany is technically Hansel and Gretel territory. We had orientation to learn about German culture and customs and yeses and nos. We girls were told to not swing our pocketbooks. That is a dead giveaway that you are an American. Also, nice girls walk arm in arm on the streets to show that they are ladies of the day instead of ladies of the night! They showed us how to hold our forks and knives and spoons and so forth.

We visited interesting sights along the way such as Johann Sebastian Bach's house. The Bayer factory gave us a very nice tour and lunch. You would know them as the Bayer Aspirin factory. We noticed that northern Germans lived in red brick houses and spoke rapidly. As we got into southern Germany, the houses were all beige stucco with red tile roofs. We saw lots of black and white cows that are named the Holstein cattle from the province of Schleswig-Holstein.

Once we arrived in Freiburg, I was assigned to the Studenten Siedlung (Student Settlement) at Sundgauallee 4 in Lehen, the village next to Freiburg. It was about a twenty-minute bike ride from the university. There was also a nice public bus. There were about a dozen dorm buildings, half girl, half boy. Behind the buildings was a nice, clean lake for swimming. Some dorms were two story, and some were six stories. Germany has a very tightly structured society with lots of rules and expectations. A knowledgeable sociologist will tell you that means there are fewer homicides compared to the number of suicides. Sadly, a couple of students jumped from a sixth floor later during exams. We were walking distance from a small grocery/butcher shop. Can you believe it, in their freezer was a white cardboard package of frozen chicken stamped Gainesville, Georgia?

I met a sweet older woman at the bus stop named Frau Ursula Marion. She invited me for coffee now and then. I was heartbroken to find out that she had lost her husband and her son in the war and had no grandchildren either. You wonder how these innocent victims were able to put one foot in front of the other and make it through each day.

My room was on the second floor of a two-story building. My roommate was Rosita from Bavaria. Her boyfriend, Hedwig, told me that I reminded him of the novella 'Der Kleine Printz' by Antoine de Saint-Exupery ('The Little Prince.') He bought me a German copy of that book, and I still have it. The favorite girls on my floor were Beate, Jutte, Waltraud and Mitzi from Michigan.

Dave from Minnesota in my group lived in the building next door. He was planning to go into the priesthood. I met a student in that building named Marwan from Syria. He was studying medicine to become an orthopedic surgeon. The first thing he ever said to me was, "I hate America, and I hate you!" Eventually Dave and I won him over with patience and kindness, and he became like a very protective big brother to me. He took me to buy a used bicycle. It was blue and silver, just my size and very nice with gears. It cost fifty Marks which equals $12.50 in American dollars. In the spring I could have ridden with Marwan to Syria and driven through Turkey. The problem was that Israel and Palestine had the Six Day War. I could not bear to tell my parents that I was going to such a hot spot in the world. They would have been worried to death. There were two fellows in Dave's dorm that went home to fight for that. One was Israeli, and one was Palestinian.

Marwan took me to Café' Schmidt in town. He introduced me to Ursula who was a medical technologist and Brigitte, a secretary. Ursula and I became best friends. She rode the train from Hinterzarten every day to work in a lab as a medical technologist. She lived in her parent's Gasthaus. (guesthouse) She invited me to spend a weekend with her. The funny thing was that I had a fake braided bun on my head. When I took it off at bedtime, she was astonished. We still laugh about that. She will always be a dear friend like a sister. We and our children visit back and forth from time to time. Her daughter, Anne, even lived with us for a semester to learn more English. Ursula's parents were always very good to me. Her dad was a bit frail since the war. He had problems with his kidneys. But her mom lived up into her nineties.

During the war, Ursula's mother worked down in Freiburg in a photography shop. One morning she waked up with fever and congestion and called her boss to say that she did not feel like coming to work. Freiburg was bombed that day, the shop burned to the ground, and the owner died. Fate and destiny and kismet are very interesting things. I heard many war stories from people I met.

Dave's roommate, Klaus told me that right after the war some American soldiers gave him an ice cream cone. He had never seen ice cream, so he took it home and put it under his bed for safe keeping. So sad was that! His father was in a prisoner of war camp in France until Klaus was three years old. Later Klaus married Princess Grace's goddaughter, Marie Odille, and he sent me a photo of Grace and Ranier at his baby's christening holding little Caroline. I was so happy that life had finally treated him well. Ursula had a dollhouse that her dad made for her from broken pieces of wood in the ruins and rubble. German children liked to play in the rubble, but it could be dangerous. One of my tutors got a broken arm that way. We have no clue how fortunate we are to not know what it is like to live in a war-torn country where you must start all over and struggle to have food on the table, clothes on your back and a warm bed.

I have another girlfriend, Gudrun. Her family lived in the eastern part of Germany. When her mother was pregnant with her, she and her father and two older sisters fled through some mountains called the Erzgebirge from the Russians after the war with only two suitcases of clothes. That was when Germany got divided into East and West.

I.E.S. had their office building on the Marktplatz (market place) where we had our tutorials. It was directly next to the famous Freiburger Munster cathedral. My favorite tutor was Herr Schneider. I called him Mr. Scissors since schneiden means to cut. The other tutors grouched at me a lot because they thought I needed to study more. I was out and about meeting people from all over the world and learning about life and German culture.

Since Freiburg has a huge medical school, international students were abundant. I met Darius from Iran who taught us to put cardamom in our coffee and tea. He became a pediatrician and settled in Basel Switzerland. Kiki was from Sweden and was studying dentistry. Kiki introduced me to clogs. Voila! The shoe that was made for my flat Nordic foot with the Dutch genes. I have worn them ever since. For years the Bjorndal clogs had to be ordered from Anna's Swedish Clogs in St. Augustine, Florida. Now clogs are so popular that there are numerous manufacturers, and they are easy to find in many places.

It was pleasant getting to know my I.E.S. classmates. We had wonderful camaraderie, and everyone was friendly and congenial and from very nice families. I don't recall any misbehavior from anyone. That is, no one got in trouble with Herr Wronka. Danielle was from Palestine. They had had difficulties getting her a passport. She was like a girl without a country. Cynthia and I really clicked and spent a lot of time together. She and Esther were pastors' daughters. Dorothy had been a victim of polio and walked with a brace and crutches. Bev, Debra and Nell were very nice gals and jovial. The fellows were Dave, Eric, Chuck, Ron, Louis, Donald, Steven, Andrew, Wayne, and Michael.

Dave found a cobbler shop that encouraged arts and crafts for their customers. He bought some scraps of thin leather. He selected forest green and black. The cobbler gave him a little paper pattern of a frog. He cut it out and sewed it together all around the edges, leaving a one-inch opening. He poured in sand to fill it loosely and then finished the stitching. Then he glued yellow glass eyes on the head. It made the cutest toy that was fun to pitch about. I made several also. Actually, Allie still has the one that I made for her. Will someone please tell me why Dave and I did not invent beanie babies? We just did not realize what a wonderful idea this was. When back home in America I realized that you could also stuff these little frogs with grits. However, that might have invited some kind of insect pest like mealy moths. Sand was much more sensible.

The marketplace was interesting, and especially buzzing on Saturdays. Peddlers sold flowers, herbs, produce, handmade wooden toys, Freiburg straw peasant shoes, souvenirs, trinkets, knitted gloves and shawls and books. I learned about some new fruits. Stachelbeeren are gooseberries. They are green translucent sweet/sour and make a tasty pie. Lingonberries are small red sweet/sour berries that make a delicious jam. I now have two pair of straw shoes that I wear as bedroom slippers. One pair has green fabric lining, and the other has light blue.

An elderly lady dressed all in black native dress rode her bicycle there to sell books. For eighteen marks or $4.50 I bought a huge, beautiful German Bible printed in Leipzig in 1905. It has brown cover and gilded pages and beautiful paintings. The cover has gold pictures of Jesus, Moses, David, John and Paul. Naturally, the font is the old German print, much harder to read. One can buy delicious sausages there in the market. The favorite is a light-colored Bockwurst made from venison. Forget about catsup, it is all about dark, spicy mustard in Germany. Don't count on finding mayo either. Horseradish is very popular.

The Munster was built back in the dark ages in the Gothic style and is very remarkable and famous and beautiful. I encourage you to look it up and see photos of the carvings, arches, flying buttresses, stained glass windows and gargoyles. Dave's mother sent him a package that had some new American products. One was Nabisco canned squirty cheese. The other was some little plastic super balls that bounce very high. I got the brilliant idea that we should climb to the top of the spire and drop off super balls to see how high they would bounce. It was loads of fun, and we were extra cautious to not drop one on anyone's head. We had a friend below to retrieve them for us. I am still in touch with many of my American classmates from that year. There is a saying: Next time we are in Paris under the Eiffel Tower, will someone please let us know where Julie is! One never knows what she might drop from a high place.

Freiburg was full of quaint, interesting little shops. I loved the Seilnacht clock shop on Eisenbahnstrasse. I still have my tiny green footed windup alarm clock from there. Later I bought Lula a real cuckoo clock and bought my brother and sister little gold alarm clocks. It was next-door to the wonderful bakery. They baked loaves of bread for children in the shape of animals such as turtles or rabbits or cats and so forth. I found a thick warm navy-blue coat in a shop. They also sold me some black leather lederhosen that came down to my knees. We still have those pants. They will never wear out. One store had pretty wood carvings. I bought Mama a tiny one of Mary, Joseph and baby Jesus plus one of an angel with her arms around a girl. I told Mama that she was my angel.

We could bike about nine kilometers across the border to Requivier France. That is a quaint French village that goes all the way back to the Roman emperor Diocletian. Around 284 CE. There is a wonderful vineyard there that makes very good wine. The banks of the river had plenty of escargot that were easy enough to retrieve. We could build a tiny fire and roast them with garlic and butter. I basically learned French on the streets that way by venturing over the border here and there. I have German ancestors that were from Saarland on the border in that general vicinity.

I wanted to introduce the girls on my floor to popcorn. I went to a small grocery store and asked the lady proprietor for some kernels. She looked at me as if I were mad, and said, "Excuse me, but corn is for farm animals." Also, there were no marshmallows or instant coffee. My mom sent me a nice big care package with those items. The girls absolutely loved the popcorn. I roasted the marshmallows over a candle, and they were astonished. Waltraud admired my large, fluffy, fake fur pink slippers so much. I gave them to her. Her mother was a poor war widow. For many years I mailed Ursula fifty packs of microwave popcorn every Christmas by slow boat. After the bombing of the World Trade Center towers, all packages to Germany had to be airmail. The cost became prohibitive. You can find popcorn in the PX stores on American Army bases.

I had some interesting courses. For history I had The Popes and the Kaisers in the high Middle Ages. It was shocking to find out how corrupt the church and governments were. Folklore and Fairy Tales literature was my favorite course. The psychology course was very hard. Dear old faithful Mom and Dad sent me a box of psychology textbooks in English. This was a very helpful supplement to help me understand the works of Freud and Jung who came from that part of Europe. Later we had a lot more German literature to study from different eras in history. The postwar writers were easier to understand because they used very few words. This was supposedly due to all of the trauma, hopelessness and brokenness that they experienced and felt like all of the Germans.

German students study hard and don't have the distractions of football and basketball and cheerleading and dances. They work when they work and play when they play. I never met any students who gave a hoot about the kinds of clothes that they wore. There were no labels on T-shirts or the desire to have certain prestigious running shoes or clothes. They did a lot of walking and biking and skiing and were very physically fit. They ate a lot of fruit and other clean, fresh food. I imagine they would use American processed cheese slices as small frisbees!

If you were enrolled in the university, it was because you had always been a bright student who applied themselves. Children were divided at an early age around eleven. If you were not truly cut out for university, you went to some kind of trade school to be a butcher or plumber or day care attendant or clerical worker. No one looked down on trade schools. If you were going to be a baker, you knew you would strive to be the very best baker in town and be proud of yourself. German learning institutions have longer breaks and holidays than we do. They get an entire month off in the spring.

The university cafeteria was very inexpensive. They had Eintopf for 1.25 marks. Eintopf means one bowl, so it was a huge bowl of stew either meat or lentils with rice or potatoes. This ancient university was there way back in the time of Erasmus, the Dutch philosopher and theologian from Rotterdam. He was born in 1466, and was one of the greatest scholars of the northern Renaissance. He wrote in Latin. His writings greatly influenced the Reformation. The interesting red and gold house where he lived is still on the Marketplace square.

There were often students on the campus peacefully demonstrating for Mao Tso Tun Chinese Communism. Many German students were confused about politics. They were kind of lost after World War II. They had lost their trust in all forms of government and were floundering to find something to hang onto and embrace. Others were simply apathetically ignoring it all. They understood that we were from a democracy, but it was hard for them to fully comprehend our America and what it meant.

At Christmas all of a sudden, my building was empty, and I got a little homesick. Mama and Daddy bought me an airline ticket to go home. I rode the train to Frankfurt, spent the night in a hotel and flew out the next morning. While shopping there, I found a bright Kelly-green wool long sleeve pantsuit from France. It was lined and very nicely tailored with covered buttons. This was slightly before women were wearing pant suits in the US. My parents liked it a lot, but when I came downstairs, great aunt Nevada commented: The Bible says that men shall not dress as women, nor women as men. Out of deference for the older aunt, Daddy asked me to go back up and change into a dress which I did. The ironic thing is that when polyester pant suits became popular here, Daddy sold a ton and a half of them to working women, and that clearly paid for my graduate school expenses later plus my siblings college degrees.

While at home, Daddy and I went to the Mercedes dealer in Buckhead and ordered a 200 D diesel with stick shift. The plan was for me to ride the train to Stuttgart to the factory and pick it up as soon as it was ready. With four marks to one dollar, it cost around $3,200 which was less than we had paid for the Chevelle two years previously. Daddy let me pick the color, and I chose sky blue. I named it "Der Blaue Engel," which means The Blue Angel. This was in honor of my favorite German singer and actress, Marlene Dietrich. Mama bought me a 33 1/3 record album of her music when I first started studying German, and I memorized every song. She also bought an album of German student drinking songs. Some of them were in Latin. I still have those albums along with an old-fashioned record player.

After Christmas I was back in Freiburg and walking in the market place and out of the blue, there was my dear friend from Oxford, Marsha. She was studying at a finishing school in Nice, France. She decided to come visit me, but did not have my address or any phone number. She said, "I knew if I kept walking the streets, I would eventually run into you." She stayed a couple of weeks, and we had a grand time. We shared my twin bed by sleeping with our heads on either end and our legs side by side. I took her on the train to Hinterzarten to see Ursula, but we got off one stop too soon and had to trek through the January snow four kilometers the rest of the way. Basel, Switzerland had a wonderful January parade, so we took the train thirty-five kilometers south and took Klaus to protect us. The nighttime parade was drummers and flute players marching down the main street with candles secured tightly to their hats. It was a beautiful sight and rather dreamlike and ethereal.

The entire month of February was a wild and crazy succession of weekend costume balls for Fasching. That is the German equivalent of Mardi Gras. Our dorms had a small recreation center, so that was a popular gathering place. I really was not into beer drinking, but most of the students enjoyed sipping the suds. My friend Jutte had the funniest costume. She cut a large hole in a black and white striped knit dress and surrounded the hole with white bunny fur. She painted her belly to look like a face with big blue eyes and red lipstick on the mouth which was actually her belly button.

We all studied hard during the month of March. We took a bus tour to Berlin, and that was totally interesting. We toured West Berlin thoroughly. One night we all went to a night club that had motorcycles hanging from the ceiling. Since I had never seen such in America, I thought that was fascinating. When we were at the border of East Berlin, guards came on our bus and rolled up the carpet on the aisle. They were looking for any kind of newspapers or magazines that might be propaganda against the Communist regime. We were all squeaky clean and had no intentions to talk about revolution there. We went to the university and talked to students who told us, "Right or wrong, we East Germans know what we believe. You Americans do not, and you are clueless." When I went to a restaurant, the utensils were such feather-light metal one could hardly use them. The saddest thing of all was the travel bureaus. In the windows there was only one poster. It said: VISIT MOSKOW. Yes, that was somewhere they were legally allowed to travel. Otherwise, they were being held captive by the Soviet Union. We were told that no one was allowed to take any of the coins with them out of East Berlin. I tucked a few in my braided bun and no one suspected. Also, you had to be back in West Berlin by 11pm. I dashed to the bus station to make it on time.

I squeaked by my exams and passed everything. When April came, Herr Wronka and our tutors took us on a bus to Italy for three weeks. Herr Wronka had just married, so he brought his sweet bride, Marlene, with us. We were studying art history. It started in Milano where we saw Da Vinci's painting of the Last Supper. We toured many towns and villages and monasteries to learn about art from the Byzantine Era through the Dark Ages and into the Renaissance. It was fascinating and really appealed to me. We learned about frescoes and sculpting and Roman and Gothic architecture and all of the artists and rulers such as the Medici family and the popes.

I learned that treating women as second-class citizens kind of started with St. Augustine and St. Jerome. When priests were no longer allowed to marry, but still had carnal desires, they blamed the women for being temptresses and decided they must be put down. Kind of like Adam, huh? "But God, the woman gave it to me to eat."

I loved going to Assisi where Saint Francis lived. Padua was so peaceful. Florence was epic. We arrived on Easter eve. All of the town was out in the streets with candles and lanterns marching to the Duomo cathedral. Easter morning was quiet as could be, and the streets were deserted. That is because in their culture the emphasis is on the crucifixion instead of Jesus rising from the dead. I hiked to the top of a hill to see the large copy of the famous Michelangelo marble statue of David. Along the way I bought sweet buns at a bakery. Florence had recently had a terrible flood. You could see the mud line stains on their beautiful bridge. The straw market was loaded with small, meaningful souvenirs. The fruit vendors made creative boats and sculptures out of melons, fruits and veggies. I bought a tiny Mona Lisa painting and a miniature statue of David and Venus de Milo.

Pisa was quite an adventure. In those days you were allowed to climb the Leaning Tower. Dave and I bought a paper bag of grapes for snacking and climbed right up to the tippy top. I noticed the priests below in their long black robes with broadbrimmed black hats were riding their black bicycles hither and yon all around. I said to Dave in a voice that he knew would lead to mischief, "Do you realize how awesome it would be if we could make grapes land on their hats?" He fully agreed, and we tried our best to no avail. Something about the laws of physics regarding time and distance and velocity was unknown to us. I wonder if he ever went to confession about those antics?

Venice was to die for! We went to a glass factory. The glassblowers threw their colorful glass scraps out onto the shore of the calm bay. Over the years the waters had polished the glass into smooth, rounded stones. That shore was very colorful and beautiful and unusual. We took a boat out to a little island. The little school girls were dressed in navy blue dresses with white ruffly pinafores. The boys wore navy blue shorts with white shirts and blue bows for ties. They wore white straw hats with navy ties around them. We were told to not accidently fall into a canal in Venice. They were badly contaminated from having so much refuse tossed into them.

Rome was incredibly interesting with centuries of fascinating history. One morning I looked out my hotel window and saw a motorcade. It was United States President Lyndon Johnson. Sadly, Vietnam War protestors threw buckets of brown paint on his limousine. We toured the catacombs caves where early Christians had hidden from persecutors. We saw the entire Vatican City and St. Peter's Cathedral with the Sistine Chapel. It was striking how much gold and artwork the church owned while so many little barefoot children were begging in the streets and on the Spanish Steps.

Street vendors sold watermelon wedges. There was hops grain soaked in brine and sold in white paper cones. Cynthia and I were at the Trevi Fountain when we met an older very polite Italian gentleman. He wanted to practice his English, so he took us to his pizza parlor and gelati store. Then we went to a Donald Duck movie in English with Italian subtitles. He was really Atilla the Fun! Dave and I walked to a hillside one day and had a picnic overlooking a shepherd with his sheep. It was lush and green and so restful. I am definitely a fan of pastoral scenes rather than partying.

Our Mercedes had been in storage in Milano. I met a friend from school there, and we started the journey to Spain to meet Daddy. We stopped in Nice to see Marsha, and she and her mom took us to the perfume factories and to eat my first helping of steak tartare which I liked very much. It is raw very lean ground steak mixed with raw egg and dill pickles. We played Bridge speaking French. Then we went to the bakery, and Marsha's mom pointed to a pastry and accidently called it a "two no trump!" Once in Barcelona we overnighted at a campground. Halfway between there and Madrid we stayed in Zaragoza. Once in Madrid we met Daddy at the American Express office. Remember, we had no phones, so it all had to be prearranged by date and time. Daddy had gotten there a day early and gone to a bull fight. He took us to the Prado Museum, and I was astonished at the tall floor to ceiling paintings of El Greco. When you see them in art books, you have no clue how large they are.

We headed back to France. There were so many little Spanish villages that looked like they were one hundred years behind the rest of Europe. Women in long black dresses with black scarves were carrying jugs of water from fountains in the village squares. There were some clay dirt roads that were very high overlooking beautiful turquoise lakes down in the valleys. In Barcelona we decided to drive down the coast to a sleepy little fishing village called Cadaques. There were winding roads lined with beautiful stone walls. The famous impressionistic painter Marc Chagall lived there at that time. Nancy Brittain (my literature prof's wife) had told me that my paintings reminded her of Chagall. I had one liter of anise liqueur to declare at the border.

We stopped in Avignon and saw the Picasso Museum. The dish I ate at a small café had cream sauce, and I got an upset tummy for the first and last time in Europe. Instead of dancing on the bridge of Avignon like the song, 'Sur la ponte, Avignon', I was under the bridge upchucking! We stopped in Nice to show Daddy the perfume factories. We went to Monaco and played three hands of Black Jack at the Casino in Monte Cristo. There were wealthy elderly women there wearing sparkly black dresses and dripping with diamonds. They looked like they had not seen the light of day for years. They had wrinkles that were deeper than their pockets and caked with a makeup color I would call "Caspar the friendly Ghost."

Soon we were in Genoa, and the Italian coast was breathtaking with unbelievably tall cliffs overlooking the crashing sea. We showed Daddy Milano. As he was driving and looking at the beautiful Duomo, he accidently ran a stop sign and was flagged down by a carabinieri or police officer. We got a ticket. Daddy was anxious to get to Switzerland, so we enjoyed that beautiful scenery and clean, crisp fresh air. From there it was not terribly far to Freiburg. Daddy loved meeting my friends and seeing the beautiful city.

I took him to the local Gast Haus near my dorm. He made arrangements to rent the top floor bedrooms for Mama, Aunt Sara, Eric and Kim to stay there all summer while touring nearby countries. We drove north to Strasburg to cross over into France and drive to Paris. We loved the countryside and quaint little shops and cafés. There were small antique shops with tiny treasures he could take to Mama and Kim. We saw all the sites in Paris and went to the Moulin Rouge café to see the can can dancers that I adored. We saw the Mona Lisa at the Louvre Museum. After Paris I drove Daddy to Amsterdam so he could fly home on KLM Royal Dutch Airlines.

Back in Freiburg Dave was taking horseback riding lessons with Herr Addig right down the street from our dorms. I signed up and thoroughly enjoyed that. My wallet and keys disappeared from my cubby, and I was pretty sure the elderly stable hand took them. He always looked at me with such disgust and hatred. I understood that he was one of those shattered persons. No telling what he had lost and experienced. Thankfully there was no passport involved.

On Sunday afternoons we all rode along the Dreisam river. Elderly people sat on benches on the banks and did topless sunbathing for their health. Germans really prefer to be outside in nature. If they are inside, they want the windows open. They constantly ask for "frische Luft, frische Luft" which means fresh air. No screens are needed since there are no mosquitos. There were the popular Black Forest cherry trees everywhere. When you are up on a horse, it is quite easy to reach the cherries on the tree. It was pleasant and relaxing.

Poor Herr Addig was very emotionally devastated from the war. He often sat in the courtyard of his stable by a fountain and wrote poetry for hours. His thin little wife was constantly running a wheelbarrow in and out of the stalls to do the mucking. No matter who pooped it, she scooped it and just always kept on mucking. Years later I heard that he had some kind of a mental illness meltdown, and Freiburg took his neglected horses away from him. It was so sad. War is horribly senseless and evil. It destroys the very souls of the people and leaves their broken hearts in ashes.

During one holiday week Klaus took us to his home in Sonthofen in Bavaria just west of Munich. What a beautiful part of Germany! The cow pastures were covered in carpets of yellow dandelions. I was told when cows eat those blooms, it makes the sweetest milk. Funny since they taste so very bitter to humans. We toured King Ludwig's castles such as the famous Neuschwanstein (like at Disneyland) and went down into Austria to see more sights. I bought a half pint of Austrian rum to take to Grandmother Hazel to soak her Christmas fruit cake. We loved Klaus' parents and sister. I think his mom wanted to have me in their family complete with my shiny new Mercedes. She said as much.

In Freiburg I was finishing up my studies. Mama and Sara arrived with my brother and sister. I got them settled in the Gasthaus zum Hirschen. The owners, Mr. and Mrs. Baumgartner, had five children. My brother Eric especially liked Werner, and they had adventures together in the barn and retrieving fresh trout from a trough for the restaurant. Werner took Eric in the attic to see his dad's army uniform in a trunk. Eric was not to let the parents know they had done that.

Mama took the car and toured Germany, Switzerland, France and The Netherlands. In Oberammergau, Germany, home of the world-famous outdoor passion play, Mama bought an incredibly beautiful hand-carved nativity set with figures eighteen inches tall with fabric clothing. I display it every Christmas on our hearth. Mama and Eric and Kim were in a taxi in Paris, and the driver was extremely rude and hateful. When Mama got out of the car, before she paid him, she said, "Monsieur, I will have you know that there is American blood spilled on every acre of your land. Don't you ever forget that!" Now that is a Sockwell/Mobley/Moore woman in the flesh. They are strong matriarchs who take a stand and assertively get their point across while remaining ladylike and poised.

When Yankee history writers visited Mama's Grandmother Mobley in Covington to get her information about the War Between the States, she would tell them, "Sir, I will have you know that when it was against the law to take a bath in New Jersey other than on Saturday nights, Georgia had America's very first women's college, Lucy Cobb Institute. I am a graduate of that college."

I finished school, and we drove to Brussels Belgium. We were the guests of Colonel Van Enthout and his wife. He had served during the war with Mama's cousin Colonel Holbrook. They took us to climb the very tall monument at Waterloo. Forty-seven-thousand died there, and people harvested the teeth of healthy young soldiers to make dentures for the wealthy.

Mumsie had instructed Mama to buy me a Brussels lace wedding veil. Mrs. Van Enthout took us to the salon of Madame Antoine who had made the veil for Princess Grace. I selected a cathedral length veil which has become a treasured family heirloom.

When walking around Brussels in the evenings, my brother asked Mama why scantily clad ladies were on balconies with red lanterns. Every morning early an elderly woman with a rickety little wooden wagon came down the street crying out for old rags. Probably she sold them to a paper company.

Then we headed to Calais France. When we got on the ferry to Dover England, it was D-day, the anniversary of the Americans landing on the beaches of Normandy to win World War II. American Air Force planes were flying in formation with red and blue exhaust. It was very impressive and meaningful. Our hearts leapt within us. Landing on the white cliffs of Dover was breathtaking and memorable to say the least. One does not forget moments like that very easily. Europe and England are another world. They make you realize that America is great and wonderful in so many ways, but is only a baby country in the scheme of things. We are more clueless when it comes to education, childrearing, caring for the elderly, work ethic, nutrition and so forth. Refrigerators in Germany are the size of dishwashers because they shop for fresh food and bread every day with baskets and reusable bags.

We hit most of the hot spots in England and found the Brits to be so friendly and helpful. They were not at all stuffy as I had heard. The ladies always said, "Yes, love, no love, what do you need, love?" Mama was not feeling very well, and everyone was so kind and thoughtful. London was simply amazing! We were staying at the Hilton, so that is where I celebrated my twenty-first birthday. They brought me a pretend key to the city. Daddy had sent a letter for me to the American Express office. It had a sweet poem he had written for my birthday. When I went into the ladies' powder room on the lobby level next to the restaurant, there were two of Aunt Lila's prints of magnolias on the wall across from the dressing tables with mirrors. Imagine that! What a shame that I did not have a smart phone to photograph that! Oxford and Cambridge were well worth visiting.

When we went to Stratford on Avon to learn all about Shakespeare's world, we stayed in a bed and breakfast with a very nice English family that had a little redheaded five-year-old boy. He came home one day in a brown velvet jacket and shorts with a white shirt all lacy/ruffly around the neck and sleeves. He triumphantly declared in his adorable English accent, 'I have been to a "buthday paaty"'. Eric and I got up before the dawn cracked a single crack and went to stand in line at the Royal Shakespeare Theater to buy tickets. We purchased four tickets to see 'Macbeth' that afternoon. While waiting there on the Avon River, at daybreak the swans were flying above the river and gliding down and sailing close to the river as if waterskiing. That was the kind of moment that takes your breath away!

We drove north to Lincoln England to catch a Swedish ferry to Amsterdam. It really did have a true smorgasbord of food in the dining room. I have never seen so many trays of every kind of food in one place in my life! We toured the city, and Kim wandered off and got lost. She was only thirteen but had the presence of mind to find a police station. When the officers asked her where our hotel was, she told them it was on a canal. Gee, Kim, how profound. Everything in Amsterdam is on a canal! Anyway, we found her eventually perfectly safe.

We took the Mercedes to the shipping company that Daddy had prearranged. It had my trunk in it. Mama was frail and sickly so I decided to put her on a KLM plane to home. Somehow, we traded tickets, and when I flew Icelandic Airlines to Iceland with Eric and Kim, I was listed as Mrs. David Datry. No one gave a hoot about that situation or questioned anything. Same story when we boarded the plane to fly to New York, and when we boarded Eastern Airlines for a flight from New York to Atlanta. Wow! Times were decidedly different when it came to passports and identity and security. Unbelievable! Hardly anyone had ever even heard the word terrorism. The western world was still innocently reasonably safe altogether. Wars and conflicts were obscurely far away from our lives. We lived in blissful idyllic peace. The world still adored heroic America for winning the war.

I took my siblings on the train to Luxemburg for our flight to Iceland. We had Mama's very heavy forty-pound, cumbersome breathing machine in tow along with our suitcases. While waiting at the airport, we were walking around outside on the grass under the trees. My brother had a tiny little gun that actually could shoot. He was going from one clover flower to the next shooting bees. And yes, you guessed it, he took that little gun on the plane with no one complaining or batting an eyelash! Can you even imagine? Years later he had beehives at his home. Perhaps he had guilty feelings about sending the poor little striped buzzers to Honey Heaven.

All the way from Iceland there was a baby that cried incessantly. I told Eric and Kim, "Would someone please tell that little kid that the war was over two decades ago?" Anyway, we arrived home in Atlanta all safe and sound and full of such happy and interesting memories. Mama and Daddy took us to eat at the International House of Pancakes on Clairmont Road at Briarcliff. Kim looked at the menu and made a very funny comment about the international burgers. She said, "Oh, I bet I know how the French burger looks. I think it probably does not have a top bun." She was making reference to the fact that when she went to The Folies Bergere in Paris, the dancers were topless. We have laughed about that for over five decades.

I started receiving requests from various groups in the community and at our church to come and speak to them about Germany and my travels. It was the perfect opportunity to be a diplomatic ambassador. There were still many people who had bad feelings toward Germany, so I could help to mediate to exonerate the average German citizens and set them far apart from the government regime that really did all the atrocities. This was really my forte'. That is why Cousin Telsa repeatedly called me Mrs. Kissinger, the diplomat of the family. I always wanted to understand both sides of every conflict to help the "conflictees" come to some kind of suitable resolution to their differences or misunderstandings. It suits my peaceful, pastoral, placating personality. Who needs petty verbal pummeling, anyway, please?

Chapter 12
Going to Graduate and
Give Back, World!

It was wonderful to be back with my family and friends again, but there was deep sadness leaving Germany behind. I now had two homelands and felt torn into two jagged pieces. I was like a stain glass window that was a bit shattered. Allie asked me to room with her, and I was a fool to say no and take a single room. My heart was grieving, and I just needed to be alone with my thoughts and memories for a while. She understood that I was going through a difficult passage in my life. It was really hard to fit in my country again. I was very different. I had lived with people who came from ancient lands and had different ways of doing life. I saw values that were eternal and rang true for me. There was logic and sensibility. They had more clues about life and running a society. This ancient wisdom did not work as well in the America that I love. Our government may be advanced, but life for me is a triangle: Church/State/Home.

I was studying Educational Psychology and Child Development and taking German literature courses and grammar. The first book was studying Goethe's novel 'Faust.' The German students highly admired me for being so advanced, but at the same time were intimidated by my superior proficiency in the language. Dr. Johnson, head of the department, had visited me in Freiburg and was determined to have me accept a three-year fellowship to the University of Georgia to get a PhD in German. It would be paid for by the state of Georgia and in today's market would be worth hundreds of thousands of dollars. It paid tuition, room and board, books and pocket money plus living expenses for three summers in Germany. I would have to be under contract to teach in Georgia for at least three years.

Emory is only a couple of miles from Decatur Methodist church where I grew up. I attended on Sunday mornings. The choir director, Mrs. Clark, enlisted me to sing in the choir. Rehearsal was on Wednesday evenings. There was so much construction going on at Emory that it was almost impossible to get a parking space when I returned to the dorm. I was having to park in unauthorized zones and hoping to move my car early each Thursday morning. But alas and alack, I got so many parking tickets! Mumsie had a dear friend from her Wesleyan College days named Mozelle. We called her Aunt Mozelle. She was a retired missionary who had spent many years in Japan plus being a dietician at Emory Hospital. She lived right across the street from my dorm in a house with a huge driveway, of all things. She agreed to rent me a parking space for $5.00 per month. That was quite a relief and cut my stress load way down. Every time I went to pay her, we had tea with tea sets she had brought from Japan a long time ago.

I spent a lot of time with Wendy and Peggy and Allie. Wendy was majoring in Psychology. Peggy was getting an English degree, and Allie was studying Sociology. Wendy's boyfriend got me a blind date with a nice older gentleman. On the first date he confessed to me that he was unhappily married and asked me if that bothered me. I promptly told him goodbye and good luck! Anyone with at least five brain cells in their head would have said the same thing. I had my whole life ahead of me and decidedly did not need to settle for such a wacked out arrangement that could only lead to desperation and heartbreak.

Emory had a new weekly class schedule. Every Wednesday was called "Wonderful Wednesday." There were no classes, and it gave us more time to study and go to the library. This started for a very specific reason to help students. The previous year there had been a terrifying horrible prank played by medical students that were really stressed-out during exams. They stole many pints of blood from the hospital blood bank and broke into Dooley's Den snack bar late at night. They scattered broken Coke bottles covered with blood all over the room. The next morning the police thought people had been murdered, and the entire campus was frightened and in an uproar. The students got caught, but the administration was merciful and decided to make campus life a little more laid back and student friendly. Also, the week of exams, many professors stood in the quadrangle and allowed students to throw pies at them and pour buckets of ice water over their heads. This was supposed to relieve tension and help the students deal with their feelings of fear or anxiety or depression.

I usually drove home four miles on Tuesday night and spent the night with my family and Lula. I mostly had my studying done by then. It was so happy to be with them and eat Lula's delicious home-cooked meals. Mama had taken up decoupage and had tables of supplies in her basement craft and sewing room. I made my sister Kim the cutest wooden pocketbook. On the sides I made miniature copies of her childhood piano sheet music and glued them to the wood. Then I put about twenty layers of the polyurethane varnish on top. The box was held together with brass hinges and had a metal handle and clasp to keep it closed. One of her pieces was called 'My Budgie.' It was about a little parakeet. Kim kept her African violet plants in that art room on shelves with Grow Lux lights.

For the Winter quarter along with German I took a sociology course that introduced me to many new concepts and was very interesting. I still like to observe society using the ideas I learned. The education courses continued. I was very fond of Dr. Ladd. Later we were all deeply saddened when he was riding his bicycle on the quadrangle after an ice storm, and a heavy branch fell on him and killed him.

Another favorite was Dr. McCandless. He introduced us to really engaging research about behavior and child development. I remember everything he taught. I even kept in touch with him when my children were born, and I had questions about things. His wife was Swedish, and he encouraged me to speak German to my preschoolers. We had no email, so I sent him letters and photos, and he always responded. This was in the very early stages of daycare centers. With funding from the C&S Bank, he started the Kittridge Center daycare on North Druid Hills Road at Briarcliff near Emory. It was a roaring success. Women were beginning to join the workforce en masse. This was much needed.

I met and befriended an instructor in the German Department named Dr. Hollweg. My heart nearly broke for him. He dated only Jewish women and eventually married one. His father had been a Nazi, and he was trying to compensate for the load of collective guilt he felt for being German and having a family that supported that regime. I cannot imagine being that tortured for a lifetime. Dr. Freud for you is on line 1!

Dr. Brittain and his wife, Nancy, took us one weekend to the old family hotel at Clairmont Springs in Alabama near Cheaha State Park. It had once been a resort near some mineral springs. It belonged to his mother's family. Then it was closed, and we had the entire hotel to ourselves. We got up in the mornings and made pancakes in the huge kitchen on the griddle. Peggy and Allie went with me. Allie and I took long walks, and Peggy did some writing. Cheaha is the highest elevation point in Alabama. Every year around September 21, Christian drummers, flute players and buglers climb to the top and play their instruments at the appointed hour to pray for our nation. The trade winds take the air from Cheaha all the way to Canada, so it is symbolic of spreading prayer across America.

When Spring Quarter came it was time for me to do my student teaching, so I moved back home for good. I requested Briarcliff High since my siblings were there and studying German under Mr. Clack. I was assigned to teach a half day at Tucker High School and half a day at Henderson High School. The principal at Tucker was Dr. Hinson who would later be the superintendent of The DeKalb Schools. There was a senior girl there named Betts who would later be my principal when I taught at Henderson Middle almost thirty years later. She married a Mr. McGinnis. Mr. Neely, the German teacher at Tucker drove me with him to Henderson every day. It is a coincidence of unbelievable odds, but when I taught special ed at Henderson decades later, I was in the exact same classroom where I had taught German. The proof was an Oktoberfest mural painted on the upper wall of the classroom! I asked my math professor cousin David what were the odds of that happening. He did the calculation and said the number was off the charts.

In May my Aunt Sara took me to church with her downtown at Trinity United Methodist. It was Atlanta's very first integrated church ever. Trinity dates back to before The Civil War. At that time, it was used as a hospital for confederate troops. The sanctuary has the beautiful original stone floors and stained-glass windows and a huge pipe organ. Sara had found out about it from Ray and Marie in her prayer group that met at the home of her teacher friend, Yvonne Rustin. Ray was the news director at WSB Channel 2. Ray asked me to help him teach a fifth grade Sunday school class. These were children from the poverty neighborhoods of Capitol Homes and Cabbage Town. I taught the children art and played my autoharp and sang for them.

The pastor, Dr. Jones, was a graduate of Emory's Candler School of Theology, so there were Emory professors like Dr. Brewer and family. His daughter, Christa had been in my class at Emory at Oxford. Dr. Jones had grown up in poverty in Florida with a single mom, so he truly had a heart for this inner-city mission field. There were quite a few Emory students there from the Theology department or others. Emory grad, Max Cleland had come back from Vietnam in a wheelchair as a triple amputee. He and I sat on the back row every week. Later he became the Secretary of State for the State of Georgia and finally aUnited States senator. There were prominent citizens who believed that we are all God's children. They had left high class churches like Peachtree Road Methodist to promote peaceful civil rights awareness.

Dr. Cox and his wife Anne were members. He was head of audiovisuals at Emory. Cox Hall is named for his dad who was a past president of Emory. Anne worked in the Special Collections library. Anne and I started a library at Trinity Methodist. I did all of the cataloging and classifying, and she did most of the selection. Many members donated quite a few good books.

Dr. Martin Luther King had just been killed in April. Sara's prayer group met Yvonne's brother Dr. Frank Roughton Harvey and his wife Hazel. He was a creative Methodist pastor graduate of Candler who traveled the United States and the world doing biblical dramas in churches and for the armed forces. He had studied biblical archaeology and had authentic costumes and props. Frank had a PhD in drama from The University of Georgia. He had a dream to build an amphitheater in Cherokee, North Carolina for the native Americans so that they would have a ministry and more income. Frank came to ask Ray to help him do a bi-racial passion play in the Atlanta Stadium to bring the races together. It had been predicted that Atlanta could be blown apart that summer by race riots since Dr. King was from Atlanta.

Ray and Frank went to the Christian Council of Metropolitan Atlanta to ask for help. The council decided this was a wonderful idea, and they committed seventy thousand dollars to the project. They decided to have the production on Sunday September 15, 1968. Sara told me she felt I should go to Frank and offer my help. I drove to his office at the Share Foundation. He looked at me and said, "You are the one! God is speaking to my heart and telling me that you are to be the property manager for our theater company." It was called 'Behold the Man.' Something clicked in my soul and spirit, and I knew I was to follow this charismatic pastor for all the right reasons. A comforting peace washed over me, and it was all systems GO! I had always wanted to do something to help my nanny Lula Mae's people. This was the golden opportunity. I am not sure how qualified I was for this job, but when the Dear Lord calls you, He also equips you! I had some theater experiences, true, but this job was mind-boggling and astronomical. I was way out of my league, but an unseen force energized and guided me. We faced many obstacles, but the desire to make the world a better place made us like track stars that could jump over very tall hurdles.

Frank gave me a list of hundreds of props that we needed. There were Roman soldier swords, shields, breastplates and helmets. I had to find dozens of plastic palm branches for Palm Sunday. There was the table, stools bowls, goblets, and bread and wine for the Last Supper Scene. There was even an authentic well for the Samaritan woman. I was to work closely with Herschel Harrington, owner of the scenery company on Tenth Street. He usually did scenery for the Alliance Theater at the Arts Center at High Museum. He made things for me like fiberglass boulders for the Garden of Gethsemane. I was responsible for benches, chairs, tables, King Herod's throne, Pontius Pilate's throne and so forth. There were giant cushions for the dancers in Herod's court.

In the Temple scene there were the Ten Commandment tablets to be made on urethane foam. Frank had me go to a holocaust survivor, Reverend Gore, at the Episcopal Church of the Epiphany on Ponce de Leon in Decatur. He had been a rabbi, and then became a Hebrew-Christian pastor. Since my Papa's family in Europe had perished in that genocide, I truly could relate to Reverand Gore's life with all of the shock and trauma and grief and loss. I still have the little half piece of notebook paper on which he wrote the commandments for me in pencil in Hebrew.

For the Palm Sunday procession, I had Mr. Bush's cabinet shop in Decatur make a canopied Roman litter. This was for a wealthy Roman citizen lady actress to be carried by four servants. I had to be sure about every detail for each of the scenes from Christ's birth to the ascension into heaven. For example, there must be enough plastic fruit and bowls and chalices for the Last Supper table along with a basin and towel for the foot washing. It was challenging fulfilling Frank's props list. It was also fun and rewarding. We had such a short amount of time to pull this off, but you know why angels can fly, right? It's because they take themselves lightly! It's all about real, unmovable faith. All the forces of evil were against us, but we drew a line in the sand and said, "We shall not be moved!" The symbol of Atlanta had been a phoenix rising out of the ashes. Now Atlanta would rise way out of the fiery flames of racism and give "Jim the Crow" a bad blow! Many feathers would be way beyond ruffled. Feathers of bigotry would fly and drift down into the flames.

I had one live prop, and that was the donkey for Mary to ride in the Bethlehem scene, and Jesus to ride in the Palm Sunday scene. He was loaned to us by a farmer in Jonesboro who very kindly delivered him to me at the stadium. I can tell you he was a typically stubborn donkey and had the habit of leaving stinky presents for me on the stadium field. This made Mr. Shirley, the stadium manager, quite unhappy with me. Nonetheless, the donkey did his job beautifully and never kicked me even once. I think it was divine providence that he was not overwhelmed by the thousands of spectators in the stands, especially since this was his first experience as a Hollywood type star donkey.

I was on the executive board of 'Behold the Man', and we had our meetings in the Christian Council building downtown on Walton Street. Dr. Wm. Holmes Borders, pastor of Wheat Street Baptist Church on Auburn Avenue near Dr. King's church, Ebenezer Baptist, was chosen to play the role of Christ. One of the pastors suggested that we invite Hollywood personalities like Sammy Davis, Jr. and so forth to give us smashingly good publicity. Another pastor protested that Hollywood was not holy enough, what with drinking, drugs, divorces and whatnot. Dr. Borders stood up, banged his fist on the long wooden conference table and said, "Jesus ate with sinners and tax collectors, and you think that we are better than him. Nonsense!"

What I failed to mention was that I was still taking two courses that summer to graduate from Emory. Thankfully, they were not that hard. One was about poetry. I already had a small notebook of poems and songs I'd written that I could submit to the professor for assignments. The other course was about educational exercise fitness and recreation, and it was literally child's play, but I had to show up to these classes. I graduated in August with a degree in German with a minor in secondary education. Once again, to keep cool, I wore a damp bathing suit under the robe. My predominantly Nordic ancestry just gives me way too many red blood cells! Then I had an entire month to focus solely on the 'Behold the Man' production.

Frank's wife Hazel made the dozens of costumes along with Jamesine Reeve, director of the Glen Players at Glen Memorial Methodist on the Emory campus. Dr. Borders gave us a huge vacant garage behind Wheat Street church to use as a sewing room. Mama and Daddy donated hundreds of nice hangers from their stores in Decatur for the costumes. There were quite a few extras for the crowd scenes. We literally took so many of them right off the streets near the stadium. Others volunteered from churches of all denominations. I truly needed some dedicated prop assistants. Of course, Allie and Peggy volunteered along with a childhood friend named Tommy. Also, my dear friend Marsha joined in, and they all worked very hard. We had our rehearsals at the fairgrounds in south Atlanta near Greenbriar Mall. Finally, there was a dress rehearsal in the stadium the day before the performance.

Dr. Bevel Jones, my pastor at Decatur First Methodist had contacted every pastor he knew in Georgia by phone to encourage them to come to Atlanta to see the drama. This is the way we were able to sell over eleven thousand tickets and pay all of our expenses with enough left over to give to worthy inner-city ministries. Countless busloads of people came from the entire state. It was a joyful celebration of love and human brotherhood. Many lives were transformed from participation in and viewing 'Behold the Man'.

In the scene where Jesus was blessing the little children at his mother's house in Bethany, it was the sweetest thing imaginable. A group of children from a Catholic orphanage were there with their nun housemothers. They danced in a circle around Jesus and sang the song, "We Are One in the Spirit. We are one in the Lord. And we pray that all unity will one day be restored." It was the kind of occurrence that has so much beauty and love and feeling that it gives you chills and profuse tears of joy.

This was the sequence of scenes: Birth at Bethlehem, Jesus in the Synagogue, Sermon on the Mount, The Temple, Samaritan Woman at the Well, Palm Sunday, The Upper Room, Garden of Gethsemane, King Herod's Court, Pilate's Court, Crucifixion on Mount Golgotha, The Tomb, The Ascension into Heaven. The scenery was arranged in a circle, and the scenes were illuminated one at a time. The mountain was made from high scaffolding covered with fiber glass cloth that was spray painted to look like rock. Dr. Borders was seventy years old, and was theatrically hung on a huge real cross. At one of the later performances the next year, my brother, Eric played the role of the bad thief, and my sister Kim sat on a cushion in King Herod's court.

Newsweek Magazine sent a reporter who wrote a very nice article entitled 'That New Time religion' that was published on September 30, 1968. He said we turned Atlanta into a city of love. *Ebony Magazine* came also and wrote an article with many colorful photos of quite a few scenes. They called it "The Miracle of Atlanta." Johnny Popwell from the Alliance Theatre played the role of Judas.

For me this was totally a volunteer job. Thus, there was no paycheck. However, when my beautiful little daughter April was born on September 15, 1972, (same date as the first performance) a little still, small voice in my mind and spirit spoke to me: Well, how do you like your paycheck from 'Behold the Man?' Extensively awesome, right? If it does not give you happy chills, you might have flatline brain waves, respiration and heartbeat!! My spiritual stethoscope confirms and affirms that, ladies and gentlemen!!! Step right up and listen to the warm!!

Chapter 13
Where in The World Do
We Go from Here?

Now I stood at a crossroads. It felt quite a lot like a busy railroad crossing with noisy freight trains zooming past constantly with lots of bright blinking lights and whistles. How was I going to get across? I was more confused than a chameleon in a bowl of Skittles! The electricity was zooming across my corpus colosseum from left brain to right brain and back at LA freeway speed.

As much as I loved teaching the German language, high school students were not that enamored with it. The majority of them were in German class because they had German sir names, and their parents had insisted on it or bribed them. Also, the boys were all a head taller than me. I had not been the mom of a teenage boy yet, so it was rather intimidating. I did very engaging lessons and activities as much as possible. I baked gingerbread. I turned out the lights and had the students put their heads on their desks with eyes closed while I read simplified texts of Grimm's Fairy Tales. I wore my dirndl dress and told the students many interesting things about German culture, geography, art and history. I also focused a lot on Austria, Lichtenstein and Switzerland. I played my autoharp and taught the kids fun German children's songs with active movements. That is called TPR or total physical response.

In an education class we had studied the research about chickens and pleasuring. If you put an electrode in a chicken's brain attached to the pleasure control center and give the chicken a choice between pushing the food lever or the pleasure lever, the chicken starves to death every time. American teens were already so used to having short attention spans and entertainment that I felt the need at times to stand on my head blowing bubbles, wearing a purple polka-dotted clown suit! This is the result of so much visual and auditory stimulation from the media.

Needless to say, I did not accept that gold-plated three-year fellowship from the State of Georgia to get the Ph D in German. It seemed prudent to take a semester off and do some soul searching and try to get my head on straight. I worked a bit in Daddy's stores. Inspired by our time on the French Riviera, Daddy opened a new store at North DeKalb Mall, and we decorated it in French country style. The dressing rooms had pale blue French floral chintz curtains, so I precisely copied an impressionist painting of a lady in her white corset and pantaloons. It was a side view of her powdering her nose. The background was a soft, fluffy light blue. We bought old wine barrels and put round glass tops on them to display jewelry and accessories. The walls were adorned with lavender silk wisteria flowers like we had seen on the gray cliffs above the ocean in Nice, France and on the way to Italy. It was a feast for the senses!

I was active at Trinity Methodist in the inner city. Dr. Border's wife asked Hazel Harvey and me to teach a homemaking class for young girls at Wheat Street Baptist. That was very rewarding. I helped Trinity start Camp Trinity. The government had given us an old Girl Scout camp up in Cartersville, Georgia on a lake for $1.00. They provided us with a lot of government surplus food such as powdered milk, peanut butter, raisins and cheese. The Marriott Hotel donated sheets and towels. We bought clothes and bathing suits from Goodwill and Salvation Army thrift stores. Toiletries were donated by Trinity church members. Dr. Syn and his nurse wife Dee provided medical care for the youngsters. These children were so in poverty that they got on our bus unbathed without so much as a pair of pajamas or a toothbrush. Their families had worked in the mills, and few of them finished school or got good employment.

I was the art teacher and a couple of times drove the school bus up to the camp. One night while walking barefoot through the woods, I stepped on a snake that wiggled out from under my foot, but I was not bitten. I have no clue what kind it was. The next year when it was time for the astronauts to walk on the moon, our pastor brought a TV, and we all watched the historic event in the picnic pavilion where we had our meals.

One day I felt compelled to visit Mumsie's dear Wesleyan College friend, Miss Odille Ousley in Decatur. She had been an author for the Ginn & Company publishers. She wrote a series of easy to read first grade books that featured the siblings Tom, Betty and Susan and their dog Jip. Miss Odille was bedridden and declining close to the end of her life. Her mind was sharp as could be! As I sat on her bed, she took my hand and said, "Honey, go to library school at Emory and get your master's degree. You will be able to use your art and music and drama talents to encourage children to love books and literature. You can do storytelling and play your autoharp and sing." Miss Odille had watched me grow up and knew me very well. She was a wise, sweet and caring lady with a sensitive spirit. Something clicked in my career box, and it just felt so right. I could already picture myself being the library lady that rocked!

By then I was living in an apartment on La Vista Road with Marsha and Gail and Emily from Emory. Marsha was a server, Emily was teaching, and Gail was a nurse. Marsha's physician dad had a favorite charity which was libraries. Therefore, he was close friends with Dr. Lawson who was the director of Emory's library school. Now how is that for a genuine "God wink"? I mean really, the Good Lord has amazing ways to bring His will to pass. I find it mind-boggling to comprehend how my Daddy God can get me to hop through a window of opportunity about the size of a gnat's eyelash! Or? You have to admit, it is amazing and hard to explain away whether you believe in God or not. Coincidences can only take one so far, and then divine providence jumps in and says, "Hold on tight! We are about to go on a wild ride!" These are not rides for which one can purchase a ticket. These events are written in our destinies, and God's providence bring them to pass.

It was undeniable that my feet were being planted on this path. Dr. Clouse made one call to Dr. Lawson and told him that I was perfect for his department in every way. Dr. Lawson was hoping and praying for creative, gutsy, innovative students that would make libraries child-friendly and fun and attractive. He did some zippedy-do-dah rush-rush paperwork, and I was solidly in and due to start in mid-January. I was looking forward to being a happy librarian that did not just slink around the library telling the children, "Don't spit in the books!"

Trinity Methodist was presenting the Giancarlo Menotti operetta 'Amahl and the Night Visitors' for Epiphany in early January. This was the beautiful story of a poor little lame Italian shepherd boy and his widowed mother. They were visited by the three kings on their way to take gifts to the Baby Jesus in Bethlehem. It had originally been a black and white Hallmark production on NBC television. Do yourself a big favor and try to view it someday on YouTube or somewhere. It will touch your very being. Can you believe that I volunteered to make the costumes and the set and gather up all of the props?

There was even a live parakeet for King Caspar's birdcage. Also, I danced the shepherdess dance with a Candler Theology student named Larry and the pastor's wife Betty. Thankfully, someone else was doing lighting and sound and publicity and selling tickets! Whew!

I did the sewing at the home of Mrs. Hutchison who was the choir director. She was singing the part of Amahl's mother, and her niece Pam, crippled from polio, was playing the part of Amahl. Dr. Hall from Emory was the King Melchior who brought gold. After Christmas, Dr. Hall and I rode around the Druid Hills neighborhood by Emory to collect Christmas trees from the streets. I had my yellow convertible with the top down in freezing weather so we could stack the trees on the back. We tied them to the altar at Trinity, and it absolutely looked like a lush green forest! Everyone loved the fragrance of balsam, spruce and pine. There was a fireplace in Amahl's tiny, humble cottage. I stapled gray cardboard boxes from Daddy's layaway department onto a piece of plywood and painted black lines on them to look like a stone chimney.

The production was a huge success and went off without a glitch. It was very inspiring to the less fortunate people who lived near the church at the corner of Trinity and Washington Streets. It helped to show them that there was a whole wide world outside of the ghettos of Atlanta, Georgia.

Right before graduate school began, Joe and Nancy Brittain took Allie and Peggy and me skiing at Beech Mountain in North Carolina. We rented a cottage. On the way up Interstate-85, I was driving Allie's little Fiat. A huge greyhound dog came out of nowhere, and I could not avoid hitting it. I was very shocked and sad and shaking and speechless. Nothing like that had ever happened to me. It did a wee bit of damage to Allie's bumper, but the car was totally drivable. I had never been a very good skier. I hesitated at the top of the mountain, so Allie gave me a gentle push and down I went. Of course, as usual, I wound up with my kizip flat in the snow at the bottom. Oh well, at least I can brag about being a wonderfully skilled slalom water skier. And please don't forget my softball pitching, skating and soccer skills! Plus, only one human being has ever beat me at Chinese Checkers in my entire life!

Library School had it's good and not so good ups and downs. Our classes were in the old beautiful white marble Candler Library. Emory has always been heavily endowed by the Coca Cola Company because Asa Candler bought the Coke secret recipe from the pharmacist Dr. Pemberton and made a small fortune. Allie's mom is from that family. Elderly Miss Satterfield who taught me cataloging and classification was a gem. She loved the way I signed my name with a daisy for the J. She called me "Daisy." She got it that I was a creative round peg person and just did not fit in all of the square library school holes. She loved the way I had color-coded my Dewey Decimal book with colored pencils. I also glued paper tabs to each chapter to make it easier to find things. She allowed me to be myself, and I thrived under her.

Mrs. Moister felt otherwise and called me out in class and embarrassed me for being different. It was as if she thought I did not know squat. Squat could wear a T-shirt with me that said, "I am with Stupid." When I did something creative, she accused me of trying to be cutesy to show off. Non creative people who are mostly left-brained just do not understand that creativity pops out of one like poppy seeds germinating on rich, dark soil. You cannot exactly hold it back. It is invasive to the garden of the surroundings of your turf. Sorry, boring people, I could not contain my exuberance. I was excited about children and books. No one was going to squelch me. I even gave Mrs. Moister my extra ticket to the Metropolitan Opera at the Fox Theater on Peachtree Street. We saw the opera 'Norma.' There was no buttering up this broad! I was just going to have to take my two IQ points and rub them together and start my own fire! She thought I was weird or not too bright and that settled it.

There are times in life when one goes nose against the brick wall. Thankfully Daddy had taught me this saying: If you are going to play football with the big boys, you will have to learn to get your nose busted. Later when I had my own elementary school media center in the DeKalb Schools, it was a joyful, fanciful place that got me grants and accolades. Georgia State's library department sent their students to observe how I ran my media center. Surely that is the best revenge for initially being a misunderstood "artsy craftsy librarian." There are times when that expression is an oxymoron!

Thankfully, when my library school career was floating at the top of the fish bowl, and my grades were shaky, Dr. Lawson intervened and slid me through to the next course. He really did get me! Young Miss Coughlin tolerated me fairly well. She even participated in the April production of 'Behold the Man' and was sitting on a harem cushion in King Herod's court where Nancy Brittain played Salome and danced in a red costume. Joe Brittain played the disciple Matthew.

Dr. Cox taught us about audiovisuals, but in those days that meant slides, film projectors, microfilm and simple things like making attractive posters…sad but true. We had no video players or computers or any such newfangled thing. My best subject was children's literature. It was fun and exciting child's play for me. I wrote a paper about the fascinating life of Ludwig Bemelmans who wrote the Madeline books. Nancy Brittain introduced me to a New York promoter, Mr. Stevens, who was raising the money for Emory's new nursing school and law school buildings. He had lived in Greenwich Village and had often socialized with Bemelmans and his wife.

My family was having some kind of a meltdown anxiety attack over my chosen career. My closest friends were married and most of them expecting their first babies. The Datrys were thinking that I might wind up being a spinster. Anyway, not everyone was meant to be married and hatching out offspring. Aren't stereotypes just the pits? I don't blame my parents for wanting grandchildren, but for Pete's sake, I had not ever been a shrinking violet wallflower. I always had very nice gentlemen callers from very nice families. I had had several proposals. My family's fears were unfounded and off a wallflower's wall! I wanted a family very much and had no doubt that would happen when the time was right.

Chapter 14
Maybe I Do, Maybe I Shouldn't.
Just Get Me to The Church on Time!

There was a dapper older man at Trinity Methodist who was the organist. His name was Tim. He asked me to have lunch with him one Sunday after church at the fancy Top of the Mart restaurant in the Atlanta Merchandise Mart. He took me to the opera, and I really liked the fact that he was so much more mature than the young men I knew. He was tall and strikingly handsome and dressed like a Brooks Brothers haberdasher. He had a stable career in housing. He drove a shiny new Buick and owned a house. Most of my friends were living with their parents or in-laws while their husbands were living in fox holes in Vietnam. This fellow liked the same things I liked like working in theater, attending the symphony and browsing in dusty old antique shops. The earth moved without Archimedes even lifting a finger or a lever! Long story short, after five dates, we got engaged. Oh, my I was so young and naïve! If someone had brought me a Trojan horse, I would have said, "Oh, what a cute pony! I will sign for that!"

Aunt Dettie's husband's former diamond merchant partner Mr. Fine, had a wholesale jewelry store in downtown Atlanta. Aunt Dettie phoned him, and we went down to look. While there I selected a 125-point Tiffany cut engagement ring with a wide gold wedding band. Tim told Mr. Fine that he wanted a perfect, flawless stone for his perfect fiancé. I suppose love is blind, deaf and has an IQ of about 65. I purchased a wide gold band for Tim and had it engraved inside. It said in Latin: Sine qua non. That means: Without which there is nothing, which was to say that I thought of him as my everything. Tim wanted to get married immediately saying that he did not want to be a grandfather to his own children. It would have been wiser to have a longer engagement to get to know each other better. Also, it is wise to let issues surface so that one can work on them before tying the knot, jumping the broom and smearing cake on someone's face.

Now Mama and I had only nine weeks to plan a big wedding for over five hundred guests. Poor Daddy had nine weeks to get over the shock of the bills for clothing and flowers and reception and everything. Daddy was friends with the owner of a bridal shop, so I could buy a lovely dress wholesale at cost. This gentleman suggested that since my cathedral length Brussels lace veil was so fancy, that my dress should be plain and simple. I chose a high-neck long-sleeve dress that had a small amount of trim that matched the veil. The veil would attach to my head with a lace-covered wire frame that gave me a couple of inches of height. It would remind you of a Dutch doll or lady of Spain with a mantilla.

Mama thought bouquets of purple violets would be lovely for the bridesmaids, and I totally agreed. Like my godmother, Mother Dennis, I loved violets completely. Daddy ordered long purple velvet dresses for my attendants. They were high-waisted like Napoleon's Josephine and had Florentine lace around the neck and the sleeves. My bouquet was to be sweet smelling gardenias and stephanotis with white satin ribbons. It was fairly small in order to fit on top of the little white Bible that the Dennis's had given me at my christening. I have never cared for gladiolus that much. They remind me of funerals. I told Fairview Florist I wanted only lush green leather leaf ferns and candles at the altar. They were dear friends of Mama and Daddy. I had worked for them for a short while between college and graduate school keeping the shop orderly and making corsages. In those days one earned $1.50 per hour for such work.

Eric's closest friend's family owned the popular Rhodes Bakery on Cheshire Bridge Road. Of course, they would make the cake. Hard to believe, but the total cost of the cake was $80.00. We were members at Druid Hills Golf Club on Ponce de Leon near Emory. The reception would be there. They charged a mere $4.00 per plate for heavy hors D oeuvres, punch and the servers. I did not want a lot of fancy flowers at the club, so I told the florist to put a few purple mums on the topiary trees by the door of the reception hall and let it go at that. There was no dancing at Methodist wedding receptions in those days. What a crying shame! There was only that long and boring receiving line with meaningless chatter when no one was really listening.

Supposedly you could have said, "I killed someone in the bathtub with an ax." No one would even notice. You drank punch and ate toasted pecans and mints.

I was living in my parents Chateau Apartments on Clairmont Road then. It was a fairly quick bike ride to Emory on level sidewalks up Clairmont and then down North Decatur Road. I lived upstairs in the middle, and Mumsie lived downstairs on the end. Mumsie kept my frig full of home cooked meals. Mrs. McKibben, widow of a Decatur Methodist pastor, lived downstairs. Mumsie's friends Pauline and Quilla lived next to Mumsie. They were elderly sisters who made the most beautiful little pastel hand towels with a wide three-inch border of tatted lace that they made by hand. They bought the toweling fabric at the Scottdale Mill next to Decatur and Avondale Estates. I still have pink, baby blue, yellow, mint green and white of those and treasure them. By the time I realized how precious tatted lace was, Mumsie's eyesight was too far gone to teach me. Nonetheless, I have an entire basket of long pieces of her tatting. Will someone please motivate me to sew a beautiful dress for the newest granddaughter and trim it with Mumsie's lace?

On the afternoon that Tim and I were to meet with the pastor for our pre-nuptial counseling session, my Chevelle would not start, so I hopped on my bike and pedaled to the church which was probably a mile or so away. Tim and Dr. Jones asked me why I did not simply take a cab. My response was that I was a frugal person and did not need to waste that money when I had a sturdy bike for such purposes. That may have been a bit unusual for a gal who came from an affluent family. I have always been a minimalist that is opposed to waste. That became even more the case after living in Germany where not one piece of string or paper was wasted. Let's change that word frugal to parsimonious that means frugal to the 10th. Power!

Friends of our family had some lovely showers and luncheons and dinners for me. My elementary school principal and her sisters gave a luncheon downtown at the Atlanta Athletic Club. Mr. and Mrs. Ball from our neighborhood had a luncheon at the Cherokee Club in Buckhead. Family friend Nancy gave me a linen shower. The ladies at Daddy's stores had a beautiful crystal shower luncheon for me at Rich's department store. The Nelsons had a dinner for the bridal party to come and see the photos. He was Daddy's closest friend since eighth grade.

My sister Kim was the maid of honor. Looking back, I wish that I had had our younger cousin, Lori to be a junior bridesmaid and my little cousin Kathy to be the flower girl. The flower girl was friend, seven-year-old Kathy. I had been the flower girl in her mom's wedding. Three roommates Marsha, Gail and Emily were in the wedding. There was also the sweet little teenage girl, Gayle from Trinity Methodist. The pastors from Trinity Methodist and Decatur Methodist officiated. Tim's sister Rebecca was a bridesmaid. She was always a very lovely person and very kind and encouraging. My brother, Eric, was a groomsman. I so wanted Lula to attend the wedding. She was just too shy to do that. Her excuse was that someone had to stay home and guard all those silver and china and crystal gifts. I would have given her a seat of honor right next to Mama on the front row! Incidentally, I chose the same Chantilly sterling silver that Mama had.

Tim was from a wonderful family. His dad had died. His mother Maggie Belle was a real scholar with several degrees. She was such a fine lady in every way. She thought the world of me and was always very kind and loving to me. She was proud of my education, loved that I played the piano, and thought I was a wonderful mother when the little ones came along. We never had an unkind word between us. I was good to write to her often with all of our news. Daddy ordered a lovely mink stole for us to give her one Christmas. Tim's brother Richard ordered one for his wife Sally.

The wedding was scheduled for Friday, January the 9th. The weather went wacky to the limit, and the temperature dropped to eight degrees. We were getting married in the old chapel where I grew up. The pipes froze, and there was no heat. It was probably fortunate that there were hundreds of people crammed in those pews. They certainly must have kept each other warm. It was lucky that the golf club was not affected by the weather and everyone was toasty warm there. Poor Eric had to drive home between the wedding and the reception because I had left the special silver cake knife at home accidently. Daddy was so nervous that he left Mama at home for a few minutes, and had to go back and get her. She was a bit steamed about that, and I hope that helped to keep her warm!

Mama wore a long aqua silk organza dress with matching jacket. Mumsie wore a sky-blue silk dress with rhinestone trim and broach. A neighbor down the street from us sewed the flower girl's dress to look identical to the bridesmaids. Daddy had ordered extra yards of the purple fabric for that purpose. There was also extra fabric to make my tall, beautiful lanky sister longer sleeves. Eric used to call her "El Bow" when describing her long arms.

I think she inherited them from Mumsie's Aunt Sallie Mae who was literally a long tall Sally! Tim's mother had a beautiful long pale pink silk dress and wore exquisite amethyst earrings she had purchased in Florence, Italy when touring Europe after graduating college.

Rebecca's husband Billy brought a giant tape recorder with large reels set up to capture the audio of the music and the ceremony. My only requests for music were Jesu, Joy of Man's Desiring and Ave Maria. We had the traditional wedding marches for going down the aisle and coming up the aisle at the end. Wouldn't you know, during the ceremony a loud fire truck went past and there was a long sound of the siren on the tape. There are those who say that was a bad omen.

If I ever have another wedding reception, there will be no receiving line. The problem is that if you are receiving over five hundred people, you don't get a single bite to eat other than one bite of wedding cake smeared on your face for the photographer to snap that traditional photo. I had not planned for any alcohol or champagne, but some of Daddy's friends wanted some brandy supposedly to warm up from the arctic blast, so Mama and Daddy told the club to serve that. In those days weddings receptions were so boring. There was no dancing. You just ate some pretty little sandwiches and chicken liver/bacon rumaki. You drank fruity punch from a 4 ounce crystal cup with a tight handle that pinched your pinky.

The big surprise at the reception was when some gentleman friends came in in black hats and pretended that they were going to kidnap me. This was orchestrated by Tim's friend, Sonny You will remember him as the actor who later played the deputy sheriff Enis in the popular TV series, 'The Dukes of Hazzard'. Sonny had complained that well-behaved people like my dad and the pastors had not been invited to the bachelor party. So he said those who were invited were the dubious "black hat" friends. I have some choice photos of those Black Hatters.

My dear Aunt Judy and her husband Tom came from Chicago and brought their youngest children Kelly and Kathy. I wore a purple crepe pantsuit for going away. It had voluminous pleated sleeves that were like bat wings. As I was coming down the stairs, my Uncle Tom shouted, "Look, she already has on her pajamas!" Yes, my Yankee relatives are very plain spoken. You always know exactly where you stand with them. There is no southern ludicrous lily-lipped loquaciousness.

Our groomsman Buddy drove us to the airport to the Air Host Inn. We were so hungry that he went to the vending machines and brought us packets of Nabisco cheese crackers and bottles of Fanta grape soda. That became a tradition. Every year on our anniversary we took Buddy some cheese crackers and grape soda. He lived right around the corner from us, so we could easily walk. We had an early morning flight to West Palm Beach. I can't say it was super warm in Florida in January, but I could swim a bit. Sorry to say I had to sit by the pool in a yellow bathing suit covered with white lace and read a lot of lessons for library school. That was the only way they would let me take off in the middle of a semester for a honeymoon.

I had an internship at the main Fulton County Carnegie Library downtown a couple of days per week. It paid $1.50 per hour. I was the assistant to the public relations director Miss Cornn. My job was to write book reviews for her to read on the radio. I was also responsible for doing attractive posters and bulletin boards. Once a month I changed the display case that housed personal belongings of Margaret Mitchell who wrote 'Gone with the Wind.' Her husband had donated things like her bone china, the champagne bottle that she had cracked across the bow of the U.S.S. Atlanta and her typewriter. I must say it was awe-inspiring to type on her typewriter just a tiny bit for fun.

On March 31, 1970 Atlanta had a massive snow storm. That day the buses were not running, so I hitched a ride with an Army General and two Colonels at the corner of Briarcliff Road and Fisher Trail in northeast Atlanta a few blocks from our house. Yes, I was a loyal employee for sure to brave it downtown like that. They politely dropped me off right in front of the library.

Later that spring when the staff artist Judy had a baby, Miss Cornn put me in her studio as the staff artist for the entire Fulton County Library System. Miss Cornn had worked with me on 'Behold the Man', so she knew I was artistic, creative and motivated and could handle that job. I made flyers, bookmarks, brochures and so forth to advertise upcoming events in all of the libraries. Directors of individual libraries such as the West Hunter Branch and so forth could request artwork from me by sending me a memo by way of the courier. I found this job to be totally fun, and I could have done it forever. I was also in charge of teaching local librarians how to make puppets and do puppet shows. Vincent Anthony the founder of Vagabond Marionettes Theater on Spring Street downtown taught me how to do this.

Also, Mrs. Parker, the Children's Director, felt that I should do a closed-circuit TV program for all of the children's librarians in the county to motivate them to do innovative and engaging activities and art projects. Sadly, Mr. Rochelle, the head director could not squeeze me out some funds from anywhere to do that. Nonetheless, I was honored that Bertha believed in me that much.

I had a long, narrow studio, and my desk was at the back facing the back wall. One day a strange mentally ill library patron fellow wandered into my office. Obviously, this was in the days before CCTV cameras, so I had to press a buzzer under my drafting table to call for security. They came quickly and rescued me before there was any incident. Another time, a delusional paranoid schizophrenic man attached himself to the outside telephone pole with an extension cord and receptacle he had installed on the pole. He claimed if the guard unplugged him, he would die. Thankfully an ambulance took him to a psych ward for proper care. I had read about an identical case like this in Dr. Karl Menninger's book 'The Human Mind' when I was eight years old. It made me feel so sad! We don't realize how fortunate we are to have balanced brains that function well without bizarre behaviors. And look at the advancements in psychotropic Rx meds!

After work I walked up Peachtree Street to ride home with Tim. He was in the Peachtree Center building next to Macy's. Of course, in those days Macy's was still Davison's department store. Tim's friend Sonny was modeling for an agency called Peachtree Models. That agency was owned by the daughter of Jamesine who made the costumes for 'Behold the Man.' Bonnie is the person who took Sonny to a Burt Reynolds movie to audition. This led to his part on 'The Dukes of Hazard.' On pleasant days, he and Tim ate sack lunches on the benches in front of their building.

Usually there were homeless men along the way from the Atlanta Union Mission. They were asking for money. It was heartbreaking to me that they were so ragged and unkempt and hollow-eyed. I decided that the best thing I could do was to take them into a tiny not so fancy restaurant on a side street and buy them a hot meal. There was never a problem with this. No one objected, and the men were very grateful and gentle. In the dead of winter with runny noses, they also needed tissues to replace their jacket sleeves.

We bought a washer at Sears and started decorating the house to suit my taste. (Still hung clothes on a clothesline.) I took the beige drapes, dyed them aqua and made redesigned ones with button tabs at the top. I found a beautiful colonial reproduction striped Dwoskin wallpaper for the dining room called "Sturbridge Village." It had stripes of white, French blue and turquoise covered in little floral designs. My wallpapers could never meander all over the wall. It had to be definite orderly stripes. The beige carpet was wool. My careful vacuuming around the edges stirred up hundreds of case-making moths, and the house needed serious treatment. New acrylic carpet must be bought!

On Audubon Drive I loved the next-door neighbors, Carol and Tommy to the left and Mrs. Bradshaw to the right facing Ravenwood Way. There were sidewalks, beautiful azaleas and dogwood trees everywhere. I threw all our kitchen trash on a compost pile but did not know to put powdered lime on it. The food attracted rats that got into Tommy's dog food bin. Oops! They were good-natured and forgave me post haste.

Chapter 15
Let the Joyful Fun Begin!

I did not take a permanent library job anywhere or even complete my teacher certification paperwork, because we were ready to start our family. I enjoyed being a homemaker and had learned a lot about cooking from Mama and Lula and my grandmothers Hazel and Lucie. Grandmother Hazel was from Dutch ancestry, so she and Aunt Judy and Lula had more than taught me how to clean just about anything to a fair ye well! I actually enjoy cleaning and find it therapeutic. I get really good ideas when scrubbing and polishing. That is why I have never hired any housekeepers in my entire life. Cooking was not as cosmopolitan in those days. Yes, we did southern cooking, traditional American meat and potatoes and simple Italian. We were so provincial that no one had even heard of pesto sauce or Alfredo sauce or capresi salad. There were certainly no Thai or Greek or Mediterranean restaurants. Everyone went to Chinese restaurants and did not cook that food. We had down to earth Betty Crocker cookbooks and a southern cookbook called 'Mrs. Dull's Southern Cookbook.' Mama knew how to cook exotic French dishes like duck l' orange and flounder stuffed with crab meat. So that was the sum and substance of it.

Tim would give me a $20 bill for the week. That covered gas for my car and groceries, not spoofin' you! Well, I mean let's face it. Bread was $.25 per loaf. A can of tuna or a box of raisins was $.39 and so forth. Our money stretched like Silly Putty and Hubba Bubba bubble gum from hell to breakfast for real! Also, there were just not many things to spend money on in those days in the suburbs. There was the occasional movie or pizza parlor night. Our closets were small because our wardrobes were very basic purchased on a need to have basis. Today the price of everything is high as a cat's back!

Things rocked along in neutral until November when I felt up-chuckie every morning and went to the Emory lab for the test. There were no do-it-yourself test kits at the pharmacy. The test cost $5.00, and I wrote a check with the memo, "pregnancy test." Our money was in the bank in a small town. Tim said, "Uh oh! The clerk at the bank will tell everyone in town sure as shootin'!" And that was precisely the case. Ladies in my family had always gone to the Ob/Gyn clinic at Emory, so that is what I did. I craved bananas, and was positive that the baby could be a chimp. I also craved cherry vanilla yogurt. The months passed quickly and were uneventful. We decorated the nursery with an antique book cabinet with glass doors for the baby clothes. We put an 1800's dark oak spool bed in the room for middle of the night nursing.

Thankfully our cousin Terry lived nearby. She had started La Leche League in Atlanta for nursing mothers as well as Birthright to discourage pregnancy termination. I went to La Leche meetings at Terry's house and learned all the tricks. I saw women nursing twins and adopted babies and realized I could definitely do it too. Nothing was going to stop me or discourage me. My doctor informed us that he would not let the baby get too large. When we got to the seven-pound stage, I needed to have induced labor, also known as "baby by appointment."

Our son David came into the world that summer on what would have been Mumsie's fiftieth wedding anniversary. She gave me $50.00 to start an education fund. Papa opened the account at Decatur Federal Savings and Loan. I knew no better than to be put under with gas, but everything went smoothly for the arrival of that little 7lb. 5 oz. red-headed fellow. He was strong as a little ox and rubbed his nose raw lifting that head and turning it from side to side to see his whole world. His face broke out in a rash, and the culprit was the Physohex anti-bacterial soap the hospital used. Fair-skinned blue-eyed children are more allergic and ticklish. There was never a more elegant lady in our family than Mama. She went to an antique store and bought a little covered porridge bowl for his cereal. It came from the dining room of The Queen Mary Ocean liner. I still have it. She also purchased a Chantilly baby spoon with his initials on it.

Another blessing was that Mama, Daddy Kim and Lula lived about a mile away in Briarcliff Woods. Plus, our dear friend and groomsman Bob was our pediatrician. His office was very close by at Toco Hills. His wife Gwen was a nurse and was very helpful with all of my questions and needs. I did not climb any stairs for an entire month and did not lift anything heavier than the baby. We had a washer, but now it was definitely time to buy a dryer. This required running a new circuit, so Tim's co-worker Tom who had been in our wedding, came over and did the electrical. Older houses were simply not very well updated in those times. The little clothesline in the basement could not accommodate the new larger laundry load. I used the Lullaby diaper service which came once per week to bring cloth diapers. Disposables had just come out, but were not perfected and tended to be somewhat leaky. Ray Moore brought us an ingenious diaper gizmo that he and Marie had used with their three boys. It was a simple sink sprayer attached to the water supply of the commode. When rinsing a soiled diaper, one needed to only spray it. It was a handy-dandy time saver.

For the christening at age six weeks, we decided to have it at home in our living room with Frank Harvey officiating. He brought a tiny glass bottle of water from the Jordon River. His wife Hazel played her autoharp and sang, 'When He Cometh to Gather His Jewels.' Afterward Mama had a sumptuous luncheon at their house, and all the grandparents, great grandparents, aunts, uncles and cousins attended.

The night before we had walked extensively at the new Underground Atlanta tourist attraction down town. I got overly tired and woke up the morning of the christening with fever and a tender breast. I called cousin Terry. She rescued me. She told me I had a plugged duct. She told me that babies have an appetite increase at six weeks, and you need to rest more and not take so much out of your body. She said to get in a warm tub and follow a procedure that unplugged it. Good that I did not heed the instructions of the Ob doctor on call. He told me to put that baby on a bottle of Pet milk mixed with water and Karo Syrup. No thank you, Dr. Gullible, who believed his med school brainwashing! Nursing babies was just beginning to catch on, and we women had to stick together to claim our rights. There were actually people that thought breast feeding was perverted! Help me, Holy Ghost!!

We drove down to Auburn Avenue to see Dr. Borders at his home inside Wheat Street Baptist Church. We wanted him to bless our baby. He took him in his arms and prayed that his life would be like a pebble tossed into a pond with the ripples spreading out far and wide. Can you believe that we rode in cars back then with our babies in our laps in the front seat? Laws about car seats were non-existent.

My boy was quite active! When we walked with the stroller, he pulled his shoes and socks off and threw them to the side. Once we were walking around

Rich's department store, and he figured out how to get under the safety straps and get out of the stroller. I had to take the elevator to the floor where sewing accessories were sold. I purchased five yards of one inch elastic and made my own child-proof stroller straps. He walked like a champ at nine months. He knew how to open the refrigerator. One day I found him at the open frig holding a huge carrot that he was chomping on. It was not long before he figured out how to open the drawer cabinet just so in order to climb up the drawers like a ladder. He actually got on top of the frig! I had to booby trap the drawers so that he could not do that again. I remembered enough about my little brother's toddler days to realize that we were in for a wild ride of adventurous challenges with a very bright child that did not understand the "n" or the "o" in the word NO. He was the poster child for Dr. Dobson's book 'The Strong-Willed Child.' Yes, Mama wished one on me, and fish fish, she got her wish! It's actually a blessing to have a son that does not sit passively in the corner. Young men need to have strong personalities to ward off bullying and strive to be successful with exuberant self-confidence.

My sister, Kim; who was seventeen. wanted to study overseas, so Daddy and I went to the library to look for good schools. The nicest one we found was Professor Buser's Daughter Institute in Switzerland. Kim agreed and went there and had a wonderful experience and learned quite a lot of German. She had studied it in high school, but this was total immersion. It totally enhanced and enriched her education.

We spent a lot of time over at Mama and Daddy's. Lula also absolutely adored the baby. The little black poodle Luvy, was like an extra nurse maid. My sister had an unusual bed that Daddy and Eric built for her. You went up two carpeted steps that went all the way around the entire bed. Then you stepped down to the mattress and box springs which was technically right on the floor. Kim had seen it in a teenage magazine and just had to have it. It was called a "conversation pit." It made the perfect giant baby bed/playpen. Luvy lay down on the top step, and the minute the baby waked up she ran downstairs and barked and jumped around to let us know to go get the baby. Some days I left David with Mama and Lula and went to the European Health Spa at Toco Hills. A couple of times I took him with me sleeping in an Amish basket that Mama had bought in Pennsylvania. I still have that basket and keep my many tiny puppets for storytelling in there.

In the meantime, there was another baby on the way. This time I craved Brunswick Stew, so go figure. We were running out of space, so we decided to finish the basement and let that be our family room. That way the den could be another bedroom for the new baby. I made two Roman shades out of an adorable, colorful child-appropriate fabric. I found the cutest long curtains at Sears for David's bedroom. They were royal blue and red and had Copenhagen Danish type soldiers on them. With plywood and Daddy's jigsaw, I cut out a six-foot tall soldier and painted it to match the curtains.

I actually painted the downstairs concrete blocks with rubbery waterproof paint. That was probably a bad decision. Today women know better than to breathe paint fumes when pregnant, and this paint was particularly noxious. Naturally one day little David stepped in my bucket of paint. Thankfully he had on only a diaper and plastic pants, and the bucket did not turn over. Nonetheless, it was a bit of a clean-up nightmare since we had not installed a bathroom or sink yet. I had to carry him upstairs to the bathtub wrapped in a small drop cloth just four weeks shy of giving birth.

This time I reluctantly switched medical groups because I wanted to be awake and participating in the birth. Cousin Terry sent me to the appropriate doctors who also believed in rooming-in with the baby instead of putting the baby in the hospital nursery. This was a much more friendly scenario for a nursing mother to feed her baby on demand. When this baby was approaching the seven-pound mark, they again scheduled me for an induced delivery. The Pitocin hormone drops that start the labor, make the pains twice as strong, so I really needed a small amount of pain meds. I mean, if you have to push a watermelon through a Cheerio, who couldn't use a little numbing?

Of course, there were no ultra-sounds used back then, so I had no clue if blue would be the color or pink. I told everyone that if we saw a full head of black hair, it would surely be a girl. That was based on past family history. I got my wish, and pink it was! The beautiful baby girl was perfect with the sweet little face of a rosebud. She did not look wrinkled and newborn in the least. We had already decided on a name. I chose April, and Tim chose the middle name, Caroline. That honored my mom, Carolyn, but Mumsie did not understand naming a baby for a month. She said she would gladly have shared her name with a great-granddaughter. She said her neighbor's cat was named April.

When we got home, David was ecstatic to have a baby sister. He was only fourteen months old, so we had not been able to tell him what was coming. He loved to hug and hug that baby and was never even the tiniest little bit jealous. Of course, when April nursed, he decided that he wanted to nurse again also. I did not mind at all. There was no way I was going to push him away. His needs for comfort were every bit as important as the new baby. He quickly tired of nursing when he realized how much easier it was to get a big cup of milk in his Tommy Tippy cup.

I did have to be careful to watch him, because he was a climber and liked to get into April's crib. That could have been dangerous. I decided for safety's sake I should employ a little bit of gentle Pavlov behavior modification. I waited until he swung that little leg over the top of the crib. I came up behind him and did a tiny poke on his leg and said, "Uh oh! April's bed bite you!" That did the trick completely, and he never climbed in there again. I have a mahogany corner cabinet that Mumsie gave us. I had to attach straight pins with masking tape to the lower cabinet door one half inch apart to keep David out of that cabinet. We called it "the bite you cabinet." He knew how to bypass child-proof latches.

When April was seven weeks old, we arranged to take her down to Auburn Avenue to Wheat Street Baptist to be blessed by Dr. Borders during the Sunday service. He had played Christ in the 'Behold the Man' production. Our family attended along with April's godparents Ray and Marie. Since Ray was the news director at WSB, the service was televised. Dr. Borders could preach like there was no tomorrow! Even though he was a scholar with a string of honorary degrees, he frequently paused to say, "Help me, Holy Ghost!" Papa said it was the best sermon he had ever heard in his life.

Mama noticed that David had an orthopedic condition called anaverion, which is a slight rotation of the hip like my brother Eric had had. Eric's was caught later, so he had to have a small surgery behind his knee. Dr. Kurtz sewed him up with the baseball stitch which he did for little boys. Thankfully Dr. Kurtz was able to prescribe a brace that David could wear at night. It held his legs in the right position so that they would grow out of the position that made him toe in on one side. Remarkably, super boy could swing his little legs with the brace over the side of his crib and land on the rug, no problem. Who knew I had brought an acrobat/contortionist into the world? The doctor noticed that April toed out, so he gave her a brace that made her legs straight. She wore it night and day for three months. Then she wore corrective high-top shoes that toed in for several months to correct her legs.

A friend of ours told us about the Sugar and Spice Center. Tim took David there twice a week so I could get a bit of rest. With one baby being an active early riser and one baby pulling all-nighters, I had gotten a bit run down. He loved it there with his teacher Mrs. Tasha. She was very loving and patient. The very day he turned two, he came home and got on the potty and said, "David go potty with big boys." There were three-year-olds in his class, and he learned from them. Wow! Who knew I would have such an easy transition with him from diapers. What a blessing!

There was a big ice storm in Atlanta when April was four months old. A medium sized pine tree fell across our driveway. We had no heat or electricity, so Tim took us downtown to stay with Aunt Dettie at the Peachtree North Apartments on Peachtree Street at North Avenue. Lula had gone to live with her. They were on the tenth floor, coincidently right across the hall from our friends Joe and Dale. Can you believe that Daddy put dozens of bags of growing soil on their balcony so Lula could grow turnip greens? Hilarious! The ground floor of this building had a huge rec room for children with slides and climbing equipment and a merry-go-round for little ones. The building was on a generator, so we were safe and secure from the storm. The only problem was that when Aunt Dettie ran out of bourbon, she told Lula to go to our friend's apartment to borrow a cup of booze. Daddy was unhappy about that and told Lula no more of that.

For David's second birthday Mama and Daddy hired a truck from a lumber company to come to our house and deliver a load of sand. Daddy had already built a large, square sandbox in our backyard. Of course, little David helped him. There were wooden seats on each corner. I still love to play in sandboxes. Face it, it is very restful and therapeutic. We did not know to put a cover on the sand, so it is a thousand wonders that none of us got any pin worms. Tim's cousin Frances who lived a few miles away insisted that we have one of her dog's puppies. We took a male, and David named him "Peep-eye."

Daddy went to Mr. Bush's cabinet shop and brought home pieces of 2x4's. He sanded the edges and wrote David's name on each block. This is a tradition in our family. We believe in old fashioned toys that promote development of fine motor skills and imaginative play. The "David blocks" provided endless hours of amusement.

I always attempted to allow the children to have lots of fun and messy art experiences. In warm weather it was a big hit to take a bucket of water outside with large paint brushes and pretend to paint the house. I gave them finger paints in the bathtub, and they could paint the tiles and each other as much as they wanted to.

One afternoon five your old April was lying on my bed facing the bathroom. She was studying the gray square tiles in the tub. Out of the blue she said, "Look, Mommy, if I count five tiles up and four tiles across there are twenty tiles in all. Does that mean that five times four is twenty?" I was astonished! This was a very bright child beyond any doubt. I've heard that musical prodigies are also good in math. No wonder she could hear me play a Beethoven sonata and then play it by ear!

We did a lot of reading and cuddling in my canopy bed every day. Early riser David came to my bed at sunrise and said, "Mommy, warm me up." April was more of a creature of the night. I went to her bed, and she sang rousing choruses of songs like 'She'll Be Comin' Round the Mountain When She Comes.' At bedtime prayers I always asked the children if they wanted to tell God anything from that day for which they were sorry. I explained to them that our conscience is like a strong brick wall that protects our mind and heart and spirit. I said that when a brick fell out, we needed to ask for forgiveness so that the brick went back into the wall to keep it sturdy and solid. We talked about the forty-nine-character qualities mentioned in the book of Proverbs. For example, the one called Truthfulness would keep their trousers from spontaneous combustion, if you catch my drift and so forth.

April took us seriously and was very obedient and compliant. Perhaps I had been so determined that David would not have the negative effects of being a first-born child that I had overplayed my hand. I told him to be himself, express his real true feelings and not feel responsible for my feelings. It seems every family requires a first child by default, so April became that. Maybe David did not take me seriously and thought I was just jaw-jacking around to hear my teeth rattle when I spoke. David was so much cleverer than his parents that he thought we were "dingledorfs" that could be ignored.

Chapter 16
Life as We Knew It Came to A Screeching Halt! We All Hit the Dashboard!

Daddy had some kind of awakening or perhaps it was a mid-life crisis or a burnout. I don't know. All of a sudden, he wanted to sell his stores and retire and move to a beach. That did not set well with Mama. She had two grandbabies nearby and was loving every moment of being a grandmother. Daddy was only forty-six years old and Mama was forty-seven. I think Daddy was just plain burned out and used up. He had shepherded the entire City of Decatur for decades. He had been the head of his family and Mama's family. He looked after everyone. He had grown weary of being caregiver to his entire world. It was as if he was saying, "This whole marriage thing has been a lot of fun, but I gotta' go now."

The other problem was that Mama was very attached to her lovely home and friends. As a three-year-old little girl, she had stood on a sidewalk in Bradenton, Florida and watched their home burn to the ground. I think that had traumatized her. She spoke of the pain and fear when she realized that her little doll was in the fire. Mumsie was expecting Aunt Kitti. A kerosene heater exploded in the kitchen in the middle of the house. Mumsie had to run to both sides of the house to carry Julian and Mama and Sara to safety. The bottom line was that Mama dug her heels in the ground and flatly refused to move. I was feeling like we were the family that brought dysfunctionality to America!

I sent them to the Atlanta Counseling Center which was supposed to be the best Christian counseling center in Atlanta. It was recommended to me by the people in my Bible study group. They went to a few sessions and then dropped out. They never told me why they stopped going. I imagine one of them was not willing to look at themselves or heard something they did not want to hear or accept. I call that "My baloney has a first name. It's D-E-N-I-A-L." I can vouch for the fact that my parents were less than skilled at getting in touch with their feelings or feeling them accurately. They were from that generation of "Children should be seen but not heard." Parents told children, "Oh, you know you don't feel that way."

The result was that in March of 1973, Daddy moved to the lake and was living in our houseboat. Mama was desperately disturbed. She could barely eat a bite or sleep a wink which physiologically dumps your neurotransmitters off the manic deep end eventually. Now I had to be a caregiver for another human being. This went on until July. Then my parents came to some kind of understanding and Daddy moved back home. That year for my birthday they gave me a GE toaster oven. Daddy said the whole thing had just been a colossal bluff to shake Mama into reality. But sadly, it did not last. The same financial and life style issues resurfaced and Daddy did not know how to assert himself over a strong matriarch, and he left for good. I felt like I just needed to check outside and see if the world had ended.

MARTA, the Atlanta rapid rail system was building a station in Decatur on Sycamore Street. The construction cracked Daddy's building. Also, they were going to take away customer access to stores for six months. Daddy hired a genius attorney, E.T. Hendon. He dug up an old English law called *incorporatimus humidarium.* That means the merchants own some of the dirt in the street, so no one can take that away. This was a great victory for Decatur.

Daddy sold his three stores and apartment buildings and houseboat at the lake. Fortunately, the lady who bought the North Decatur store has been my sweet, caring friend ever since. Her name is Nisha from Bombay, India. She and her husband live three miles away. We would do most anything for each other. We have the most comforting bond of love and trust.

Daddy was a minimalist who had a dozen pairs of black socks and a dozen sets of white underwear the same. He had indulged Mama to the limits and spoiled her royally. She rode with the white knight, but he never made her clean up after the horse, so to speak. Daddy let people stir the poo poo, but then he licked the stick until he didn't.

Mama managed to stay in the house four more years. When the divorce was final, she had to move. The house was on the market. She was not facing this reality and was still busy planting petunias and cooking fancy stir-fry and such. I told the realtor that I needed some help to light a firecracker under her, so he sent me two ladies that did estate sales, and we got the job done. Eric told me throw all the paper work into a dumpster, but I knew I would have to go through each thing one by one. Mixed in with Rich's, Georgia Power and Davison's bills that went all the way back to 1956 were priceless photos of family. It fell on me to be the curator of that museum!

I met a lady Mama's age named Adina at Mama's estate sale. She bought a pair of silver candelabras. She was from Tel Aviv Israel. Her husband Robert who was originally from New York was a biologist working at the CDC to help find a cure for Legionnaire's Disease. She was on leave from assisting the Minister of Education in Jerusalem. We just really hit it off and loved to spend time together. She came to my Sunday School class and showed very interesting slides of flowers of the Holy Land. One was actually perfectly shaped like a menorah. She translated an entire children's picture dictionary into Hebrew for me.

It inspired me to go to the Jewish Community Center on Peachtree Road in Buckhead to study Hebrew. I found that it opened up the Old Testament so much for me. Adina explained the symbolism which is quite interesting. Just before she was to return to Israel, she asked me take her to Dr. King's church, Ebenezer Baptist, to worship. It was a moving experience to stand close to the people and sing and sway back and forth. Adina told me that since Jews had been slaves in Egypt, they really identified with the African American people totally.

Adina and Robert had such an interesting courtship and marriage story. He was an American soldier stationed in Egypt after World War II. He went on leave to Israel and met Adina. They fell madly in love. The problem was that the British were controlling Egypt and would not let him bring Adina and marry her. True love is a swift-moving river that cannot be dammed up, I think. Would you believe that he smuggled Adina to Egypt somehow under a load of Jaffa oranges? They lived in Robert's New York for a while before settling permanently in Israel.

Finally, we got all of Mama's furniture and books and dishes into Bekins boxes and into storage. Mama had been going to First Baptist downtown on Peachtree Street. She entertained the foreign students in her home. A young student from Singapore named Joo Ann rented a room from her. He taught her a lot about Chinese cooking. My favorite was sticky rice with dried fruit. There was an east Indian theology student named Kris from Trinidad. These young people were all very fond of Mama. Kris was from a well-to-do family that owned the trash collection business on Trinidad and some pharmacies. He arranged for Mama to go and stay with them for several months. This was wonderfully therapeutic. Mama could reach out her bedroom window and pick avocadoes from the tree. She was able to get relaxed and get her head on straight.

Daddy met Shay at a singles dance. She was a couple years older than him and had two grown children. Gere was head of the library at Mercer University in Atlanta. She had graduated from my same Emory Library School. Buster was a dentist. He had gone to Emory at Oxford two years after me. Then he graduated Emory and went to the state dental school in Augusta. Shay worked at the CDC on Clifton Road near Emory and lived in a condo across the street from her job. Her sweet elderly mother Florence lived with her. Daddy married Shay, and we called her mother Granny Shannon. They were from Newnan, Georgia.

Shay had no grandchildren, so she adopted all of us and loved us like her own children. She retired and spent all her time doting on us and doing fun activities. She loved to do arts and crafts with us and bake cookies and go to movies and pottery classes. She was the all-time best and most affectionate stepmother that ever lived! She had the patience of Job and the sweetest smile. You could never meet a more generous person with a smoother personality.

Daddy and Shay built a beach house at Alligator Point, Florida. That is a tiny peninsula shaped like an alligator about forty-five miles south of Tallahassee. We typically spent five or six weeks there every summer. The house was on the bay, and Daddy had a small Drascome British sailboat and a motorized boat for fishing out in the gulf and waterskiing. We had seine nets for shrimping. Alligator Point is a quiet community with only a KOA store, campground and a marina. Florida State University's marine biology lab was nearby, and the children could participate in all kinds of activities with baby sharks and sea urchins and horseshoe crabs and such. They were allowed to play in Jack Rudloe's private tanks. He wrote articles about sea turtles for National Geographic and sold specimens to universities.

We could drive west on Highway 98 out onto St. George Island or to East Point where they gathered oysters by hand with old wooden paddles. Carrabelle was the shrimping town. They had an old-fashioned drug store with ice cream parlor and antique ice cream tables and wrought iron chairs. Daddy contacted the president of the Izod company and enlisted him to help build a building for the volunteer fire department. It had a large community room on top for social events like crab picking and eating. There was a large wooden Izod alligator above the door. If you drove east you wound up at Wakulla Springs where many of the Tarzan movies were filmed. I even took the children up in a fire ranger tower, but David got a bit of scary vertigo coming down. Tricky, sticky wicket but we made it!

The children collected aluminum cans on the beach. We would dump them in the carport and run over them with my car. They put them in plastic trash bags to take home to sell at the recycling plant. Also, there was an artist in Carrabelle who had a gift shop. She liked to paint beach scenes like palm trees and sea oats on sand dollars. We had an overabundance of sand dollars right in the bay. David and April bleached them in Clorox water and sold them to the lady for $.50 apiece. Yes, Datrys have the blessings of Abraham when it comes to business. We all know how to earn a buck, and most of us know how to hold onto those dollars and invest them wisely. Then you have funds left over to share with those who are less fortunate.

Eric and his wife Pam and daughter Alycen built a magnificent house on an extra lot that Mama had next to her former home. Eric designed it, and it was unique, beautiful and unbelievable. He built an architectural studio over the garage where he could design structures and draw landscape architecture plans. The house was so stunning that it was fully featured in an architectural magazine. Eric was managing his construction projects, and it became very stressful. So, he took flying lessons and got his pilot's license and bought a small plane.

Mama had a friend named Agnes who had moved to Myrtle Beach, South Carolina. She invited Mama to come and visit. Agnes was managing her brother's motel and gave Mama a room. Mama decided to stay at the beach. Isn't it ironic that both Daddy and Mama wound up in medium-size beach houses but one in Florida and one in South Carolina? Oh, what tangled webs we weave even when we are not even trying to deceive! She bought a two-bedroom condo and had all of her belongings delivered. I flew up to visit her to help her get settled.

She was attending a full-gospel church. The pastor, Owen, was a former professional baseball player and a barroom brawler. When he accepted Christ, he felt called into the ministry, and was truly a wonderful pastor who had a thriving congregation. At Owen's church, Mama met Jimmy. He was a very handsome man thirteen years her junior. He looked quite a lot like the football star Joe Namath. He had been married to a former Miss South Carolina and had some children. Jimmy was jovial and upbeat and owned a thriving car dealership. Mama asked me what I thought about him. I told her that he really seemed to make her happy. He was a complete gentleman and very gentle with Mama. They eventually got married and lived in Jimmy's nice house on a canal in North Myrtle Beach. Jimmy was from Henderson, North Carolina. His family-owned furniture stores. They liked Mama a lot. They recognized that she was a fine southern lady who kept Jimmy grounded.

Mama had started a small business which was a tanning salon. It was called Sun Fun Tan. She also sold Neo Life health products and other vitamins and food supplements. I have to say that Mama with all of her many talents and abilities was not a very good business woman. She had never even had to write a check when married to Daddy, so naturally she did not have the experience or expertise to make good business decisions. She truly had no clue how to manage cash flow and things like that. She spent way too much on the décor and supplies. Sun Fun Tan was not fun when Mama was losing money, so it closed for good.

It was fun to visit Mama and Jimmy. They had a deck where the children could jump safely into the canal. The fishing and crabbing were good. There was a neighbor friend who took David and April on long golf cart rides. Myrtle Beach is a beautiful resort with plenty to do for the whole family. Many Canadians typically come there to spend the winter and do a lot of golfing. One day Mama was in the local hardware store, and a Canadian couple asked her to please show them where to find the grits seeds. They thought grits grew on bushes or something with no clue that they were made of ground dried corn!

Jimmy had dyslexia and was ADD hyper and kept wild hours. He was up and down all night. He lacked impulse control. Due to his manic tendencies, he was the kind of man who could make a million dollars one day and lose it a week later. Mama did not thrive on this emotional rollercoaster. She hung in there for several years, but the wild ride was taking its toll on her nerves. He was a dear, sweet guy who did not gamble or drink or take drugs or chase skirts. He was a perfect gentleman. He would never have hit her or yelled at her or made fun of her in a million years, but she could not handle the lack of stability. She tried so hard that she took him to a specialist in New York City, but he was not able to get with the program of listening to the doctors' orders and calming down. They finally separated, and she went to live with some friends Anne and her mother Mrs. Cook.

Mrs. Cook's house was a huge mint-green stucco. She gave Mama a large garage to store her furniture. Mama had an entire wing of their ranch style house. They loved having Mama there because she did such wonderful cooking and sewing. She was kind and helpful. Mama had lots of friends at her church. Her social life was fun and busy. Agnes by now owned an antique shop. She sent me an 1850's long white cotton nightgown exactly like the one Melanie wore in 'Gone with the Wind' in the scene where Scarlett shot the Yankee soldier, and they cleaned up the blood with the nightgown. I now keep it displayed on my Governor Winthrop canopy bed, and I wear it when I do a Santa Lucia skit and song for children during the Christmas season. I wear the battery-powered candle wreath on my head.

Cousin Melanie in Mama's family was getting married, and she wanted April to be the flower girl and David to be the ring bearer. April wore a long blue organdy dress with a white embroidered bodice and lace trim. David had a light blue three-piece polyester suit. They were almost the same height and wherever we went, everyone thought they were twins. They were old enough to follow instructions well and did a very good job.

At home David had a riding toy called a Green Machine that was much like a Big Wheel. We lived at the bottom of two steep hills, and he or April could start at the very top and zoom down the hill. They used the three large, thick bushes by the driveway for brakes. I must say that there were older ladies on our street that could not watch them do that. They got heart palpitations and too scared. But the neighbors loved the sight when I made giant pretend lollypops, and April and her friends had a lollypop parade on the sidewalk. The lollypops were made from paper plates covered in red and blue and green cellophane attached to a wooden dowel. They were filled with candy and small toys and were quite a hit with the girls.

At another one of April's parties, I thought of an idea for party favors. I bought navy blue umbrellas from Daddy's store and painted designs on them with white and yellow and red acrylic paint. I painted teddy bears and balloons and rabbits and flowers and you name it. On rainy days, it was a sight to see when all the little girls arrived at the school door with their painted umbrellas!

David was really skilled with needle crafts. When baby cousin Alycen was born in 1977, he put my sewing machine on my bed and made what he called a baby dress for her. It was cut out of one of my old white sheets. He loved to do counted cross stitch with me. His fingers were so agile. We even designed some of our own patterns with Bible verses. I had them framed, and they hang in our house to this good day.

One afternoon right after his seventh birthday, he was intensely watching Shay make a macrame' pocketbook. He came home and said, "Mommy, can you please take me to Michael's craft store? I need forty-six yards of macrame' thread and a handle. You can pick the colors because I am making you a purse." I was very skeptical, but not wanting to dampen his spirit, we went to Michael's first thing the next morning. I chose a beige color with a plastic tortoise-shell handle. By the middle of the afternoon, there was my bag almost. He could not quite remember how Shay finished the bottom, so we drove over and she showed him. I still use that purse every summer. After that he went around the neighborhood taking orders. He custom made purses for family and friends in navy, white, shamrock green, red or whatever they desired. He charged $20.00. Everyone was way beyond astonished at this clever, industrious boy!

In later years David's hand-formed pottery was so good, it was displayed at the High Museum at the Atlanta Arts Center. His black ink drawings were remarkable. I had them framed to go over the sofa.

April's art was brightly colored whimsical graphic designs. She enjoyed hand formed pottery and ceramics. She had watched me do all kinds of needlework, but that did not seem to interest her at all. She gleefully baked my chocolate chip crème de menthe cake. When company came, she made special fruit plates. She arranged the fruit in symmetrical designs. She was an organizational wizard. She always did her projects and book reports at least two weeks early. Her homework assignments were consistently done carefully and handed in on time. Her brother was famous for doing his homework and leaving it by the toothpaste. The gifted teacher Mrs. Lisela said his IQ went off the top of the chart like his sister, but he had difficulty getting it all together like a true absent-minded professor.

Chapter 17
Our Genetic Wonders Bloom
and Blossom!

Tim's cousin Olga called us about a house down the street that was larger and had a garage and a large flat turn around driveway. She said we probably could use the extra room, and that was correct. We moved the summer David turned three. The house had a basement that we later finished and made a bedroom, bath with shower and a sitting room. The upstairs had a large living room and dining room and family room paneled with real mahogany. Next-door lived a nice lady that had gone to Decatur High School with Aunt Judy. We furnished it with our abundant supply of interesting antiques. We had a spool bed, pine chest, pump organ, spinet desk, Duncan Fife sofa and oak tables, dressers and chairs. At the former house I had put a beautiful teal blue/French blue/white striped colonial wallpaper. Thankfully, the Dwoskin store still had that in stock. I took my matching Waverly fabric drapes and had the walls papered in the new dining room.

Our dear friend and pediatrician declared that David and April were astonishing genetic wonders. They were bright as new pennies, handsome and beautiful and incredibly gifted and talented. Their expertise covered academics, art, music, drama, sports and people skills. David was more athletic and active. April was more inclined to sit at her desk and draw and paint. David could write his name beautifully by his third birthday. His preschool teacher Mrs. Cherry at Oak Grove Methodist was astonished! Her great grandfather had often been a violinist on weekends on the town square. We both had rich gene pools for expressive arts and academics with the long twitch muscles of athletes.

Papa was failing fast. He had Burger's disease which is typical in Ashkenazi eastern European Jewish families. That is poor circulation in the legs and feet. He also had an aneurysm in his chest. There were no procedures then for inserting stints and so forth. He died in his sleep 1976, and it was quite a shock to me. I was very attached to my grandparents, and they lived not far away on Clairmont in an apartment. I took it really hard and had trouble sleeping for a couple of weeks. I could not even go in his bedroom for over a year.

I had already scheduled a trip for David and me to fly to Cleveland to see Papa's family, so the timing was perfect. Papa's sisters and nieces really enjoyed seeing us, and we had a wonderful visit. I met many new cousins and learned so much about the family history. Aunt Mildred wrote down great Gramma Fanny's bedtime prayer for me and some German children's songs that Papa had sung to us while bouncing us on his knee.

Aunt Ellie drove us down to Cambridge, Ohio to visit Frank and Hazel's farm. They were just starting the process of building their amphitheater for performances of 'Behold the Man' which they renamed The Living Word Theater. There was a natural bowl in the land that Frank had seen from above while landing his plane after traveling somewhere to do a Bible drama. It is a completely remarkable Godwink that they had bought that piece of land without knowing that on the front end! God's powers and will and infinite wisdom can just blow you away.

The bitter cold Ohio winters were eventually too harsh for Frank's tubercular hip, so they moved to Lexington, Kentucky for the winters and spent every summer in Cambridge, a sleepy little college town. The theater was staffed with students, and busloads of people came from many states. That theater is still in operation forty-six years later. It is an amazing place to visit. Many of the props are ones that I had gathered for the first production in 1968 in the Atlanta Stadium.

From that time on I was providing Grandmother with most of her transportation since she did not drive. It was no trouble at all. She was such a good, pleasant person. I never heard her gossip or say an unkind word about anyone. If she heard criticisms, she always said, "Well, to each his own." She was fiercely independent and cleaned her apartment and always cooked nutritious meals. About once per month we went out to lunch, and I took her to a movie. The children loved her. She would get down on the rug and play cards with them for pennies or M&M's. She took them to the railroad track behind her complex to put nickels on the track.

Our April angel was born with the most generous little spirit I had ever seen. At six months she began to sit up in her highchair. If I gave her a cracker, she broke it in half and gave me half. Then she broke her half in half and gave me half of that. Also, at age four, she collected some of the used wrapping paper from birthdays. She wrapped up small toys and treasures in her room and put them in a pile by the windows. If someone came to visit, she took them by the hand to her room, showed them the wrapped gifts and said, "Pick a pwesent!" She is still that thoughtful and is forever giving us meaningful gifts and helping the poor and needy and treating her students like her own children. She is the kind of sweet high achiever that can collect awards and scholarships like coins or stamps.

My mom definitely wished a strong-willed child on me, and she got her wish with bells on it! David was the most determined child I had ever seen. He had his own way of interpreting whatever we said. We speak, and what does he hear? It might as well have been backwards talk or dolphin squeaks. He always had elaborate explanations for his choices and did not want to take responsibility for them. I told him, "If you predecease me, I am putting on your tombstone: But It Wasn't My Fault." Of course, this will of iron enabled him to achieve magnificent things by sheer determination.

The children sang in the cherub choir at church and were always given the solo parts. This was also true when they started Sagamore Hills Elementary School where they sang solos, played the lead roles in the plays and were put in the gifted program. At first April did not test as gifted, so I told her teacher to test her in the afternoon. (She is not a morning person.) Then her score went off the chart. In second grade David won the blue ribbon in the science fair even competing against seventh graders. He made microscope slides of insect wings and compared them to slides of winged seeds. He was a tough little soccer player and did well in basketball and softball. April took ballet and tap and clogging lessons with girlfriends.

Our elementary school had wonderful teachers. Debbie, the art teacher was exceptional. She had a master's degree in art therapy and deeply cared about every child. I later became Godmother to her daughter Michelle who was born against all odds. She has given me three new God babies to love.

Volunteering at the school media center was relaxing. That included shelving books and reading picture books to the younger children. When I heard that the San Francisco public library had falsely banned the Mary Poppins books for racism, I suggested to the media specialist that we have a book parade for National Library Week with me leading the parade dressed as Mary Poppins. This was lots of fun and a huge success. Each class dressed up like the characters of a popular, well-known book. We did a Mary Poppins skit in the media center and David and April were Jane and Michael. A theology student from Emory agreed to be the chimney sweep. The DeKalb News Sun came and did an article about this. I was able to explain with documentation why the Mary Poppins books were not racist. Then I sent an editorial to the Atlanta Journal with my proof and a call to ban censorship.

It was very fulfilling doing projects for the Parent Teacher Association. One year at the request of the principal, Mr. Shivers, we gathered together some artists to paint scenes on plywood partitions that he wanted to use in the cafeteria. Another year it was the PTA scrapbook, and it won second place in DeKalb County Schools. David's teacher Ms. Reams asked if anyone's mom would dress up like a pumpkin for the Halloween party. David proclaimed, "My mom will!" So, I bought some orange fabric and made a pumpkin costume. It was big and round because it was stuffed with plastic dry-cleaning bags filled with air. Now that can make you get a little sweaty! Newspaper or packing peanuts from then on!

David joined Cub Scouts and April became a Brownie Scout. I was not one of the leaders, but helped out whenever I could. For refreshments we baked a gingerbread boy as large as our oven and frosted it to look exactly like a Cub Scout. We then made one for April's troop to look just like a Brownie Scout. I helped chaperone if a troop went on a field trip or skating or to Six Flags or whatever.

We made a big deal about Halloween every year, and I usually made the costumes. There was a Peter Pan one and a scarecrow and so forth. Every Christmas we made a German stollen coffeecake filled with almonds and candied fruit. We baked challah bread and braided it into the shape of a round wreath, and that was our Advent wreath with candles. We made gingerbread and cookie houses also. There were fun Easter decorations that I had made in a ceramics class. Home birthday parties were more of the norm back then. Thankfully our children's birthdays were in pleasant weather months, so we could have engaging outdoor activities. I attached treats and small toys to shrubs and trees for treasure hunts. We had a Go Fish game on the patio. An adult hid underneath in the tool storage room and put goodies on the fishing line with a clothes pin and then tugged on the line.

Being a stay-at-home mom, I decided to have a small home business to help fill the hours. I think homemakers probably need to have some "butter and egg money" to keep in their sugar bowl, so to speak. Grandmother had done that because Papa liked to bet on poker at the Elks Club, and that made her a little nervous. I had met a lady at a wedding who was there to take the bride's bouquet home to preserve it. That sounded fascinating to me, so she told me to buy a certain book that would teach me the method. I bought about fifteen pounds of silica gel at a craft store and put it in airtight metal Charlie Chips containers. One needed green floral tape, wires and some craft spray paint. Soon after mastering this art, I advertised with some local florists and started getting customers.

The finished dried bouquets were secured in large brass and glass boxes from Mexico. When my neighbor flew his plane to Mexico to watch whales run, he brought me plenty of boxes. There was also a source in Birmingham that could ship them to me. I called my business "Keepsake Corner Flowers." It was a joyful endeavor that made people so happy. My slogan was, "I will preserve everything from christening corsages to coffin covers." One lady even brought me flowers from her dog's funeral at a pet cemetery! Now you may want to call my flower business a "Little Shop of Horrors!"

About that time, there was a class to learn to do stained glass. It was fun, and I made some lovely sun-catchers and Christmas ornaments. Actually, my skills were not all that good, and that meant tiny cuts on my hands and fingers. When I taught my neighbor Carolyn how to do it, she excelled and could even make windows. I had taught her how to preserve flowers, but she said it was too tedious and would make her crazier than a Brussels lace maker! It was very delicate work. That is why my motto was, "Only God can make a flower, but I come in for a close second place." Carolyn was gifted in art and did beautiful water colors of flowers.

The children loved outdoor play. There was a creek and plenty of woods. They could ride their bikes everywhere. It was safe for them to walk the half mile to school and back. We never heard about any crime. The neighborhood had good sidewalks. We had a tree house that was over a very deep eight-foot pile of oak and hickory leaves. Children came from around the neighborhood to jump into that leaf pile. Everyone was safe and sound all the time, but once little Amy from down the street broke her arm. No lawsuits were necessary back then. Isn't that amazing and unbelievable? Children stopped at our house after school, because I made "snow ice cream" in the blender with milk, sugar, vanilla and ice. I also spread a clean white sheet on the floor from time to time and popped popcorn on it, and the children ate it off the sheet.

We had a roll of newsprint paper given to me by the Cranes at the Decatur News. I rolled out twenty-foot lengths, and neighborhood kids drew trains and long dragons or puppy parades or whatever at our "imagination station." The garage was filled with brightly colored shelves with toys, games, sporting equipment and science and nature experiment supplies that neighbor kids could borrow from our quasi-learning center. They were put and take shelves: You bring one back, you borrow another. I called it "The Learning Cave."

David and April displayed exuberant self-confidence in everything they did. They were spontaneous and fun-loving and enjoyed life. They were always encouraged to express their real true feelings in an appropriate manner. Since kids really do say the darndest things, I kept a book of all the cute things they ever said. We called it the Funny Book. Even when they came home from college for holidays, they wanted to plop on my bed and have me read to them from that book. The all-time funniest one was when April was singing the Sunday School song about Zacchaeus. The end of the song says, "Zacchaeus, you come down. For I'm going to your house today." April sang, "Zacchaeus, you come down! You know you don't have permission from your mommy to go to a parade!"

Creative children can really be a hoot. April would stand on top of a sturdy wooden coffee table and holding a map book would give weather reports. She would say things like, "There is going to be a storm, and it will be a terrible, terrible thing!" She also liked to stand on the table and preach sermons with her deep, booming voice. The funniest one was when she shouted, "And the Lord said, David, mind your mother!" She recognized that her brother was a challenging hand full that did not understand accepting authority. I mean really, I told him he was my little shepherd boy, and that someday he would lead a great flock. That communicated to him that he was "King David." Uh oh! Guess I overplayed my hand.

David was fascinating and along with that comes mothers with gray and white hair. The summer he turned seven we were sitting in church on the far-left side by the aisle where the bright sun was blasting in on us. Behind us was Mrs. Price who would soon be his second-grade teacher. I did not notice that he had brought his tiny magnifying glass from his stamp collection. You guessed it! I saw a red Methodist hymnal almost catch fire. Well, by gosh and by golly, the icon for the Methodist Church is a cross with flames that represent the Holy Spirit. How do you discipline a kid for doing something so appropriate to the scenario? No wonder he had insisted that we not sit in the balcony that Sunday! Sweet Mrs. Price said, "Don't worry. I have a grown son named David who was this kind of little boy. I understand him and know how to teach and nurture him." Whew! What a relief to my mental state of consternation!

By the time he was in fourth grade we were sitting in the balcony on Sunday. At home he had made a paper airplane and concealed it in his jacket. Very athletic children are super coordinated, but it baffles me to no ends wondering how he made that aeronautical piece of Mead notebook paper land precisely on the top of the nearest white Ionic column. I kid you not! That airplane sat on that column until the church was repainted years later.

Around this time, a German couple joined my Sunday School Class. Armin was studying at Candler School of Theology to get a Ph D. Gudrun was an elementary school teacher and was taking two years off. It was wonderful to have someone to speak German with me. Also, she took our Richard Scarry's 'Best Word Book Ever' and wrote all the words in German for my children. She was a lot of fun. They lived in some apartments on Clairmont behind Emory. She would invite us over to bake German cookies and gingerbread.

The children's pre-school at Oak Grove Methodist asked me to paint some murals for the walls. We decided to focus on displaying character qualities. Gudrun was a very good artist, and she offered to help. She did a wonderful job. We did 'The Little Engine that Could' on a full sheet of plywood. This was for the entry hall. I took an old door and turned it sideways and painted a little girl having a tea party with her dolls with her head bowed saying Grace. I painted her face to look like April, and she looked so pretty in a pale blue dress with white lacy pinafore.

Gudrun was surprised to discover that an unplanned baby was on the way. They had wanted to start their family when back in Germany. I had a beautiful hand-made canopy cradle that my brother Eric had had made before April was born. Even though we did not know "boy" or "girl", he was determined that I would have a baby girl. I loaned this to Armin and Gudrun. The Sunday School class helped with all the needed clothes and baby equipment. They had a little boy and named him Jan. Years later when I visited them in Germany, they had a daughter Astrid and one more son, Jonas.

My dear friend Lachlan in the neighborhood had grown some lovely green bells of Ireland flowers, and I so coveted them and wanted to have some in my garden. One March I bought some seeds, put them in little plastic starter pots and kept them watered and in the window. Normally in Atlanta one can put annual flowers in the garden on April fifteenth. By then the days and nights are warm enough with no more frost or ice. Sadly, my seeds never even sprouted. My thought was to not let that potting soil go to waste, so I tossed all of it in my neglected garden by the driveway. One day I was walking in the yard and noticed green bells of Ireland plants blooming with their upward stalks of little green bells. All of a sudden it hit me. For decades Mumsie had always said, "Just let go and let God." Somehow, I had never really related to that saying or put it into practice in my life.

However now, something quickened in my spirit and it all made sense. It was a beautiful feeling to know that the Dear Lord had reached down from heaven and touched my heart with some genuine truth. I will never forget that day! And some years later at another home after a really long chain of years of traumatic events and ungodly stress, I was astonished to discover bells of Ireland blooming in my garden by the driveway. Peace and joy washed over me like a waterfall, and I just knew that I knew that I knew that Mumsie and some angels must have come there and planted them. I cannot prove that, but no one can dissuade me from believing it! That's why people say that there is no comfort like the kind that heaven brings to us.

Lachlan died from an aggressive kind of liver and brain cancer. I wrote a beautiful poem about her. She had been such a gentle, loving friend. Thankfully they had a strong extended family with an attentive grandmother and aunt nearby. Human life is so fragile and temporal. We must be thankful for every day that we have on earth and with loved ones.

Mama had given us her little black miniature poodle, Luvy, when she moved. Luvy had been my dog when I lived in an apartment on LaVista Road when starting graduate school. Her real name on her pedigree was Enfant d'amour de Soleil et Pluit. That means love child of the sun and rain. We first called her Pluit which means, it is raining because she made little pitter patter rain drop sounds with her toe nails and puddles until she was house trained. Later, since she had been born on Valentine's Day, we called her Luvy. Once she had five beautiful puppies which we gave to family and friends. They were born on Halloween.

In the middle of a cold, dark January night, a little black and white tuxedo cat came to us as a stray. We named her Dunkleheit which is German for the darkness. That was for the dark night when she came. Somehow, she bonded with Luvy and decided that she was a poodle. She cried at the porch sliding glass doors when she wanted to go out. Yay, no disgusting Fresh Step or Martha Stewart Pretty Litter needed! Luvy chased her playfully and they were great friends. She did only one naughty thing which was jumping on the cabinet, but our vet, Dr. Gordon told me to gently spray one squirt of water on her. That was the perfect cure and worked right away.

Chapter 18
Preteens and Pretending Parents

The children were continuing to flourish. The Oak Grove Methodist choir was presenting the Giancarlo Menotti operetta, 'Amahl and the Night Visitors.' David sang the part of Amahl, the little Italian shepherd boy. I did the publicity and had posters made at Toco Hills Printing. Mr. Buffaloe, the choir director played the part of Caspar who was one of the three kings traveling to Bethlehem to take gifts to the baby Jesus. It was performed two nights, and The Atlanta Journal sent a photographer who wrote a very positive review.

A talent scout from the Alliance Children's theater came and did everything in her power to recruit David to join their group. She told us that David was the best child actor and boy soprano in Atlanta. Someone also came from the Atlanta Boys' Choir. They said the same. David's opinion was that he wanted to just be a boy and stay in scouts and play soccer and be with his friends in the creek and trees. We did not push the issue. We wanted him to enjoy music and acting on his own schedule without being shoved and prodded by stage parents.

This production left sweet little April a bit in the dark and overshadowed. She was every bit as talented but felt kind of left out. Being an avid writer, she kept my typewriter on her desk. A week after the Amahl production, I found a piece of paper in the typewriter that said:

APRIL STARS AS MRS. WONDERFUL!

No matter how close and loving siblings are, I believe there will always be sibling rivalry. It's just human nature to want to be special and noticed. Anyway, she soon got to play the part of Aunt Polly in a chorus production of 'Tom Sawyer.' The next year she was the Queen of Hearts in 'Alice in Wonderland.' Things have a way of balancing out if you keep encouraging your children to pursue their leanings. I tried so hard to communicate that life is harsh and cruel and unfair at times. But I read the book. We win at the end! Children need to know that timing is best left to the clock of Heaven. Things have a strange way of working out for the best.

We continued our summer beach holidays plus visiting Aunt Kitti and Uncle Truman in Jacksonville, Florida. Cousin Lori had a little sky-blue Volkswagen that she called "Bump Bump." She and Cousin Glen took the children on rides and swam with them in the backyard pool. They had an adorable little Cocker-poo named Pamper. Uncle Truman had to spread tobacco dust on the front and back lawns to keep the fleas away. Florida's mild winters yield large populations of bugs like mosquitoes. The palmetto bugs are the giant flying roaches that I say are so militant that they carry machine guns and leave grocery lists on the frig.

At home Aunt Sara was active in our lives. She loved to take the children to the North Georgia mountains. They stayed at the York House Inn near Clayton where Mumsie and Granddaddy had gotten engaged on the porch swing. The inn was not really in operation very much, so the owners gave Sara an entire room to use as an art room. She taught the children a lot about painting and sculpting. They went up the road to Franklin, North Carolina for gem hunting. They explored waterfalls and went to the top of Black Rock Mountain. Sara was wonderful at making good memories for children. She believed in spending quality time with children. She was all about building self-esteem.

Sara had a dear friend from art school named Hilda. Many years previously when Hilda's brother Walter came home from the Army, he had fallen off a truck and gotten a head injury and developed aphasia. That is when you kind of lose your words. Sara was a teacher who specialized in helping children with special needs. She worked with Walter until he was able to communicate fairly well even though on disability. He had also been in the Navy during the Korean War. They went their separate ways but later reconnected and fell in love.

Walter was always very quiet and shy, but when he spoke you recognized that he was quite intelligent. He and Sara decided to marry at Belvedere Methodist Church in Decatur. This was the church that Mumsie had started in her living room when I was a small child. Tim played the organ. David and April sang 'O Perfect Love.' Mumsie walked Sara down the aisle. I made all of the corsages and flower arrangements. Kitti catered the reception. It was a sweet wedding, and we got a wonderful uncle.

Walter was really good to Mumsie and my mother. He drove us all so many places. He was always available to help family members move or whatever. He was patient even though Sara was an incorrigible back seat driver. Sara and Walter bought a nice little two-bedroom cabin in Mountain City next to Dillard, Georgia where Kitti and Truman had a mountain house. It was a fun place to visit with a cozy pot-bellied stove for heat. They also bought three lots on a mountain in Tiger, Georgia with the hope of retiring there and building a home and having an art school for poor mountain children. Sara went to the Salvation Army thrift store on many Wednesdays when things were half-price and bought carloads of clothing and shoes to take to the mountain people. She had a heart of gold and was generous to a fault with everyone. They often brought us bags of mountain apples and such.

The children spent seven weeks with Aunt Kitti and Aunt Sally one summer, and I had a one-month trip to Italy and Germany. First, I visited friends in Freiburg where I had lived. Ursula and Alfred drove me to all the familiar places with their three-year-old Anne. Their second child was just days from being born. Baby Julia came a few days after I left. I realized how much I had missed Germany. There was definitely a Freiburg sized hole in my heart.

Then I took a train to Sonthofen in Bavaria to see other friends. There was a summer version of Oktoberfest, so we danced and got icing decorated gingerbread hearts on a ribbon to go around our necks. I caught a train to Munich to get to Rome. There was a young Italian man in our sleeper car. He told us to lie down with our backpacks behind our heads and our legs raised so that we could kick any robbers hard. That was a bit unsettling, but the trip was uneventful. I was dressed like a vagabond backpacker to look poor instead of a tasty morsel of "Lady Plushbottom."

In Italy I visited my friends Rosalind and Helmut who lived next to Vatican City in Rome. I took a bus tour of southern Italy and visited Sorento, Naples, the Isle of Capri and so forth. It was a wonderful visit, but we had to be very cautious with our money. One day after Rosalind and I rode a very tightly packed bus, she found her key on the floor of the bus which meant someone had been in her jeans pocket. The banks of the Tiber River were littered with hypodermic needles. Drug dealers were behind every bowl of pasta! Even carrying a shoulder bag was a no no. Thieves zooming past on Vespa motor bikes had shears for cutting the strap and speeding away with a purse.

I had a ticket for Germany on the day Italy won the world championship soccer match. It seemed that the entire population of Rome was out in the streets in little fiats standing up through the sun roofs waving Italian flags that were as big as the cars. They were banging large pot lids together like cymbals. My taxi driver had to go backwards up a one-way street to get me to the train station. I jumped on the train as it was literally starting to move.

I was headed to Frankfurt to visit one more set of friends before flying back home. My sleeper car had five American college students that were working their way through Europe as street entertainers. They were all hungry, so I bought them breakfast on the train. They told me about all the cities they had visited and did some singing and dancing for me. They knew well-known clowns in Atlanta whose act was called "Lenny and La Banana."

In reality Tim and I were not a very compatible couple. When one plus one equals zero, you don't need Pythagoras to tell you something is wrong with the equation. Marriage is typically an uphill "hellofavator" ride that is known to be a struggle. But it should be a glorious struggle. He said that he had married me because I had peanut butter crackers and tennis shoes under the seat of my car so that I could go on a picnic on a whim whenever. He thought that I could teach him to be carefree and spontaneous and whimsical. In reality, when I was me, it threatened the holy bejebus out of him.

We were from different generations. He had lived through the Great Depression and World War II. His teacher grandfather needed to be so frugal that he made his shoelaces out of squirrel hide. They lived in a small rural town that was a century behind when it came to accepting people with different races or religions. When we visited there, I usually wound up sick with a cold or sore throat because the oppressive racism affected me that way. I don't mean to attend an "All You Can Eat Character Assassination Buffet" here. The people were provincial due to lack of exposure to the wider world. The family liked me because of my gold-plated education and prominent family and treated me very well, but the culture was toxic for a gal who had been a peaceful civil rights worker.

I admired Tim for being a dependable hard worker and good provider. He was diligent about caring for the yard and the house. He was a brilliant musician and used his business degree well to be a higher-up executive with the government. On paper we had a lot in common and should have been ultra in sync. We were educated Methodists who loved theater, music and antiques and enjoyed family and entertaining. Sadly, even with prayer groups, Bible study groups counseling, tapes, seminars, books and so forth, we just could not make things work. The entire marriage unraveled, and he moved to an apartment nearby. I felt like a "lame" chop slathered in fail sauce! He was dutiful to take David and April every other weekend and spend a lot of quality time with them.

We won Academy Awards so to speak pretending to be the ideal happy family, but the picket fence had been eaten by termites and dry rot. It just was not working. The children were picking up on the tension and toxic vibes and showing strong signs of stress, depression and anxiety. Somehow, sadly, the romance and relationship had evaporated into thin air. It was hard for an older dad to be patient with normal children's noise and confusion and behavior. His patience was tried to the limits.

That spring David was Winnie the Pooh in the school musical. I made his costume out of honey-colored fake fur. Oh my, that was challenging to sew that thick fabric on my sewing machine. Of course, we did not understand the copyright laws very explicitly. It was against the law for me to make a red t-shirt that had the name "POOH" in yellow letters. That was the Disney version of a Pooh costume, and it was a big no-no, but no one realized or complained. That costume is the size for a twelve-year-old kid, so it still fits petite me. I wear it if Halloween night happens to be very cold. It also came in handy for school book parades when I was a school "LiBEARian" in two DeKalb Elementary Schools. Once I wore the costume minus the t-shirt to do a story at the Dunwoody Library. It was an Aesop's Fable called 'The Bear and the Crow.' It required me to wear a frying pan on my head. Look that story up and see for yourself! The book was illustrated by Arnold Lobel, author of 'Frog and Toad are Friends.'

Chapter 19
A Challenging New Life into
The Dark Unknown

Ninety-year-old Mumsie moved in with us. We gave her closet space, and she purchased a lovely light blue velvet sofa bed for the living room. Even though her sight was basically gone from macula degeneration, she was very helpful and totally willing to help cheerfully. We enjoyed her sweet disposition, and she was a lot of company to me in the daytime when David and April were at school. She could empty the dishwasher and chop fruits and veggies and nuts. She always ate nutritious meals and was very healthy, so there were hardly any doctor appointments.

She did have enough vision to sit sideways in the family room in front of the TV and get a bit of the newscasts. When she did that, I took down her snow-white bun and gently brushed her very long hair that came down to her waist. Her old neighbors from Midway Road lived right across the street! Mrs. Bradshaw was so good to take Mumsie to their garden club meetings and to the church ladies circle meetings. She would dress up so nicely and wait by the mailbox for her ride. My next-door neighbor Miss Anne said she looked like a regal duchess.

The funniest thing with Mumsie Lucie was on school mornings. She insisted that David have a fried egg for breakfast. Usually, he was on the way out the door to the bus, and she had to put it on a paper plate with plastic fork. He had the really quick-witted funny personality of a stand-up comedian. He took that famous country song, 'You Picked a Fine Time to Leave Me, Lucille' and changed to the words to: You picked a fine time to FEED me, Lucille. When I was teaching him to drive and said, "On, James" like British aristocracy say to their chauffeurs, he would reply, "But I am Bartles." That was a take-off on the brand of wine called Bartles and James.

One morning at around 2am I was awakened by Mumsie's loud coughing. She was not conscious. Something in me perceived that she was dying. Then I saw a tiny flicker of light like a butterfly flicker from her chest. I got on her bed and kept saying, "Mumsie, don't leave us. We need you." She sat up, coughed one more time and said, "What is the matter, honey?" I tried to forget the little light. It had to be my imagination. However, later my friend Linda shared with me that she and her mother had seen this same light at DeKalb Hospital the moment her daddy died. Since then, I will always believe that I experienced the existence of the human spirit.

We lived at a corner. There was a produce truck that went around that corner every morning. Sometime it went a little too fast and things like grapefruits or whatever rolled onto the grass by the mailbox at the driveway. The most unusual gift we ever received from a truck rounding that corner swiftly was a stack of Playboy, Penthouse and Hustler magazines. Whoa! David and Chucky and Roger discovered them when walking home from school one day. I heard them giggling in the storage room under the porch and went to see what all the commotion was about. I did not act shocked or indignant or like a Bible thumper or say anything that would make that dumpster trash seem like desirable forbidden fruit. I simply said, "Fellas, how would you like it if those photos were of your mom, grandmother, sister, aunt wife or daughter?" They said they would not like it. They threw them in the trash can by the garage. David says that cured him. He never again wanted to see anything like that that degrades women or girls.

David gave April a little black rabbit for her birthday. She named him Bun Bun. This was so much fun for us that David decided to start raising rabbits. He built a cage and got a white rabbit. My sister is an exceptionally brilliant photographer. She had a photography client who was the Uptown Clown. He dressed in a tuxedo with top hat and red bow tie. Sometime he borrowed the white rabbit for a magic show. David built another cage by the driveway and had some beautiful Dutch lop ear rabbits.

One frosty January morning I looked out my window and saw a large brown dog in the rabbit cage. I went down and grabbed it by its brown suede collar and dragged it into the garage. The dog had no tag. We called Animal Control. When the truck arrived, the gentleman said to me, "Lady, do you know what kind of dog that is?" I said, "No." He said, "That is a pit bull, and you are lucky to be alive!" Again, there were over-worked angels asking Saint Peter for more coffee breaks 401K plans and four-day work weeks!

I advertised our downstairs in law suite at Emory's off campus housing listing. There were no computer websites or emails or texts, so everything had to be handled by landline phone and answering machine. We found a super nice theology student from Minnesota named Dan. He paid $200.00 per month and was allowed to use our washer and dryer. There was a sink, small frig and microwave for simple cooking. Since we had the little tuxedo feline named Dunkleheit, I put a sign on his door that said DANIEL & THE LIONS DEN. He spent a happy year with us, and we really enjoyed him.

There were other renters continually. Can you fathom that we all shared the same phone upstairs and in the apartment? We were too backward to even realize how inconvenient it actually was to not have mobile phones. Thankfully there was an answering machine sent to me by my Uncle Tom from his electronics store. Unbeknownst to me the children put this outgoing message: You have reached the castle of Dracula. At the sound of the beep please leave your name and blood type. Sorry we are not here, but this is such a fly-by-night operation.

Most of the tenants were polite and pleasant and cooperative. Every once in a while, someone came who was a real pain in the kizip, but that is historically the nature of the landlord/tenant scenario. Some people do not want to accept authority and follow any house rules. They tend to have stinky attitudes about everything no matter how kind and reasonable you are. You learn a lot of tricks along the way. It is good practice in being patient, tactful, assertive, forbearing and wise.

Daddy had always taught me that you get more flies with honey than with vinegar. True, but there are times when one must lower the boom, enforce the boundaries. You either pour out some vinegar, or the opportunists will put you in a pickle! I had a short, simple list of reasonable house rules tacked to the wall at the bottom of the stairs. That was helpful to delineate the parameters of the expected adult behaviors.

We had a friend who was the medical director for AT&T for the southeastern states. He had taught psychology and medicine at Johns Hopkins. He was from Italy. One Sunday afternoon I drew him a cartoon which was a take-off on 'Caesar's Commentaries' that we had read in Latin class at Decatur High. This was the scene where Julius Caesar was deciding whether or not to cross the Rubicon River to go back to Rome. I drew the Roman soldiers standing at giant boiling pots over open flames. The pots had red dye in them, and they were dyeing their uniforms. The authentic caption said: Alea jacta est. That is Latin for "The di is cast." It is talking about one di, whereas in today's world we cast a pair of dice. I did a play on words to show them dyeing cloth.

Anyway, Victor was so amused and fascinated and asked me if I would do a color Rorschach test. Naturally I wanted to do that. He said I saw more things in those ink blobs than anyone he had ever tested. He said my creativity approached that of Buckminster Fuller who invented the geodesic dome. The Good Lord made me that way, so I don't claim any credit.

Our stepmother Shay's dear ninety-five-year-old mother Granny Shannon died, and it was so sad to lose her. She was alert and vibrant and loving to all of us. She always listened to Atlanta Braves baseball games on the radio. Shay was been an only child because her parents had had several babies die. She was very close to her mother. She went into kind of a deep depression. I noticed that she had lost interest in cooking and dusting and traveling. She was quiet and sullen. Her sunshine personality had dulled to barely a glimmer.

Daddy was just not in the habit of actually dealing with conflicts or asking for help or going for counseling. He wanted instant grits, instant coffee and instant happiness. He abruptly filed a divorce, and we were devastated and saddened. The only good thing was that Shay's love for us never ended because it was genuine. She continued to spend quality time with us and never forgot us on birthdays and holidays. Her affection for us was so deep and genuine. She made a new life for herself and regained her joy and sweet smile.

David was on the eighth-grade football team. One day after school during practice, he was working out in the weight room. Another player was using the leg press machine when it jammed. David went over to help him, and the worn-out pin flew out and sixty pounds of weight fell on David's right hand. Due to some kind of massive stupidity, the school did not call an ambulance. They called me to come get him. April and I found him in a dazed state of shock. They had wrapped the hand to stop the bleeding.

We got him to the car and drove to the Toco Hill Doc in a Box clinic. The doctor gave him a shot for pain and made x-rays and told me that we needed to drive to the very fine hand surgeon Dr. Whitson by DeKalb General Hospital. It was a five o'clock traffic nightmare! Once I got there, the doctor asked me for the x-rays. I had forgotten them and had to drive all the way back.

The hand was crushed and two fingers were all but severed. Dr. Whitson was a miracle worker and reconstructed the hand so beautifully. When David was able to return to school, students were cruel and thumped on his bandage. The school did nothing to protect him. The science teacher gave him an F because he could not write and do his work.

In those days schools were immune from law suits, so they got away with murder. The hand finally healed almost completely with only one slightly crooked digit on the pointer finger of his right hand. Allie's orthopedic surgeon dad told us that tincture of time was on his side. But the physical pain was often unbearable. A shaman doctor in a rain forest would have given him psilocybin mushroom tea or edible Mary whose middle name is Jane. Sadly, our government wanted him on opioids and pharmaceuticals for migraine. The emotional scars of Post Traumatic Shock Disorder and Hateful Humans has never gone away. I tell my children: Life is short. Heaven is long. We have to take our share of suffering to learn to be strong, more patient and smarter. We just have to stay "Far from the Madding Crowd," Thomas Hardy!

Daddy eventually remarried. Sadly, this stepmother practically controlled every aspect of their existence. She never could adjust to liking or loving us or truly wanting us to be part of Daddy's life. We became mostly excess baggage and were tolerated at best. Does the cold shoulder/criticism combo come with fries and a medium drink? This toxic relationship lasted for over thirty years until Daddy died. It does not matter how many books you read about family or counseling sessions you have or pastoral care ministers you see. When "dueling dysfunctionals" dig their heels in the ground and refuse to be loving, the only thing you can do is forgive so that you don't drink the poison of bitterness and scar your psyche and damage your spirit.

We have to personally come to a point where we agree that in life, we must share in the Good Lord's sufferings to be molded into His image. Life is often a test of harsh, cruel unfairness. It nearly breaks your heart into pieces. I was always polite and never reacted to cruel, unkind words, false accusations or envy and strife. My philosophy is the solid belief that the Karma Bus has a really good GPS that knows where everyone's driveway is. It knows when to dump blessings and when to dump "alottadoodoo."

I have a way of politely saying that famous quote from the film 'The Garden of Good and Evil.' Two tears in a bucket and mother duck it. Quack! Quack! I believe it ain't over 'til the chubby angel gives you your wings! Right, all you stoic philosophical icons of reason? Just don't put your tomatoes in the frig, or you might be visited by a mobster who is not from Red Lobster! (But rather from southern Sicily)

Around this time on a Saturday morning, I was home looking forward to a quiet day when my neighbor Carolyn called me. She was signed up to help chaperone April's Girl Scout Troop at Six Flags over Georgia. Her son Rob was sick, so she asked me to take her place. Six Flags is one of my least favorite places. For me it was Six Flags over Hell! I hated the crowds and noise and confusion and did not like to ride the rides. I hate the smell of hotdogs and mustard mixed with roasted peanuts and popcorn with too much salt. The honky tonk atmosphere gets on my nerves. "Step right up, ladies and gentlemen and win a free headache to go with your nausea!" Anyway, out of loyalty to Carolyn and Juliette Gordon Lowe, Savannah founder of the Girl Scouts, I went.

I was sitting on a bench watching the girls on a ride. Next to me was an extremely handsome man, more handsome than Omar Sharif the Egyptian actor who was in the famous movie 'Doctor Zhivago.' He asked me a question about the map in his lap. I could tell English was not his native language. I would have guessed him to be Italian, but he had been born in India to a Persian daddy and Kurdish mom. His name was Mahmoud, and his American name was Michael. We had a pleasant chat. He asked me for my phone number. That was a no no! I did not give it to him because I had been raised to believe that you should meet people at church. So how did that work for me the last time? Maybe not! Nonetheless, he gave me his number and told me where he lived. It was very close to our neighborhood. I tucked the slip of paper in the bottom of a bedside table drawer.

Several months later I did actually call him. There was just something hauntingly fascinating about this man. He seemed to have such a poetic nature and gentle spirit and very intelligent eyes that revealed a beautiful, warm soul and spirit. Though highly motivated and responsible, he had the childlike playful nature that matched my whimsical spontaneity so well. Peter Pan and Petera Panera had met their soulmates but just did not quite know it yet. A match had been lit, and Lady Kismet had struck a spark on her tender box for sure!

Michael and I started spending a lot of time together. He was fond of the children and was very loving and had a happy, upbeat personality. We played games like Master Mind. He liked that my intellect was sharp and really challenged him. He taught me to cook the most delicious and healthy fresh Indian and Persian foods. He loved picnics and going to the park or Stone Mountain. He was super intelligent and British educated as an electrical engineer. While in India trying to get into medical school after being a paramedic in the Shah's army, his famous actor cousin Aghra tried to get him to be a movie star. He told him with his feather bone frame, he could be a wealthy race horse jockey. Nonetheless, he valued education more than anything. He had loved delivering babies and sewing up wounds in a mountain village near the Soviet Union. Sadly, the medical school was full.

He studied for and passed the Georgia state electrical contractor exam and started his own business called Pars Electric. Since I had no job, I became the office manager and answered the phone by way of call forwarding from his home. One day I was actually up on my roof with my AT & T cordless phone strapped around my neck with an ace bandage. I had a bucket of tar and was spreading it around the chimney with a large paint stirrer. I answered a call and scheduled an electrical job and wrote everything down on the pad that was in my pocket. All in a day's work, right? Super Girl where are you? That would be me, and here I am!

This was a very hard business to establish. It was difficult to collect the money for jobs because there were so many dishonest people who knew all the tricks about slipping out of lawsuits like greased lightening. Once in ninety-eight-degree June heat he wired a patio at a restaurant digging channels to bury the conduit. They did not pay the bill so I went over to collect the money. I noticed there were six hotel rooms by the parking lot. My gut level feeling told me they were for prostitution. The gentleman in charge reeked of mafia vibes. I went home and said, "Forget about that money. That is the kind of man who would come to your house in the middle of the night and burn it down with you in it!" Several months later we were watching the 11pm news when that very man came on the screen. His own son had gone to his two-million-dollar mansion in Stone Mountain and machine gunned his Lincoln Continental and literally burned his house down to ashes!

So, there you go. Listen to your gut! Women really do have intuition whether the world likes to admit it or not. The Dear Lord has ways to warn us to protect us and keep us in His loving arms. If you need money just believe that you have the Blessings of Abraham. If you do your part, work hard and share with the poor, Daddy God will do his part to help you have your needs met. It's all about the faith that can move mountains of invoices and bills from Georgia Power or Atlanta Gas Light or VISA.

My sister Kim had been a photographer and reporter in Hilton Head. She moved to Padre Island next to Brownsville, Texas to sell real estate. She got her Texas license. I went to visit her. We were right on the border of Matamoros, Mexico. At that location the Rio Grande River was only a trickly creek of water. People walked freely back and forth to work. The average Mexican wage was only $2.00 American money.

I loved the shops and atmosphere, but most people were driving really beat up cars. It made me realize how blessed we are in the United States. We really should never complain about anything. In America people sell hot dogs, popcorn, peanuts on the street. In Mexico there were women walking around holding up large trays of roasted sweet potatoes for sale. There clearly were no health department regulations being observed. The people of Latin America eat a lot of tomatoes, and you seldom see someone wearing glasses. Lutein nutrients seem to be the real deal!

I bought two Oaxaca Mexican embroidered dresses and a serape shawl and one huipil dress from Guatemala, where each village has their own embroidery design. I still wear those dresses and treasure them. They always get washed in cold water and never go in a dryer and still look almost new. The cotton and handwork are top quality. People say that I am very ethnic. In fact, I would call our home an ethnic-eclectic-art nouveau museum with textiles and pottery and hand-tooled metal and wooden artifacts from many countries. Who needs disgusting plastic things anyway? This is my way of celebrating the amazing diversity of this planet. Let's promote the idea that all people are valuable and interesting and worthy of love and respect and praise.

David was such an interesting kid to watch. He was all over the place with ideas and activities. He joined the photography club at school and built a small darkroom in the basement. He independently hopped on the #30 LaVista bus to go to the photography shop at Cheshire Bridge Road to buy supplies. In the laundry room I saw a tiny motor attached to a ball point pen cartridge with a sewing needle in the middle. Thinking it was probably a science project, I asked him about it. He raised his sleeve and showed me a tiny one-inch tattoo of a cross. OK, Mom, that's what you get for asking a dumb question. He loved to hunt squirrels so no surprise when he served us boiled squirrel for dinner one evening. He took it out of the pot and stood it up on a plate. Gag! Not wishing to dampen his spirits, I choked it down hoping and praying to not get sick. When he skinned a squirrel, he attached the hide to a piece of plywood with pins and covered it with salt to preserve it. He was my certified Daniel Boone mountain man!

He even raised some chickens in a pen in the yard. We thought they were all hens, but when a crowing rooster waked us one morning, the neighbors complained. Next morning David had to go out and shoot it. We ate delicious chicken that night. The hens laid the cutest little brown eggs. Eventually, when spring came, Miss Anne next door said she was getting too many flies, so they all had to go. I knew of an elderly lady with acreage on LaVista Road behind the African Methodist Episcopal Church who kept chickens. I drove to her house at dawn one morning to see if she would like to have them. She told me she stopped having chickens when her husband died.

There was only one solution. Dr. Walton, the vet at Oak Grove Road would surely want them. He was not open that early, so April and I left the crate on his doorstep before dawn cracked. Months later my brother, knowing about the foul fowl play, asked the doc if he ever had any funny happenings. He told Eric about finding the crate of chickens. Eric asked him what he did with them. He said, "A delivery man saw the chickens and asked if he could take them to his farm in Tennessee." Mystery solved!

I decided to complete my teacher certification. This required two courses. One was a computer course which I took at Georgia State University. The other was a course about students with special needs. That was available free through the DeKalb County School System where I would be employed as a media specialist. During this time, I did substitute teaching for DeKalb five days a week for seven months. I got excellent evaluations from the principals, so the personnel department interviewed me and loved my unique portfolio. They said I could have any school in the county if the principal agreed. They sent me to interview at Peachcrest Elementary. The principal hired me on the spot. My sister had done some wonderful photos for the portfolio to show all the educational things I did with children and youths.

My sister came back from Texas and moved in with us. She was offered a job at a high school friend's real estate agency but decided to be a full-time photographer with a makeover salon called Glamour Shots. She was really doing well and meeting celebrities and musicians who wanted photos. She expanded and started doing weddings. There was something magical about her photos. She had a gift to capture the very essence of a person and make them look better than any other photo they had ever had taken. I can compose an interesting scene for a photo but don't understand all those F stop gizmos and such. I say, "The F stops here with me!"

I really loved my school and did lots of decorating in the media center to make it child friendly. I enjoyed doing beautiful and inspiring bulletin boards, so the principal had me do them around the building. She applauded my creativity and gave me free range to express myself to promote learning and reading. Story time was the most enjoyable part of each day, reading to kindergarten through third grade. I sometime wore costumes or played my autoharp and sang.

It was fulfilling to me to create original non-scary clown characters that delight children. I wisely copyrighted them in my deposit account at the Library of Congress called 'Learning Tower of Peachtree.' The motto is: Educate and Entertain. That is the way to teach without being didactic like an old fashioned 'Goody Two Shoes' book or a knuckle-rapping grumpy teacher from 'Little House on the Dreary.' It felt like I had visited Mount Parnassus, the Greek Mythology home of the muses. First came Candy Lauper also named Sugarlump. She is a bejeweled baker/candy maker who teaches the children how sweet it is to read and learn. She carries a giant red heart-shaped box to give out treats. The box says "Candy Lauper."

Once the day before Halloween, I had this costume in the living room to be ready to hand out candy. My girlfriend Dawn came over for lunch. She saw the costume and the candy box and asked, "Is that a take-off on Cyndi Lauper?" I said, "Duh, yes! Candy was born while I was riding in my Chevelle one night and her song 'True Colors' was playing on the radio. I was watching traffic lights and car head lights and taillights. Voila! Candy popped out of my imagination!" Dawn whipped out her phone. She had three numbers for the real Cyndi's home, mobile and manager. She called her and left a message which said, "Cyndi, baby, do I have a surprise for you!" They had been very close friends in Burlington, Vermont one year. Cyndi's little dog, Sparkle, had even chased a skunk and come into Dawn's house, and you know the rest of that story!

Anyway, later, Dawn took me to meet Cyndi twice, and it was so special and loads of fun. I glued small jelly beans in the shape of a rainbow inside a heart-shaped box. I typed the chorus of her song 'True Colors' and attached it. She was overwhelmed with joy and gave us signed CD's and we made happy photos with her. Later she sent tickets for her Tony award winning musical in New York, 'Kinky Boots.'

Next is Cleana Turner. She wears a rainbow-colored Tina Turner wig and carries a feather duster and a bottle of Shout. She tells the children, "Clean up your homework. Clean up your room. Clean up your mouth. Otherwise, you are just Dusting the Wind. Baby you're just Dusting the Wind". (a takeoff on the song 'Dust in the Wind' by Kerry Livgren of the American rock band Kansas)

Petera Panera is a female Peter Pan who is learning to be more grown-up and responsible.

There is a leprechaun named Marney Blarney in her emerald green clothes with sparkly gold vest who talks about being honest while following your dreams for that pot at the end of the rainbow. So does Choo Choo Can Can, the Can Can dancer who dreams of being in the royal ballet. She is dressed in black with pink accessories and props.

Further down the cast of characters there is a traditional girl clown in a lime-green polka dot suit. Her name is Up Down Clown. She gives palatable advice on dealing with anxiety, loneliness and depression.

Irma Firma is a real hoot! She comes in wearing a long white granny gown carrying a two by four and singing: How firm a foundation, ye saints of the Lord. I can't have peace 'til I'm thin as a board. She helps girls and women have positive images of their shapes to end body shaming.

Holly Parton sings that she will always love God, and God will always love her!

There is certainly nothing wrong with the traditional age-old storybook characters. My Pied Piper character walks children around in a circle holding hands and singing John Denver's song 'Follow Me.' This is to promote friendship and trust. 'Wizard of Oz Dorothy' has a good modern message. Some sixteen or so other characters costumes and props are in the closet and have their helpful themes and subtle, non-preachy messages with songs and poems.

Toward the end of the year there was a major shakeup in the county regarding putting the more experienced teachers in the lower socio-economic neighborhoods like Peachcrest. So, I was sent to the plush Chesnut Elementary

School in Dunwoody. Since it was so highly endowed by the parents, they gave me massive funding to decorate the media center like an enchanted forest with clouds, trees, flowers and animals like display rabbits and birds. I had a plan to build something called "A Learning Tower." It was a small structure that had tape players inside for individual learning. The inside walls were covered with art postcards brought from Germany with art from caveman days all the way up to modern artists like Salvador Dali. It had an opening large enough to serve as a puppet theater for regular puppets or shadow puppets. We purchased a five-hundred-gallon white plastic milk storage container from a dairy farm near Macon, Georgia. My brother brought it on his truck. We painted it to look like gray stone walls. It was so fun and fantastic, that it was written up in the newspaper.

The Learning Tower led to my receiving some more grants to buy extra books and audiovisual equipment and special video tapes. I went to New York City to visit friends. A girlhood friend Ellen had become a world-famous artist/photographer, and we stayed in her loft in Greenwich Village near her gallery. We went to see Mr. Stevens in Little Italy in the village. He had raised millions for Emory University to build their new nursing school and law school. I sat for hours at the 42nd. Street Library down in the Children's Department and wrote down titles of beautiful fiction and non-fiction books for children.

Our media center became well-known. The library school at Georgia State sent students to observe me and the atmosphere. My wonderful clerk named Marge who loved to do creative things was such a great help. We made attractive, memorable bulletin boards and displays.

Our principal Mr. Standifer supported me wholeheartedly, and the career blossomed and flourished. The teachers were congenial and liked what was happening in the media center. They got as much personal attention and academic support as possible. They knew that they could request all the materials they needed. We did ethnic displays to celebrate diversity using things brought to me by parents from all over the world.

Also, I had met some glassy-eyed hippies at the Omni at a concert with my son. They sold tie-dye t-shirts, so they gave me their catalog and we opened a wholesale account and the teachers ordered a few dozen shirts. How fun was that when we all wore them on teacher work days! A second-grade teacher named Amy even ordered tie-dye table cloths for her son's Bar Mitzvah luncheon.

The year the State of Georgia cut our book budget, I proclaimed, "Not happening in our media center!" I started a little personalized stationery business to earn money for us. There was a poster with ten different attractive designs for boys and girls. The parents paid me $5.00 to make the children a packet of twelve letters and envelopes of their choice. They sold like hotcakes, and we made a lot of money. Don't ever tell a Datry "No." They will write the word "Yes" in the sand underlined and forbid you to put even one toe over that line!

Various people asked me to do volunteer storytelling for charities and at the Dunwoody Public Library and for the Girl Scouts. Everyone enjoyed the costumes and thought it was all very engaging and productive. I could often make costumes to go with various books. There was the 'Egyptian Cinderella' for example.

My goal was to guide children to love to read and to become life-long learners. This could be achieved by knowing the children personally and observing which kinds of books they gravitated to the most. For example, there was a little boy from Russia named Mikhail that we called Misha. His English was limited. He shared that he wanted to grow up to be a clown. I drove out to Eddie's Trick Shop on Memorial Drive and bought Misha 'The Complete Book of Clowning.' It was his to take home and keep. That wide smile of sheer delight on his face was worth every penny that came out of my pocket! It really motivated him to learn English.

There were students who came to my office before school and chatted with me. One boy saw me in the back office all alone reading my Bible. He wanted a Bible, so I gave him a copy of 'The Living Bible' which is written in every day easy to understand language. An incorrigible boy named Larry came to see me on a workday. I was determined to help him settle down and learn and behave. He could rock all the way backward upside-down in my rocking chair. I showed him how I could do a front walkover flip. He told me that he loved snakes, so my cousin Doris Gove sent him an autographed copy of her book 'A Water Snakes Year.' She was a biologist at The University of Tennessee.

I worked with a little girl named Tara who liked to write poetry. She was in the behavior disordered class because of some elective mutism. She had been severely abused by her mother and step-brother. She really opened up and made progress and began to talk. She sewed me a tiny bright pink pillow stuffed with cotton and tissues. Her teacher let several students come to me for fifteen minutes each on Friday afternoons. I prayed for the insight and wisdom to know what these children needed and how to get through to them. It was so rewarding. I could have worked seven days a week and not gotten tired of it.

One day I was downtown at the Marriott at a library seminar. During the lunch break I walked across the over-street tunnels to a building called Inforum. There was a large exhibit from Saudi Arabia. I chatted with King Fahd's artists Othman and Ali, and we immediately clicked and struck up a friendship. They invited my family to come have dinner with them at the Peachtree Plaza Hotel. That is the famous seventy story hotel designed by John Portman. He lived in our neighborhood when everyone thought his ideas were outlandishly insane and off the wall. In those early days he was so poor that he could not pay his wife's bill at Daddy's store.

April did a beautiful and interesting drawing that symbolized the relationship between America and Saudi Arabia. The artists were fascinated and adored it. Since eccentric Othman carried with him a briefcase with his watch collection, we ordered him a watch with that very design on it.

The artists needed assistants to set up exhibits in other cities, so my nineteen-year-old April and I met them in Toronto that summer. Before the meeting date we backpacked all the way to Quebec and stayed in youth hostels. One had been a nineteenth century prison, and we slept in Cell #2. In Toronto we had a room at the Hilton and an Italian chauffer to drive us to stores to get art supplies and equipment for the artists. One night April wanted a cheeseburger and looked on the room service menu. She said, "Othman, I am not paying $15.00 for a cheeseburger!" He said, "April, you get a many cheeseburger you going to want. King Fahd, he going to pay for it. He don't Mind." What an adventure we had there!

But it all came to an abrupt end when Sadam Hussein attacked Kuwait. The Saudi artists were immediately called back home, and the exhibit was postponed. Othman's wife was expecting a baby. I called his home in Riyadh on the due date and could hear Scud missiles exploding in the background. Scary! For the first time in my life, it made those middle eastern conflicts all too real and personal for me. We are ultra blessed to have the peace that we enjoy in our country.

Ali's art was mostly large long murals in public buildings and shopping centers. He used a palette knife for raised texture and chose warm shades of yellow, orange, brown, white and metallic gold. Othman had his own unique art style. He did vibrant somewhat abstract water colors using cool colors like purple, blue, green, turquoise. Then he drew things on top with shiny enamel from paint pens. His artwork was quite striking. I wrote a symbolic poem about the artists and their styles. It is called 'Oasis Revisited.' It was translated into Arabic and published in all of the Saudi papers. Othman sent me an original copy.

Othman truly wanted to have an art show in the United States. He was famous enough that he had done a painting for Princess Diana. He showed us a photo of them together at the presentation. I had a tenant who was the boxer Evander Holyfield's promoter. They frequently went to Las Vegas for fights. Michael told me he could help arrange for Othman to have an exhibit. Sadly, Holyfield began to get a truckload of bad publicity, and Michael switched gears and became Leon Spink's promoter and moved away. We were all so disappointed. Oh well, doubtful that I would have liked the noisy, confusing Las Vegas with too many bright lights. My, aren't the grapes sour today?

Chapter 20
Is A Little Tulip About to Bloom?

Mahmoud and I were talking about having a child of our own. It seemed like a long shot; I mean we were both forty-five years old by then. What were the odds? What would happen to my smashing career? One morning on the appropriate day I did a fertility test which said that was the day. I went to the family room and read my devotional book for that day. The scripture was from the book of Song of Solomon and said precisely: Your vineyard is in blossom. Your fig tree puts forth leaves. Well now, you can't get much more specific than that, or? I felt the presence of something very holy, and a peace washed over me like the Balm of Gilead. Somehow, deep down, I knew that I knew that I knew there would be a child.

Sure enough, it happened. The Word says that God's ways are not our ways, and His thoughts are not our thoughts. Things don't really always go the way we planned. I dreamed that that baby was a boy with dark curls and blue eyes. I named him Gabriel Luca. The famous Ob/Gyn doctor Dr. Christiane Northrup who wrote the book 'Mother-daughter Wisdom' says that women know things like this. She can't explain it, but she experiences it with women all the time. Six weeks later in July I lost that baby and was totally bewildered, saddened and disillusioned.

Nonetheless, according to my obstetrician Dr. Kral, on September 15th. Another conception took place. This was April's birthday and the anniversary of the first production of that play in the Atlanta Stadium, 'Behold the Man.' There is no timing like angelic timing. It's never too fast, never too slow. Rolex and Timex and Apple Watch, move over and take a bow before the clock of heaven! Well, Hemingway, for whom does the bell toll? This time it was definitely for us. I believe that Gabriel watches over Haleh.

The funny thing was that the previous year Dr. Kral had done an ultrasound because of pain in my right ovary. He was expecting to find at least a small cyst. There was not one. I laughingly said, "Well, I guess there is just one more baby in there kicking and screaming to be born." Be cautious what you say. The Good Book says: Life and death are in the tongue. If I were a betting woman, I would put big money on it and say that my youngest Haleh came from the right ovary.

Mahmoud had a serious accident at his job due to the carelessness of a co-worker. He fell twelve feet onto concrete hitting his head and fracturing his right hand. The emergency room doctor told us that given all of the physics circumstances, he could not figure out how he survived. He is just the grand puh bah of accident survivors. I think he could go to the 9 Lives Olympics and beat out all the cats for the gold medal. He should have died or been profoundly disabled. Nonetheless, there was a traumatic brain injury that needed to heal. Death lost, and Life won! Events like this help one to understand what is really important in life. It gives you the perspective to be thankful for your blessings and make the best of every day that you live. Navigating one's path on this planet requires a lot of blind faith.

We got a lot of flack about this baby from a few people that thought this child should not be born. It was as if they were saying, "Oh, yes. This is going to come up in the insanity hearing!" They said I was ruining my career and would be in PTA until I was old enough to croak. They acted as if we had gone to the Stupid Olympics and won gold medals. We stood firm knowing this child was a gift from heaven and meant to be. I told the scoffers in plain English that they just needed to McGet It and back off and take a hike!

I was strong and healthy all through that school year. The only day I missed was for the amniocentesis. That test came out perfectly normal and told us that we were having a girl. At my age with old eggs there was only a ten percent chance of having a healthy baby. This baby was meant to be and was surrounded by angels for sure. At first, we were going to name the baby Laleh which is Persian for tulip in honor of my Dutch ancestry and an important Persian symbol. Later we decided on Haleh which means halo of an angel.

She really has filled our lives with bright light since the day she was born. She is so loving, generous, caring with such a gentle spirit like her brother, David, and sister, April. There were older relatives that did not particularly like the name. They called her "Holly," I said, "If I had wanted to name my baby

Sticker Bush, I would have named her Sticker Bush. Like her siblings, she is very gifted, highly motivated and a high achiever. She is an Energizer Bunny like me, racing around at break neck speed. That is why I have always called her my little hummingbird. Haleh and I hold seminars to teach bunnies how to be energized."

Mama came for the birth. On the evening of the due date around 7pm, she was rubbing my back saying, "Come little baby, come!" The water broke, and we were off to the hospital. We were all in the delivery room. Mama and Mahmoud were eating Taco Bell food and watching a cowboy movie. I asked them to turn the volume down. My labor had stopped at one point, and I was given Pitocin nasal drops to start it back up. That made the pains very intense, so I had to give up on a natural birth and have a saddle block.

Everything went smoothly, and petite Haleh came into the world at 7:01 the next morning at six pounds four ounces. She had a beautiful little sweet face and was very alert. She had been so active in utero playing soccer it seemed that I would have expected a boy perhaps. She took to nursing immediately and was a content baby. Mahmoud stayed at the hospital with us all night. My lifelong friend Alison came with her young son Beau. He had picked a tiny teddy bear dressed in a clown suit of pastel baby colors. We named him "Baby Teddy", and Haleh still has him. When Beau's wife Ana had a baby boy, Haleh sent him a tiny blue baby teddy.

We were very fortunate to have Aunt Sara and Uncle Walter living walking distance from us. It was about a mile with sidewalks. We spent so much happy time with them. Sara was beginning to have serious problems with her eyesight from macular degeneration. I was able to organize all of her medical receipts and file her health insurance claims and pay the bills. She was grateful for all of the large reimbursement checks that started arriving.

I think I can safely say Haleh was pretty much awake the first four years of her life. Thankfully I had resigned from my job to stay home for a while. I was so sleep deprived that the daily forecast was "unproductive with a chance of napping." She was so active and agile that she could pull up on her crib and walk around the sides at age six months. If I did not have that on video with the date stamped on it, I doubt anyone would believe me. Dr. Bob said I had gestated another genetic wonder. What a blessing! But I knew this would be challenging. We went on many walks with the stroller so I could keep in good physical shape. I could have truly used a trip to "Mount Sleepmore."

Mahmoud built us a beautiful house on some land we had previously purchased at an auction. My very talented landscape architect brother designed a beautiful landscape plan with emerald zoysia turf and very attractive shrubs. Mahmoud hired someone to do the framing and the roof, but he did literally everything else with his own hands. He was expert with plumbing, trim carpentry, painting, tile work and electrical. I could put Haleh on my back in a Gerry Pak and serve as the sweeper and clean-up crew quite a lot. The house should have been finished by spring, but there was a historic blizzard in Atlanta. The roads were blocked for four days. When we were finally able to get twenty-four miles to the house, the burst pipe in one upstairs bathroom had caused a leak that made the kitchen ceiling fall in. There was no furnace yet, so it all just had to dry out.

It was Easter before David and April could help us put in the new ceiling. That was the day Haleh took her first steps. This pushed our construction time frame into the very hot summer. Thankfully we could soak the baby in cool water in the deep kitchen sink and then put her down on a blanket on a cool tile floor for play or a nap. We managed. In life you do what you have to do to survive and move forward.

It was joyful to finally move in right before Thanksgiving. The family came, and we had a wonderful time in the spacious, open downstairs. Everyone was so happy for us. It was a very comfortable house with every energy-saving feature known to man. The hardwood floors were easy to clean and prevented dust. I had an island in the kitchen with Italian floral swimming pool tile on top. We had a 15'x20' walk-in stand-up attic that was so convenient. There was a huge storage room behind the garage. I especially loved the gas logs fireplace that had a toggle switch. One push and you instantly had the fire going. It was so cozy that my relatives came back for Christmas.

After the former Soviet Union fell, a Christian television network was asking people to send dolls and trucks to be sent to the previously communist countries. They attached a simple story of the Gospel in the native languages to each toy. My heart was strongly moved to participate. I went to Target with baby Haleh and bought a cartful of small dolls. As I was heading to the checkout counter, there was a pleasant middle aged mulato lady standing in the aisle with her arms by her side. She had no purse or cart and was simply smiling at me. She had on khaki pants and a red shirt that had an onion dome building on it, and it said, "Moscow." A lot of joy and warmth and peace washed over my spirit, and I will always believe that she was an angel sent to show me that the Dear Lord had noticed what I was doing and was pleased. It makes no difference that I cannot prove it. Sometime you just know that you know what you know, and that is sufficient.

We found two days a week pre-school for Haleh at the Berkmar Methodist Church. She was happy there. I have the cutest video of her rolling pumpkins down the sloped front lawn of the church right after Halloween. The next year she went to Bethesda Methodist. I was there one day when she was playing at the indoor table sand box. The teacher asked her what she was making. She said it was a cake. The teacher asked her the kind of cake. She said, "It is a fish cake for "pwotein"". This child had knowledge and a vocabulary that just would not quit!

We were riding down the road with Haleh in the back seat with a sippy cup of ice water. She asked regarding the water drops on her cup, "Mommy, is this condensation?" I might have been surprised enough to run off the road! Where did this kid get her ideas? She had a mind like a steel trap and absorbed knowledge like a little sea sponge. I might add that she hated her car seat and protested vehemently because the safety straps were too confining. Oh dear, I had birthed another child with a will of cast iron!

We had a method of discipline that was kind of a cousin to "time out." It is called "nose against the wall". The child that is misbehaving or mouthing must go to a wall and touch their nose to the wall and stay still there for three minutes. If you do not think three minutes is a very long time, ask an egg! If the child protests or asks how many more minutes are left, then they must stand on one foot with their nose still touching the wall. Also, another minute is added to the time. For a perpetual motion child like Haleh, this was a very effective behavior modification. Our little hummingbird hated the nose/wall scenario enough to pretty well straighten up at the very mention of this medieval dungeon torture.

Around this time Mama had some young friends Bob and Muffy in Myrtle Beach that were moving to Panama City, Florida with their small children. They begged her to move with them and live with them. She decided to do this, so Aunt Kitti and I drove to Myrtle Beach to help Mama get organized and packed for her move. Kitti was always so good about helping family when needed. She is high energy and so upbeat and a fun companion. She had come to stay with us when we were building our house, and she did some painting and watched Haleh a lot.

Haleh had no siblings at home. Hers were twenty and twenty-one years older and in college. The thought occurred to me that I could register with a nanny service and provide my little girl with playmates and earn a little money and get out of the house. A lady with a private agency interviewed me. She was impressed with my education background and observed my parenting skills with Haleh. She told me that she could sense that I would never harm a child physically or emotionally. She could tell I knew the difference between right and wrong.

She placed me with a family who lived in an upper-class neighborhood in Peachtree Corners. Dawn and John were both Emory grads who paid me top dollar. We adored their little three-year-old girl Nicole and two-year-old boy Mikey. The parents gave me free range plus their debit card. I could take the children to the Zany Brainy toy store and purchase all kinds of books and puzzles and toys for gifted children. Haleh loved it there and bonded so closely with the little ones that she still keeps up with them on Facebook. We went to playgrounds and took nature walks on the creek in the woods behind the fifty-three-million-dollar mansion on Old Alabama Road that now belongs to Tyler Perry. We had picnics and learned about bugs and snails and plants and birds and so forth. I did arts and crafts with the children and taught them songs.

Mama came to visit us and went to work with me one day. She immediately noticed that Mikey had a very froggy voice. She knew beyond the shadow of a doubt that meant there was a problem with his adenoids. This is very serious and dangerous and causes sleep apnea. Mama insisted that Mikey see a pediatric ear nose and throat specialist that day. Dawn took him to Emory, and they admitted him promptly to remove the tonsils and adenoids. They said he was in grave danger. No doubt about it, Mama saved that child's life.

Nicole simultaneously had chicken pox, and she gave it to Haleh. Mikey came home from the hospital, and April came to visit him and bring him a gift. When she asked him how he felt, he had a delightful child's interpretation of events and said, "A mosquito bit my tonsils, and they hurt." Then the poor little fellow also got the chicken pox. There was no vaccine in the mid-nineties that we knew about.

Haleh had the sweetest little spirit that had great depth for a young child her age. She possessed a sensitivity that was inspiring. I had a small white

Bible. Haleh knew how to write her name. She wrote her name in my Bible and said, "Mommy, when I grow up, I want this to be my Bible." Aunt Sara had given me a purple Methodist hymnal with my name engraved on the front in gold. Haleh said, "Mommy, I want a hymnal just like yours." I promptly went to the Cokesbury book store and ordered one for her.

One day in April when she was almost four, we were driving in Conyers down a narrow, deserted country road lined with trees coming from visiting my friend Debbie. There was a thick fog that was kind of moving toward us. It was very peaceful and ethereal, so I stopped the car, and we got out. After half a minute Haleh said to me in amazement, "Look, Mommy! It is God's breath!" I had never thought of fog that way. How poetic! How profound! This was no ordinary child. She would grow up and do something valuable for heaven's kingdom. I bowed down to the ground. I don't remember taking off my shoes, but I knew I was standing on holy ground in the presence of the Living Lord. It is so vivid in my memory that it seems like just yesterday.

Realizing that we would be on retirement incomes when Haleh went to college, we started buying rental properties and using the rent to pay them off. I could probably name you ninety-nine weird, crazy beyond belief things that tenants can do or say or fail to do. I could give you ninety-nine excuses that they use. Some will lie when the truth would sound better. It would take hours to tell about the off the wall experiences over the years. We got really wise and perceptive and learned all the clever tricks. I could for sure write a long book about it! That book would be a tremendous service to clueless landlords. I am the good cop that rents the houses, and my spouse is the bad cop who enforces the rules.

Chapter 21
Time to Get Back to The Teacher Work Force? Phases I & II

By now Haleh was four and eligible to attend Pre-K at an Elementary School. I went to apply for a media specialist job with Gwinnett County. Haleh got a slot in their Pre-K program. This was very fortunate. The school neighborhood was affluent, and I liked the teachers and parents and children. It was not very many miles from our home and a fairly easy commute through residential neighborhoods. The downside was that the principal would not let me bring Haleh to school with me in the early morning even though she was a very quiet and well-behaved child. I had to find a babysitter near the school and pay her to watch Haleh and bring her to her Pre-K class on time. What a pain to have to get up a half hour earlier and fight more traffic!

The principal turned out to be a real pill. She was so controlling and unreasonably picky, that the best nickname for her was probably "Teeny Mussolini." No one ever told her that you get more flies with honey than with vinegar. In fact, it seemed that she believed that you get the most flies with manure! She could rip into staff members like Tiny Tim on a Christmas ham! The teachers were scared of her harsh criticisms. If she was absent, they sang quietly under their breath, "Ding dong, the witch is dead!" But no house fell on her.

There are people who can't have friends unless they carve a Pinocchio out of wood like Geppetto! The job was exhausting. My clerk was only half-time. Her father was dying, and she was out a lot. It seemed like she was absent more than she was there. Not only did I have to do her job and mine, this school had a pilot program in a studio. I was supposed to plan custom curriculums at the teacher's requests using a company in Phoenix, Arizona that had special videos and lecturers and actors to depict things to do with science or literature or history. In addition to that, the principal told me that I was fourth in command at that school, and she expected to see me there on weekends. She told me to forget about my husband and child because my new life was at that school. The only advantage was that I saved my salary, and it enabled us to make a down payment on a new dream house later.

I asked for a transfer, but there were no openings, so I thought about going back to DeKalb County. I had loved working there, and the door was always open for me, but it was just too far to drive early morning with a small child. I tendered my resignation and decided to have an interim hiatus again as a nanny/governess until something opened up in my field. Mopey, mopey, pouty, pouty, let's just get over it!

An agency placed me in a ritzy gated community with the five children of a world-famous sports celebrity. The children ranged in age from five months to thirteen years old. It was a fun job with many advantages and really excellent pay. I enjoyed helping the two older children with their homework and book reports and projects. The only downside was that I was on constant alert to guard against kidnappers. I always checked the bedroom windows to make sure they were securely locked. In gated neighborhoods there is a constant stream of trucks and vans of painters and yard crews and other assorted handymen.

Also, when you work for a famous person, people seeking autographs sneak to the door now and then. Houses were on a golf course with endless rows of bushes where burglars and other sleazy persons with malintent could conceal themselves until dark. I had the phone number of a famous Atlanta Braves pitcher named John who lived around the corner. He had a bowling alley in his basement. The mom of my family had a miscarriage and became frail and unwell. I told the family that they needed a live-in nanny, so they found one.

I was driving across the Chattahoochee River one morning on Pleasant Hill Road. Something quickened in my spirit, and I had an overwhelming desire to live on the river. I told Mahmoud, so we started looking at land and houses from Sweetwater Plantation to Peachtree Parkway. There was a lot that belonged to the Gwinnett Historical Society that was quite reasonably priced. The only problem was that the neighborhood covenants said a house would have to be built in the Charleston or Savannah or New Orleans style. That was not for us, but I picked up a little white duck feather at that land, and that little still, small voice said to my heart, "You will be living on the river someday. Think of this feather as an angel wing." Wow! I truly believed this with my whole heart.

Yes, skeptics would probably say that was Ju Ju Magumbo going on. Mahmoud saw an ad in the Atlanta Journal. We looked at that house on the river and truly loved it. It was a bit too expensive, but Mahmoud figured out how to do a first and second mortgage at the same time. The mortgage broker bought the idea and said it was ingenious. The house was for sale by owner and had been on the market for three years. We gave a ridiculously low offer, and they accepted it.

At the time a couple was renting the property. The wife was a decorator and had redone the paint and wallpaper to help it sell. Every room matched our furniture and lamps and rugs and pictures perfectly. Amazing! We could just move right in. The master bathroom had beige wallpaper with some white fluff design to it. Funny, but many years later I was sitting in there on my dressing room stool and noticed something that nearly knocked me off the stool. The fluffy white design on the wallpaper was white feathers. Oh my gosh! Why had I not seen that before? I remembered the day when I had picked up that duck feather at Sweetwater Plantation and knew beyond the shadow of a doubt that we would eventually live on the river.

Another very fine agency placed me with a family in Peachtree Corners with a girl Haleh's age named Stephanie, a girl one-year younger named Kelly and a little eighteen-month-old boy named Thomas. The children were adorable and so sweet. They loved Haleh. Both parents, Brad and Laura, were physicians, and they gave me a paycheck that was way beyond generous all the way over to spectacular! I never missed a day of work or made Laura late for her hospital job.

We did so many fun educational activities. I taught them how to make paper and how to dye cloth with plants and berries. You can even make a dye out of Kool-Aid powder even though I would never give that disgusting artificial drink to a child. We did a lot of cooking. Kelly liked to make small cakes from scratch. They absolutely loved to make peanut butter balls with powdered milk and honey or syrup or cocoa powder or raisins. They enjoyed rolling them in powdered sugar. Once Thomas accidently locked himself in his room. Thankfully it was shortly before the dad came home. He told me to push the pacifier under the door, and that did the trick!

Years later the mom called me and asked me to come over and make peanut butter balls with the big children. They remembered this so fondly but had forgotten the recipe. I have kept in touch with this family all through the years. The dad even saved my life once when I was at death's door in a coma from a drastic reaction to a medication. Later when our grandbaby Violet was a preemie, the neonatal physician mom gave me unlimited information and great encouragement.

So, it really was not all that bad that I left the awful nightmare media specialist job. Things have a strange way of working out for the best. That is why the Good Book says: All things work together for good to them that love God and are called according to His purposes. That is why we are instructed by the scriptures to praise God in all Circumstances. Heaven weaves beautiful tapestries of our lives, but down on earth we cannot see the big picture from a distance all at once. That is why some of the threads and designs don't look right to us at times.

I stayed with this family for a couple of happy years with never an unkind word or misunderstanding between any of the adults or the children. It began to dawn on me that I had only five years in the TRS, Teacher Retirement System. You need ten to be vested for a retirement pension and health benefits when you reach age sixty. I decided to go to a DeKalb Schools job fair one Saturday.

I was standing in the line for media specialists when something overwhelming came over me. I felt my feet under me moving me across the room to a line for special ed teachers. Oh, my goodness, what was happening? There was a principal and assistant principal sitting at a table wanting to hire a teacher for a Severe/Profound physical and intellectual disabilities class. The lady in front of me had seven years' experience in the field. When my turn came, they asked me a couple of questions about classroom management for this type of student. Words came out of my mouth. They liked the words, and they hired me to teach at Henderson Middle School. I really was suited for this job. After all, I did have a profoundly disabled sister, Davilyn with autism. A state certification lady there told me I would need four courses to get certified in that field. I needed to take one per year.

I signed up for the first course at Brenau University's branch on Peachtree Industrial not far from home. The professor, Dr. McGregor was wonderful, and she praised my creative projects and notebooks and gave me top grades. I had a lot to learn about the state and federal paperwork for handicapped students. A special ed supervisor taught me to write the IEP (Individual Educational Program). Once per year I met with parents to go over the IEP and get their feedback and suggestions.

I had seven students and two paraprofessionals to help me. Some of the teens were in wheelchairs. One girl had a seizure disorder. One adopted boy born from a crack mom had cerebral palsy. Two students had Downes Syndrome. One boy had autism. Two boys had Angelman's Syndrome.

I decorated the classroom with very bright rainbow colors and moving clouds hanging from the ceiling. Color and music and movement make a brain limbic to use both sides and enhance learning. Even though the teens were non-verbal, I had music activities during the day. I believed that a large part of my job was to encourage the parents who were often feeling hopeless and downtrodden. Even children with IQ's below twenty-five can have gifts and talents. It was my mission to find these abilities and promote them.

Kimberly could watercolor with both hands and do puzzles. Brian was very musical. Matthew liked to sculpt things. Reid brought my teacup, water and teabag to the microwave at precisely 2:45 pm right before the bus came. Who knows how he got that timing right? Fatima from Somalia nurtured the wheelchair students. She had been born in a grass hut and had tribal markings tattooed on her legs. Little Nicholas had three life-threatening syndromes. The nurse taught me to tube feed him. We went on a community or shopping trip twice a week to practice good behavior in public. Our bus driver, Mr. Harold and his wife were so patient and loving.

Rashanda was a very tall girl who could run like the wind. She was an escape artist, so I had to jam the door shut with a folded bath cloth. She always won the races in Special Olympics. She and Brian were crack babies. Little Manuel from Mexico had horrible stomach disorders. I told his parents what to feed him to detoxify his digestive system and had them make an appointment with a gastro doctor. He improved dramatically. They brought me a lovely gift from Mexico after Christmas. Fatima had sinus problems and a congested nose. Surprisingly the school nurse allowed me to purchase boxes of Claritin for her. When she graduated, the family brought me flowers and the sweetest card that said I was her best teacher ever. I felt a bit sad, because I knew they could not really afford that expense.

From time-to-time parents asked me to keep their handicapped child for a week or more so that they could take a leisurely vacation. One couple went to San Francisco. Another family went to Spain. I stayed with just my student or all of their children. It was fun to cook for them and play games and take them to a playground. When you have a non-verbal child, it means the world to be able to leave them with someone who would never be abusive in any way. You need someone who genuinely loves your child completely and is protective.

Chapter 22
The Art of Reaching Out Comes Knocking on My Heart

One day the Gwinnett Daily Post Newspaper had an interesting article about an art exhibit that was about to open at the Jacqueline Hudgens Children's Museum by the Gwinnett Civic Center three miles from our home. The artwork had been done by traumatized children who survived the long siege in Bosnia-Herzegovina. This intrigued me, and I thought it would be a meaningful experience for Haleh. It would have been more convenient to go on a Saturday morning, but I thought she would enjoy the Thursday opening night with refreshments. We went. I bought her a black velvet stuffed dog in the gift shop.

Then a lovely blonde lady came over to talk with me. She was Susan, the founder and director of The Art Reach Foundation. After about a ninety second conversation, she said, "You are the person I am looking for to go to Bosnia this summer and do the music." Something really clicked in my inner being, and I said YES! She asked me to email her a brief bio about my educational information and achievements just as a formality to show to the board of directors.

In the meantime, I was helping Mahmoud writing dozens of letters and faxes and emails to help bring his nephew and two young children from a refugee camp in Germany. They had gone to Istanbul, Turkey to immigrate to Sweden to work with some cousins. The plans fell through. Long story short, they walked along rivers to Sarajevo through mine-infested mountains and got on a train to Germany and were caught without any papers. The camp was in Karlsruhe, Germany. By then the pastor I had helped decades before at Emory was the director of the Methodist Seminary in Germany. Dr. Besserer put Pastor Ursula in charge of our desperate family there. She took them to parks and church and helped them get an interview with the American Embassy in Frankfurt.

I had pastor friends in Colorado who had a ministry to middle eastern persons trying to come to the US. Pastor Ibrahim and his American wife Marie did pretend interviews to prepare our widower nephew Behruz to do his interview well. Pastor Thomas took Behruz and daughter Tannaz and son Amir to Frankfurt, and they passed the requirements. The World Relief organization got them tickets on Delta for a couple of months later. They arrived in the United States and moved in with us until they could get their own place.

I joined the ArtReach team and went to the seminars to prepare for the work. They were led by Dr. Kempler who was the head of the psych department at Emory. He was a Polish survivor of the Holocaust and had been sneaked out of Poland by his German nanny who dressed him as a girl. His older sister and parents also escaped. His wife taught pottery in Emory's art department. His sister is the famous Caldecott winner Anita Lobel. Her deceased husband, Arnold Lobel wrote the 'Frog and Toad Are Friends' easy-reader books. Their daughter, Ariana wrote and produced a delightful Broadway musical called 'A Year with Frog and Toad.' Bernard sent his sister one of my children's stories, 'The Princess and the Sneeze', and she loved it and has helped me get it published. She says, "Your voice rings true for the fairy tale genre."

Our team arrived in Sarajevo that summer. We had a bubbleologist named Bo who entertained the children and teens by enclosing them in giant bubbles. There were art therapists who worked for Red Cross disasters or had private practices for traumatized adults and children. We had the well-known Atlanta photographer Mrs. Bunnen who has a gallery at the High Museum named after her. Susan arranged for a journalist named Liz from London to be with us for two weeks with a video crew paid for by the Coca Cola Company. We were to work in a town called Gorazde on the Mosta River.

We stayed in a comfortable hotel with delicious meals. The only problem was the lack of laundry facilities. I devised a method whereby I put my dirty clothes on inside-out, got in the shower, soaped them down and squeezed them and rinsed off. It was permissible to hang them on the railing of the outside balcony. Then I made friends with an elderly lady in an apartment next to the hotel. She let me use her washer, and I bought her huge boxes of laundry detergent. I sat with her drinking tea, and we communicated with simple words and gestures.

Kind people do not have to worry about language barriers. My uncle Dr. Phillip Gove who was the editor of the Merriam Webster dictionary most of his life always said: Language is communication. Of course, this drove the English teachers batty. They probably would have joyfully run him out of town.

Bosnian Christians and Jews and Muslims had lived peacefully side by side for generations worshipping freely in their churches and synagogues and mosques. These three groups lived together in harmony and did business together and went to school together without incidents. It was so obvious that outside perverse politics had stirred Christian Serbs up against Muslims and started this bloody genocide. My mom always had a saying for this kind of trouble. She called it the spirit of antichrist.

Evil does certainly exist in this world. We know that. We see that. We shudder about that. We hate that, but I always say, "Life is short, but heaven is long. Just pass your years as peacefully and kindly and lovingly as you can on the rocky path to heaven." We may arrive there bruised and bloody, but fortunately, we will not need a username or password to get in!

I was assigned to work with the special needs children and pre-teens. Some of them had elective mutism from shock and grief. We bought a set of drums for a little boy that was terrified of noises. That way he learned that there were noises he could control. One of our translators had dragged her wounded mother across concrete while dodging sniper bullets. Fortunately, many Bosnians learn German in school, and I could communicate with those people.

There were moms who had given birth on days when there was no water. Then they had to cut up their clothes to make diapers. We climbed through a tunnel by the airport that had been used to bring in supplies and take out wounded victims. There were previously in there electrical cables to provide some power. It was very dangerous to go through there when tramping through puddles! We drove past some land that had been a school. It was burned to the ground, children teachers and all!

Another on-going problem was the Russian Mafia. They were trafficking women. We were working closely with US Ambassador Miller and his wife Bonnie. They had bought a safe house for any women they rescued. These women were making and selling little dolls to support their children. I have three of those dolls. Eventually the Millers were transferred to Greece because that mafia was threatening their lives. We spent some of our leisure time at the embassy in Sarajevo. It had an indoor swimming pool. Ambassador Miller grilled meat for us while walking around barefoot in shorts and t-shirts. The Millers were such down-to-earth caring people for sure. Bonnie had been an education professor in Washington, D.C.

We went on some field trips on weekends such as to the interesting market place in Sarajevo. I actually met a soldier from the United Nations peace-keeping force who was from Moultrie, Georgia. Many of the goods came from Turkey, and I bought some beautiful metal trays for family. I found unique earrings, brightly-colored satin shoes and a porcelain tea set.

The most memorable trip was to a tiny village called Luco Mira on the top of a mountain. These people lived and dressed just as they had for hundreds of years since the Middle Ages. It felt like we were in a National Geographic film. They were shepherds with cows and sheep and lived in small concrete block houses with a kitchen/sitting room and fireplace and a loft for sleeping. Every little window had white curtains beautifully embroidered with colorful flowers. There was a cooking kettle on the fire. Men and women wore black felt blousy knee pants with colorful knitted knee socks. I have a pair hanging by my stairway. Their white embroidered shirts had wide leg o'mutton sleeves. The women wove rugs to sell for cash money. There were no cars or electricity. If someone got sick, they put them on a stretcher and walked for miles and miles to get to a doctor. Our guide, Ismet, was a doctor who had hiked up these mountains with a heavy backpack during the siege to deliver medicines to the people.

The Bosnians really appreciated everything we did for them. Even though they were poor and had survived indescribable losses and horrifying experiences, they knitted and crocheted things for us like bedroom slippers and doilies and pillow covers. I treasure the gifts the children gave me. They took a green wine bottle and glued colorful tissue paper to it like a collage. Light shines through it so nicely. They also made for me a tiny, varnished wooden hut made from popsicle sticks.

There was a lady there with a five-year-old son. Her name was Vela. She had not a tooth in her head! Her little boy was the product of rape by a Russian soldier. One of our translator's moms worked in a dental lab in Sarajevo. I made arrangements to send the money for Vela to get some dentures, and I bought her little boy a scooter. She wrote me sweet letters for a couple of years. She sent me eight hand-crocheted white cotton doilies. A Bosnian lady at my school translated her letters for me. That tiny donation gave me a hundred million dollars' worth of joy!

It was very hard to come home to hearing Americans jammer that they could not get a close parking place at the mall when going to Macy's for a one-day sale on fur coats! After seeing such devastation, it was hard to adjust to living in an affluent country with no war-torn cities. The sidewalks in Sarajevo had lots of round damaged places from mortar shells. The people painted them red and called them Sarajevo roses. I would never be the same again.

The country of Bosnia gave me an honorary teacher's certificate. I was supposed to go back to Bosnia the next year. Susan was going to rent a large house for our team, and I was to be the chef. Sadly, when the World Trade Center bombing took place, our plans got completely mixed up, and the team had to postpone the schedule for fall. Susan sent a team to New York and started Project America for veterans to help prevent suicide.

The school system obviously could not let me take two weeks off from work, so at best I could only continue to help ArtReach raise funds. When the Bosnian project ended, Ambassador Miller introduced Susan to a Greek philanthropist named Aliki whose husband was French. They owned a small palace and island near the island of Rhodes. Susan with the help of Queen Noor of Jordan arranged for teachers from Iraq, Lebanon, Israel and Syria to come to this palace for seminars on art, music, dance, recreation and writing therapy. Then they could go back to their war-torn countries and teach all of the other teachers how to help their students and parents.

ArtReach soared from zero to WOW in a very short time. American, Continental and United Airlines had three-minute inflight videos of our work in Bosnia. The director Susan told me one of the favorite clips was my ribbon dance in a circle to the tune of 'Follow Me' by John Denver. CBS Television had a Sunday morning program called Breakfast with the Arts. We were featured on that program once. Prince Charles gave money for us to rebuild the community center and soccer field in Gorazde. A United States Army plane volunteered to fly our art supplies to Sarajevo. I had a friend who told me that our work was just a drop in the bucket in this mixed-up suffering world. I told her, "Maybe so, but by golly, it is my drop!"

Susan won an Artemis award. The Greek goddess Artemis was a nurturing protector. It was presented to her by Shirley Franklin, the mayor of Atlanta, at the Roxy Theater downtown. This was after a formal dinner with Former Ambassador Andrew Young giving the invocation and blessing. We were so proud of all of her accomplishments and dedication.

Chapter 23
Rolling on Down the River of Life

Rafting down life's river is challenging bouncing over swift rapids, but it beats being up a creek without a paddle in a leaky rowboat. We had our ups and downs, traumas and ins and outs, but altogether, we were making good progress in life and acquiring enough rental properties to be able to keep our lifestyle when Haleh went to college. She liked her school and teachers and enjoyed friends and family.

We went on beach trips to Hilton Head and Destin and toured parts of eastern and western Canada a couple of times. In Toronto we saw an outdoor performance of the kid's TV show 'The Comfy Couch.' We walked for miles in the underground tunnels that were like shopping centers. In Vancouver we had a bus driver and bus all to ourselves, and he drove wherever we wanted to go for hours on end. That's where we drank our first bubble tea ever in Chinatown.

I started a small book business called Lily's Library to create beautiful book collections of award-winning titles for prosperous families. People who live in gated and affluent communities usually have professional decorators. So, I designed custom picture book lists that matched the décor of every room. That way the parents could leave the books in plain view to provide that print rich environment that makes children lifelong readers. I opened a wholesale account with a book distributor. The proceeds from this venture could then be used to buy books for needy children or to give dozens of inspirational books to adults who were having struggles in their lives.

David married beautiful sweet Kimberly whom we all loved. She was a whiz in chemistry and quite the artist. She painted beautifully and constructed intricate torn paper mosaics that are quite tedious to make out of torn magazines and Elmer's Glue. When Haleh was older, she successfully taught her how to make them. The special outdoor country wedding featured Haleh as the trainbearer. She and Kimberly rode to the aisle on the back of our family yellow Chevelle convertible. We really loved Kimberly's family and soon became very close to them and enjoyed being together.

As a wildlife biologist specializing in birds, David designed and helped build fascinating plantations for hunting quail, turkeys, ducks, deer and doves. He took the old Tuskegee air base and turned it into a marvelous bird plantation. On the side he raised the very exotic little spotted fallow deer. He got a national award for his research that succeeded in breeding quail in the wild. All the biologists in the world had said that this could not be done. It took him seven years to pull it off.

Once the governor of Alabama took him to Auburn to meet President George Bush, Jr. David invited him to his annual September dove shoot, and George Jr. accepted. They agreed Airforce 1 could land on the old runway from World War II that had been redone. Out in that wilderness no one other than the Secret Service would know he was there. Sadly, that was the year of 9/11, and obviously the president had to handle the tragic United States crisis and forget about a fun dove shoot.

David became the thirteenth Air Force certified BASH specialist in the United States. That stands for Bird Airport Strike Hazard biologist. He learned how to keep any airport safe from any kind of bird strike. It takes one year to fully study an airport and securely complete this task. One must also deal with jack rabbits or iguanas or such depending on the locale. Because of his Homeland Security training from the Defense Force, he could train airport employees to do that also.

We were all so happy when my brother Eric married wonderful Carolyn. She is just right for him in every way, and she does so many kind and helpful things for our family. We have good understandings.

April lived with us for a while. She had an executive job with a computer corporation three miles away. She was the PR director for all of their customers in the world. She had started out as a customer service rep specializing in helping clients from German-speaking countries. Having a master's degree in English, she took the company's user manuals and made them user friendly. The president recognized her motivation and intelligence and gave her the fun job of leading tours and wining and dining clients. She created Power Point presentations and did other publicity. She worked on her own time schedule and sometime took Haleh with her and taught her all about computers.

Haleh had watched her order things on E-bay and had memorized her charge card number. That's the problem with brilliant gifted children with minds like a steel trap! April once took Haleh to an Avril Lavigne concert, so one evening Haleh ordered a music CD of the concert songs. April told her that she must never do that again without permission. Even though the seller was overseas in Macedonia, the CD did arrive a week later. Surprised the heck out of me!

Mahmoud's lovely, sweet daughter Deeba gave us three incredible granddaughters. Akleema finished graduate dental school, and is a maxillofacial surgeon. Kubra and Neeba are in medical school. The three girls will build a clinic together soon. They bring us great joy and immense pride.

April bought a nice two-story stucco house two miles from us. Mahmoud helped her negotiate the deal and saved her ten thousand dollars. She and Haleh were very close, so Haleh spent a lot of time with her. There were no booster seats, so Haleh rode in April's Isuzu Trooper sitting on two cases of Diet Coke, no problem. Eventually April got a Mustang convertible and a kind gentleman caller named Randy. They were not totally suited for one another, but he took her great-grandfathers Stradivarius violin to the local Huthmaker string shop and had it strung and bought her a case for it.

She met handsome, intelligent Rick at work, and they dated for about a year, got engaged and married on St. Patrick's Day with Haleh as the flower girl. She and the bridesmaids wore long emerald green dresses and carried daffodils. The happy couple honeymooned in Hawaii.

My neighborhood swimming pool had an aerobic swimming instructor Belinda for many years. I bought the deep-water belt and foam weights and try to swim any day that is not raining. My genetic report says I have the long twitch muscles of an athlete. Thus, lots of physical activity is very enjoyable. The 7pm peacefulness of water, sky, birds and green trees melts away the stresses of the day.

Age sixty-five gave me a free gym membership. The greatest thing of all was the Zumba classes. We had teachers that taught hip hop, Bollywood, Egyptian, pop, Tango and Latino dances. I made a list of over sixty songs that especially appeal to me and make me emote. They are readily available on You-tube and easy to pull up with the microphone on a smart TV. Also, Music

Choice on TV has a soft rock channel and on oldies channel with 50's 60's and 70's songs from my youth.

We find it interesting that in twenty-five years no one has ever seen a poisonous snake in our yard or by the river. We know that there are copperheads and moccasins in the area. The probable reason is the abundance of black racer snakes and king snakes. I have seen a gray rat snake, and that is good. Their bite is not poisonous and only requires some antibiotic ointment and a band-aid. We saw one huge decay snake, and that is desirable. Yellow jackets come now and then, but it is easy enough to find their nest in the ground at dusk when they go in there. A little gasoline and a match take care of the danger. We had one bear twice in the night on the deck eating birdseed. Naughty little raccoons tear up the screens, so the birdfeeder needs to stay in a garden.

We were sitting on the blue leather sofa in the family room one evening during a ferocious thunder storm. Mahmoud was closest to the window and in his Pajamas with no metal buttons or zipper. We saw blue lighting come through the window and hit the phone line right next to him. It did not touch him! Being a licensed electrical contractor, he just went to the basement and got some phone wire and fixed it. Sadly, that same bolt of lightning hit the house four doors down in the attic, and the roof caught on fire. The firetrucks got to our street quickly and damage was relatively small.

Haleh was consistently a child with very creative play ideas. We got some pet mice in a wire cage. When babies were born, they escaped, and I found them in a bag of chocolate chip cookies in the pantry. When she had the pet mice Lily and Target and K Mart, she sewed red Christmas dresses for them that were shiny lame' fabric. She decorated their aquarium cage with red and green ribbons and glitter. She bought some tiny hats at Michael's and made Easter bonnets for them. She took them up on our catwalk balcony in a wicker basket attached with a twelve-foot piece of white nylon twine. She hung the basket over the side and lowered it and raised it and said that was their Six Flags amusement park.

The funniest event of all was on a Saturday when she and her friend Kylie put a mouse in our mailbox with a walkie talkie. She and Kylie hid behind the bushes. When the lady postal worker opened our box, the mouse "talked" to her, and she jumped back and yelled with fright. The next Thursday I got a formal letter from the Postmistress of Duluth, Georgia. It said that she knew the little girls meant no harm, but that I needed to tell them that it was against the law to tamper with anyone's mailbox. I put that letter in Haleh's baby book, and it is still there.

Haleh was a diligent and well-behaved pupil in school. She was very motivated and made excellent grades and was liked by her teachers. She started some ballet lessons, but it was pretty boring for her standing at the barre'. She was much more of a fast-moving child that needed more action. That's when we started gymnastics which was a real hit. Her body shape was just right for tumbling, and she worked hard at it, was very agile and enjoyed every minute. I bought her a purple velvet suit with silver diamond medallion at the neck.

The tumbling led to a real desire in her heart to be a cheerleader. We eventually signed up for that, and it was a wonderful activity. She totally loved the purple Duluth uniforms and pom poms. At times she had been a bit of an absent-minded little professor, so showing up at a football game on time with all her gear was good for her. She really learned to get it together. Of course, that was not the case in the mornings before school. It was a mad chase to get her to the bus on time. She was more of a night person like her sister. I wonder how many times I drove to the last stop in the neighborhood to get her on that bus! Under a cushion in our living room there is a light remainder of a stain from her spilled "wake up" cup of tea one morning.

Haleh joined the chorus at school and thoroughly enjoyed that. Cheering was fantastic for three years running. Once she started to blossom into a very beautiful young lady, there were a couple of mean, nasty girls on her squad that got jealous. They had ways of quietly saying some really ugly and hurtful things to her, and she just had not yet learned the art of either fighting back or simply ignoring.

We should have reported that bad behavior to the dear coach, Miss Charlene, but we just tried to get past it. Haleh had the delicate facial features of an Audrey Hepburn with olive complexion and long wavy dark hair. Tender-hearted sensitive children can be bullied in sly, covert ways that adults in charge don't always notice. But when you smell Limburger cheese in Copenhagen, you know something is decaying in Denmark! Also, she was distraught that the county had changed the school districts. She would have to go to a different middle school and leave all of her close friends like Anastasia.

Even though she was super active, Haleh was not an early riser or morning person by any stretch of the imagination. It was a bit of torture to get her out of bed for school. Then she had an arduous routine for straightening her long hair with a flat iron. The bus literally stopped right at our driveway, but getting her on it on time was a daily challenge. The best description I can think of for her mornings is "a snail on Valium."

In the meantime, DeKalb Schools had transferred me to Austin Elementary in Dunwoody to be a German teacher in a state model program of total immersion. I was sad to leave my beloved special students, but the new job was ultra-fun and exciting. The principal and teachers were outstanding. I was allowed to be as wildly creative as I could. We sang and danced in German class. I had puppets and costumes and played my autoharp. You could compare it to a German 'Sesame Street' in a lot of ways.

Daily I had second, third and fifth graders. I wheeled my cart full of props and posters around to the different classrooms. Every Friday my computer-generated German word-search puzzles related to what we were studying or some season or holiday. The kids had a saying, "Frau Most Rocks!!" As a teacher my mottos were: BANISH BOREDOM and EDUCATE AND ENTERTAIN.

I was there for two very happy and enjoyable years until a strange hearing disorder in my left ear forced me take an early retirement. The vestibular neuronitis affected my balance, and I even fell over a school desk one day. Whatever my right ear heard was delayed in the left ear and sounded like I was holding a conch shell next to that ear. Bizarre, right? The ear nose and throat doctor tried a plethora of treatments for months to no avail, though lowering my sodium intake did take away the conch shell effect.

The sum total of these events made us decide to take a year off from Haleh's public education and do home-schooling and educational travel. I got copies of all of the textbooks for her grade level and preceded to take charge of her education. It was not ideal, but we made it through the year and had a wonderful trip to Minnesota to visit friends. We participated in watching the birds of prey spiral up into the thermal winds to migrate south for the winter. This fascinating event takes place at Hawk Ridge in Duluth, Minnesota every September 21st. People stand there all day with chalk and blackboards and count hawks, falcons, eagles and so forth.

Going to the Mall of America in Minneapolis was a memorable treat. This mall has three oval levels, each with a one-mile perimeter. Our favorite things were Camp Snoopy in the middle and the Rainforest Café on the lower level.

It had a jungle canopy with animated electric monkeys and beautiful plants and flowers. I loved that café so much that I wrote to the corporate headquarters in Texas and begged them to build one in Peachtree Corners where they could make a fortune. That never happened. Maybe someday!

In reality it was actually a God wink blessing that I was retired and Haleh was homeschooling precisely when she was. April and Rick's baby girl Violet came three months early, and they truly needed us to be there with them for the help and loving support. April was by then a college English professor, and she had to keep her job so that baby Violet in Emory's neonatal ward would be insured for unfathomable amounts of medical expense. It was another example of heaven's calendar trumping ours, and everything working out for the best. It was indisputable proof in the natural that our lives fall into place in well-ordered patterns that we ourselves would not have been able to create so beautifully.

There was one more little side benefit for Haleh in all of this upheaval. She was no longer a little cookie-cutter preppy girl in middle school, so she developed her very own style and ways of thinking. Good-bye to shopping at The Limited, American Eagle and Abercrombie and Fitch. (Some people call it Grab a Booty and Pinch.) Later when she applied to Oglethorpe University, she got a huge, magnificent scholarship primarily for being so unique. She loved ethnic clothes and jewelry and sandals and had really become her own person, assertive and self-assured. It even led her away from the fast-food junk food culture of our land. She became interested in natural cures with herbs and essential oils and fresh clean food.

We had been members at Duluth Methodist where the pastor was a college friend of mine. Haleh announced to me that her friends were attending Sugarloaf Methodist. It is always important for teens to be in church and youth group with their buddies, so we switched the membership. Sugarloaf sticks right with the scriptures, but is more of a rock and roll church with guitars. Blue jeans, bare feet or ball gowns with spike heels are just fine! It is all about the love of every single one of God's children.

Pastor Mark had a way of summing up the gospel so succinctly in such plain English that was easy to understand. You hold up four fingers and say, "God loved, God gave, I believe, I receive." You can't get much clearer than that, and there is no need to debate about how many angels can sit on the head of a pin or any such nonsense. If you want to read the writings of Josephus, Saint Augustine or Saint Jerome, go for it! Laissez faire!

Mama had been living in Decatur at the Phillips Tower retirement high-rise building not far from my brother. After about seven years, Eric expressed that he was burning out and needed some extra help caring for her with the aging process, so we moved her in with us. She had developed diabetes and needed help managing calendar, diet and medications. She gave her car to her pastor in Decatur, and we provided all of her transportation. She brought her living room furniture, china, some lamps and pictures and so forth and gave bedroom and dining room furniture to David and Kimberly. We did not need extra furniture, but we wanted her to feel at home. Our house was large enough to accommodate everything, so that way she did not have to feel as if she had lost her entire lifetime of possessions. She joined Sugarloaf Methodist and made some wonderful new friends who often took her to lunch and came over for tea or took her shopping.

One Sunday Mahmoud decided to go to an auction at a Marriott Hotel. They were advertising silk Persian rugs. He had left beautiful ones behind when he fled during the Iranian revolution. If his brother had tried to ship them to us, they would have been seized at the Atlanta Airport and given to the Smithsonian in Washington. Auctions make me very nervous. The problem is the noise combined with my spouse's impulsiveness. He arrived home with seven silk rugs, several large Japanese Satsuma vases and some Limoges candlesticks. For everything he had paid around $13,000. That would be the cost for carpeting our house twice, but these rugs would last longer than a lifetime.

Try walking on a silk rug barefoot and tell me how heavenly that is! I asked him how in the world he got everything at one tenth of its value. It just so happened that people were there to bid on Mohammed Ali's watch and South African gold Kruggerands coins. No one was interested in outbidding him for the rugs. This was divine justice. He had suffered so much grief and trauma losing his family and home and career. It says in the Book of Joel, "I will restore the years that the locusts have eaten."

Haleh's World History teacher had an interesting assignment. You picked a famous person and did some kind of video to represent some part of their life. I suggested the lovely actress, Audrey Hepburn. Haleh did a scene from Audrey's movie, 'Breakfast at Tiffany's.' She sat in a window with a white hair wash towel on her head and did the scene with the beloved Johnny Mercer song, 'Moon River.' She was playing a guitar, and Ana taped the scene with dubbed in music. It was an A+++ assignment.

Chapter 24
Possum Blossom Beats the Odds-Bloom Baby, Bloom!!!

April's water broke thirteen weeks early, and she was in the Gainesville hospital on complete bed rest for several days. Little Violet was crouched down in breech position inutero utilizing the small amount of amniotic fluid that was remaining in the womb. I saw her on ultrasound the day before she was born. Her tiny feet were tapping like an Irish dancer. It was beyond belief and inspired me to write a song to the tune of 'What Child Is This?' When Violet's blood pressure and heart rate plummeted dangerously low on the morning of February 5th., April was wheeled into the delivery room. Violet was taken in a flash by caesarian section before the anesthesia could kick in. Brave April felt the full intensity of all of that pain. She said that at one point she was actually out of body looking down on the delivery table.

I can't explain all of that, but I can tell you the whole event was terrifying. It was Super Bowl Sunday, and I think April deserved an 18carat gold trophy and ring! Violet was one pound and eleven ounces. Her tiny hand was literally the size of my thumbnail. I arrived when they were preparing the baby to go in an ambulance downtown Atlanta to Emory Midtown. This is the same Crawford Long hospital where I was born. They have the best neo-natal unit in metro Atlanta.

It is very noteworthy that The Upper Room devotional page that day was called "From Broken Strings." It was about a violin with broken strings and bridge that did not sound right. The owner took it to a skilled luthier who made the necessary repairs. Then it made beautiful music. The author compared our grief and broken hearts to violins that need a special craftsman to make the right adjustments. Our heavenly father knows us completely and can mend well our brokenness and make us whole. The scripture for that day was from

Isaiah 61 verse 1. "He has sent me to bind up the brokenhearted." Scoffers will call this a coincidence, but we were all deeply comforted by the timeliness of these words. It truly inspired hope and faith in our family.

April had to stay in the hospital to recover, but the ambulance took her breastmilk daily to Violet and tube fed her one teaspoonful at a time. She was hooked up to so many tubes and wires she looked like an AT & T phone box of sorts. They ran any number of tests and discovered that she had three heart defects. There was a tiny hole. She also had a condition called pulmonary atresia which means her heart and lung valves were reversed. This could all be repaired with a Renzuli patch, bovine pulmonary aorta and a human pulmonary valve whenever she reached around sixteen pounds. Until then she got a stint, and we gave her eight medications three times per day.

Violet was too tiny and undeveloped to open her eyes yet. Therefore, I called her "Possum Blossom." We did kangaroo care with her. That is when you put her skin to skin on your chest. This is something that babies need psychologically and physiologically to facilitate the bonding process that makes us human. It enables the baby to feel secure and nurtured.

For many years I had regularly given blood at Red Cross donation centers. Daddy had always done this, and that was my inspiration. I have currently given 4.5 gallons, the interesting thing is that my common A positive blood has a special factor. I am cytomegalovirus negative. That means that along with only 5% of the world's population, I had never had that virus. What it equates to clinically is that my blood is needed for preemie babies and organ transplant recipients.

Having the preemie granddaughter, the words good and karma pop into my mind. So, what blood goes around my circulatory system comes around through the veins and arteries and helps keep tiny little ones alive. Kind of warms your heart, doesn't it? It is always special and meaningful when our lives have extra purposes. It motivates me to take exquisite care of my health in every way possible so that I will be able to give blood until I take my last breath.

April and Rick were exhausted, but they drove the fifty-eight miles each way every day to be with the baby and worked all week. One Sunday afternoon at age three weeks the doctors told us Violet had a serious infection and might not live until Monday. I was not going to accept those words! After all, when April was five years old looking at my wedding photos with violets she said,

"Mommy, when I grow up, I am going to have a baby girl and name her Violet just for you." This baby was meant to be. God would make a way for it. No one was going to tell me anything different.

I went into her tiny room. She was lying on her side with her little arms down beside her legs. I softly sang Brahams Lullaby to her in German. When I got to the word "Gott" which means God, she pulled her little arms up and folded her hands under her chin as if in prayer. At that moment I knew beyond any doubt that she would live. I felt the presence of angels, and a peace washed over me body, mind, will, emotions and spirit. There is barely any way to describe in human words when we are "Touched by an Angel", Mrs. Roma Downey!

You certainly cannot prove it to anyone, but it does not matter. You never forget those moments and the feelings of intense comfort and joy and peace that you experienced. That Monday I went straight out and bought a birthday card at Publix for a thirteen-year-old girl and a lavender calico floral Laura Ashley dress in size 8 from Wellspring thrift store. I think we should always back our faith up with actions that clearly underline in red what our spirits are speaking to our minds. There are times when we simply must go out on a limb and take some risks to proclaim what we believe. How else can we share the indescribable beauty of the spiritual things in life that help us to encourage others.

Most people are really hungry for this kind of encouraging news, so I systematically ignore the scoffers. I never argue with non-believers or believe what I hear or read from doubters. I think it is better to focus on what I personally have actually experienced. There is such a thin veil between heaven and earth. When angels peel back just one little corner of that veil, it gives us the knowledge and inspiration to keep believing and moving forward. At times it feels like we are crawling across broken glass to catch a fly ball that has gone over a barbed wire fence! It reminds me of the old, old book from 1678 by John Bunyan, 'Pilgrim's Progress.' Mumsie gave me my Uncle Julian's copy from his youth.

Violet came home in June, and I kept her four days a week. She was bright eyed and alert and was already tapping things rhythmically when she heard music. The doctors had warned us that she might be a tedious, fractious baby because of all she had suffered being poked pricked and prodded for six months in the NICU. Nothing could have been further from the truth. She was happy and calm all day every day. To begin with, they had only given her a 10% chance of even living. The footnote to that was: If she lives, she would not have much chance of walking, talking, hearing, seeing or thinking. This baby had beat all the odds!

I sang nursery rhymes to Violet every day and spoke a lot of German to her. When she was fifteen months old, Haleh and I were taking Ana home and out of the blue Violet sang, "Twinka twinka litta stah. How I wunda what you ah." I nearly ran off the road! She was not even old enough to talk, much less sing a song! Before very many more months she could sing twenty-three songs on perfect pitch. Did this little kid have her mom's music gene? I would shout a resounding "Yes!"

Violet was doing so well overall that Emory's pediatric department wanted to study her a bit. I took her there from time to time, and they did various tests. She was not walking due to delay of her large muscles, but her fine motor skills were noteworthy. She could take tiny half inch cubes and stack them way high. She was very verbal and alert and understood adult conversations. The Emory pediatrician told me take her home and have her crawl the stairs to loosen her hip muscles to facilitate walking. The minute we got home, she went straight to the stairs and started doing that. She walked not long after.

We made a new purple velvet "Funny Book" for Violet's cute sayings. She had absolutely as many as David or April or Haleh. If she was perplexed, she said "Oh, shoe pickles!!" Daddy thought this was hilarious and endearing. There were gray doves nesting in the fake fern basket to the left of our front door. None of our household or lawnmower or chain saw noises disturbed them or frightened them away. It definitely symbolized the peace that we had found.

Life is seldom a big party when the earth splits open and dancing girls jump out of cakes! There are so many difficult challenge mountains that seem to be insurmountable. Somehow a tremendous amount of good/ groundbreaking/ gamechangers comes out of the gory/ gut-wrenching/ gaping wounds of life's tornadoes/floods/ mud slides/ forest fires and volcano eruptions.

Chapter 25
An Hourglass, Some Sand, & The Time Goes Slip Slidin' Away!

Haleh started high school and things were going better. She had made new friends and was very involved with her youth group at Sugarloaf church. Aaron the youth pastor and his wife Kimberly were really dynamic. They helped the teens bond into a solid group. Every summer they took some students on a mission trip. Haleh's first trip was to Chicago. She discovered that she had a passion for working with homeless people in shelters. She especially was drawn to the little children and loved to read to them. She was fond of all the youth counselors. Her second mission trip was to San Francisco, and the third one was to Philadelphia. The counselors said that she was very dedicated and did an awesome job with great tenderness and sensitivity. To this day, if she sees a homeless person, she buys them a meal.

The church was building a new sanctuary, so the old building became the attractive and innovative youth department. I went to help them paint the walls. Unfortunately, I had gotten into some poison oak by the river. There was a huge, furry vine on an oak tree. I thought it was plain ivy and was chopping it down. Thankfully I was wearing long sleeves and pants, so it only got on my face and hands. It required medical treatment with steroid pills and strong prescription strength cortisone cream. I would call that "cortisone on steroids!" Pun intended. I persevered until the job was done.

I had joined an adult Sunday School class called Breakfast and a Movie. We took turns bringing breakfast foods. After eating we watched some Bible related movie about history or geography or inspirational famous people of faith. It was very interesting and engaging compared to the typical lesson one might have had in the past. Our teacher Erik was really on the ball to facilitate rousing discussions.

Most of the people in the class were somewhat younger than me, but it did not matter. I made some wonderful friends. Every fall, the first Saturday of October, the class came to our house for a campfire picnic by the river. When our neighborhood pool got new furniture, I asked for the old tables, chairs and chaise lounges. I could seat sixty people comfortably in the woods. This event was a real hit with the class members. People brought guitars, and we sang amidst the smores.

I made a pathway to the river with large flat rendered stones. Lining the path on both sides were four-foot-tall poles with green bottles on top. When entertaining at night, we put tea lights on top of the bottles. There was also a circle of poles and bottles around an area for creative movement and dance. It is truly beautiful after dark. I also made an area for music, one for art and places for people to sit and read or write or meditate.

Mahmoud had built a two-story playhouse for Haleh which Violet loved. It became her school, laundry business, theater, and store. We call the entire backyard area Violet's Vineyard. The path is Possum Blossom Alley. She has an outdoor cooking area and café and brick oven bakery plus flower shop. There is also a slide, a sandbox and a swing. The lawn has room for a badminton net and croquet game.

Our yard is full of beautiful flowering shrubs and lilies, roses, tulips gardenias and such. The yard is not fenced, so it is a constant battle with the many deer. Our home is next to a national park. We have discovered that deer do not like any fuzzy, plants or flowers or poisonous bulbs like daffodils. That means they stay away from spider lilies and furry lambs ear plant. They are not at all keen on the fourteen varieties of lilies that we have.

 Daddy gave us miniature perennial small Candlestick and Lady Jane tulips. We started out with a dozen, and now they have multiplied into the hundreds. They keep spreading without any digging up or separating. The only care they receive is a good dose of bone meal after they bloom. Those must be sprayed with a disgustingly repulsive repellent called Repels All. It does not hurt deer or other animals, but it is made from the most stinky organic things imaginable plus dried blood. I am sure that even skunks would not like it.

Mahmoud my "Moo Moo the Magician," built amazing terraced gray stone wall gardens with four tiers behind the driveway. He cut the stones by hand and built a stone stairway. On the other side of the house, he made a sloped stone sidewalk with beige hexagonal shaped stones that makes it easy for older people or wheel chairs to get to the backyard gardens and picnic tables. He built a new brown deck from a material that will never rot or get eaten by insects. Also, it cannot come apart because all of the boards are joined with sturdy screws. Our old deck, builder grade G for garbage had no flashing against the house. This shoddy workmanship allows the large bolts to rust and pull away from the house. So dangerous! We did hardwood flooring in a couple of bedrooms, but we needed to hire someone for the rest of the job. Stairways and balconies are a bit too tedious and hard to do accurately.

Popsie's tile work is flawless, so he tiled the master bathroom and put marble in the powder room. He has a city of tools. I try to keep things organized or not? We aim for fewer mistakes. He is the "Fibber McGhee" of basements and garages. I call his office the Disheveled Den of Doom! I constantly have to remind him that I am the mistress of the house, and "You want to put WHAT in my kitchen. Holy caramba NO because I am the mommy, and I said so!!!!"

I faux painted the seven Roman arches on our main floor and the five cornices in the breakfast room to look like Italian marble. We put green Silestone counter tops to match. Daddy gave me Grandmother Hazel's green antique secretary with two Medici women hand-painted on the bookcase doors. The live-in kitchen and fireplace have the look of the Italian Renaissance era. Small statues, paintings and artifacts from Italy set the stage. In general, we have so many beautiful things from around the world, that it is legitimate to call our house an ethnic-eclectic-art nouveau museum!

Haleh got a job at Burger King and saved her money to pay toward a car. She worked there three years. When there was an economic slump, car prices plummeted to beyond belief rock bottom. We found a three-year-old leased Lexus in perfect condition for 15k and put it in the garage until she got her license. She lacked only a couple of credits to graduate, so her senior year was a breeze. She took pottery, jewelry making, and other practical useful courses that were relaxing.

Haleh finished high school with honors and went to live on campus at Oglethorpe University with a very generous scholarship. This was a wonderful choice for her. She had very small classes of eight to twelve students or so. The first couple of months she drove home to visit a lot. Then she adjusted to living away from home. The professors were very involved with the young people and were constantly in touch with them. They invited them to their homes for pizza and cookouts or to watch films. She really thrived there.

Oglethorpe is said to be the Princeton of the south. It was heavily endowed by William Randolph Hearst and was a Presbyterian school. The campus is beautiful and the buildings look like Harry Potter style or Oxford University in England.

Haleh decided to major in accounting. Her daddy longed for her to study medicine, but I pointed out to him: She barely passed biology, and she almost faints if she sees blood, so maybe not! She tutored students and got an award for teaching. Dr. Benson, head of her department told her to get her master's degree and CPA license and work five years in her field and come back to Oglethorpe to teach. He said they would pay her a CPA salary. That university is heavily endowed by the Atlanta business community. She went to Georgia State for the master's degree and had all kinds of good job offers with large, prestigious accounting firms.

English professor April was chosen by the University System of Georgia to go to Mississippi and lead a literacy seminar with the famous actor, Morgan Freeman. Her job was to show the English teachers of America how to use art, music and drama to encourage reluctant students to love books and reading. Now that was several feathers in her cap, and we were all so proud! It reminded me of the time when she took a neighborhood child named Jared under her wing. He had Asperger Syndrome. She encouraged him to write and illustrate stories and read them out loud. What a gentle, sensitive soul she is!

Mama was not doing very well. She could not manage her diabetic diet or medications, and I was often away from home working on rental properties and running errands. She went to stay with Sara and Walter in Gainesville for her birthday and wound up in a diabetic coma. We got her to the Duluth hospital. They did a three-day evaluation with doctors, nurses, physical therapists and social workers. The end result was that she would not be able to live with us anymore and would require a specialized nursing facility. It had become almost impossible for her to climb our stairs to her bedroom. It was a very sad day for us. We had enjoyed her so much, and she was so loving.

Nonetheless, she was placed in a beautiful, spacious home that had a chef and wonderful activities. I visited her weekly and brought her laundry home. She had lovely clothes, and I wanted to wash them in cold water and hang on the line to dry. Her church friends visited her often and took her places. She did Garden Club, arts and crafts and Book Club there and had bird feeders.

Daddy had always been very active and healthy and spoke wellness over himself. He ate clean fresh food. Unfortunately, he had been a heavy smoker and developed COPD, chronic obstructive pulmonary disease. He was susceptive to pneumonia and needed to use a breathing machine several times per day. He had a three-acre garden full of flowers, vegetables, blueberry bushes, muscadine vines, herbs and gorgeous flowering shrubs. He built a potting shed. There were over one hundred varieties of irises. Daddy was president of the National Iris Society. They entertained with tea parties in his garden to raise money for the Vines Botanical Garden. They had stone benches, a gazebo, lovely statues and decorations and a fairy garden like the ones you see in Ireland. It had little ceramic elves and dwarfs and fairies. It became harder for him to work outside, but he tried.

I needed a heart mitral valve repair. The Emory surgeons put a tiny white plastic ring around my valve to hold it together to prevent leakage. The procedure was done by a Da Vinci robot. It hit my femoral artery, and I lost three pints of blood. The doctors naturally feared a lawsuit, but I said, "Okay, so Leonardo failed to maintain lane and hit the guardrail. I just hope chianti was not involved! Not a problem. I am alive."

Then oddly the nausea meds made me hallucinate. The blue asphalt tile floor down in x-ray looked like a Caribbean coral reef with fish and undulating plants. The blue walls in my room were ruby color with black Chantilly lace moving off the wall toward me. I have never taken any street drugs or illicit substances, but for the first time in my life I actually understood why people do. Thankfully I have a delightful natural high that my internist says makes me the envy of all the cocaine addicts in Atlanta, Georgia!

Violet and I did a lot of gardening. I taught her how to plant an avocado seed to grow a tree. The funniest thing was when we planted zinnias on the deck in a long planter. They bloomed, and we had red, orange, pink, yellow and white. One day we saw a tiny Billy bee on a zinnia. I showed it to Violet and told her all about it. She marched straight into the house and got her picture book about insects. She took a little stool to the deck and placed it next to the flowers. She opened the book to the chapter about bees and started reading it to the Billy bee. I chuckle every time I think about that. That girl is so full of life and ideas and unique cleverness. She never ceases to amaze us and amuse us.

Haleh married Bobby, and that was a joyful thing that was very fortunate. We had known him and his family since she was three years old. We loved them all so much. It was truly a blessed marriage. Bobby is eight years older. I would have predicted such for Haleh because she never was satisfied with young men her age. She was too mature, and they bored her and were immature. She told one young man from a very wealthy celebrity family, "You know, I like to study with you, but I don't want to date you. You are majoring in drinking, chasing skirts and wrecking your truck." She had values and standards and would not budge to bow down to the false ideas that our society likes to trumpet about and worship. Just feed her plain steak without the gobbledygook gravy our culture calls cool and necessary.

Violet and I enjoy going on vacations most summers. We usually went to Destin to visit Cousin Kelly and Tania's family. Their son Chandon is close to her age. Our first big trip was to New York, Connecticut, New Jersey, Pennsylvania and Ohio. We visited Cousins Jon and Dona and toured Jon's world-famous digital sculpting studio and the sculpture garden built by the famous sculptor Seward Johnson. He was an heir to the Johnson & Johnson band-aid fortune but told them where they could stick their bandages! He was born to sculpt.

We did a lot of historical sightseeing in places like Philadelphia and Gettysburg. The Hershey chocolate factory was a big hit. We toured Amish country in Lancaster, Pennsylvania. We went to the Living Word Theater in Ohio that I helped found. When it was time to leave, I told her to come to the car. She said, "Momsie, please give me a few more minutes. I am talking to the Lord." This child has a profoundly deep spirit for sure. Lastly, we spent some days at the grass-fed beef ranch belonging to our cousins Tara and Luke and family. They have a barn that is a lovely wedding venue.

I am truly blessed with fun, caring cousins and brother and sister who literally text almost every day and send an abundance of photos of everything they are doing. We enjoy spending time together traveling or at our homes. Chris, Jon, Mike, Kelly, Cynthia and Kathy are like extra siblings to me. I adore their spouses, and their children and grandchildren are such sweet bonuses also. The bond of love and loyalty is an enormous gift to me and my family and is priceless. They are all such interesting personalities and so bright and vibrantly alive.

During the years we lost Aunt Judy, Uncle Tom, Aunt Sara, Daddy, Uncle Walter, Uncle Truman and Mama. It does not seem that one can ever prepare for these deaths. There is no way to comprehend how the grief will feel or know how to trudge through the sorrow to the other side. It was especially hard with Mama because of Covid-19. You always think when a parent dies, you will be at their bedside holding their hand and telling them how much you love them. We were not allowed to see her.

The morning Mama died I dreamed we were having an outdoor luncheon with bright blue placemats on the white tables with vases of bright pink roses. The morning after she died, a scraggly, neglected, aphid-eaten rose bush that had not bloomed for two years produced two very large bright pink roses, and I knew everything was alright. Peace washed over me like gentle spring rain.

You just keep on trucking fueled by the sweet memories in your tank. You constantly think of their wonderful wise sayings, and the things they taught you. You try to pass all of this on to your children and grandchildren. There are times when it seems they are almost on your shoulder in a strange, indescribable way. Or you have such a warm, happy vivid dream and you know somehow, they were there. It does not even matter that you cannot prove it to anyone. Comfort abides as you realize heaven is close by.

One summer Violet and I did a grandparent tour of Ireland with Road Scholar. Our group was very small which made things easy to manage and gave our tour guide Kate more time for us. It was amazing and beyond beautiful and fulfilled my lifelong wish to visit there. I have some ancestors on Granddaddy Moore's side that lived in Dublin, County Cork, County Limerick and so forth. Violet made some friends that she still contacts from time to time.

That country was so relaxing and is truly an endless expanse of lush green everywhere. I will never forget hundreds of miles of beautiful stone walls across the entire country. There is hardly any crime, so you rarely see policemen or their cars. Even the police do not have guns. Since Violet and I had taken family Zumba classes for several years, she especially loved going to the Riverdance Theater. The library at Trinity College was something to write home about as was the large Dublin soccer stadium Croke Park where Garth Brooks had two weeks of concerts previously.

The following summer we were signed up to go to Greece, but the Covid-19 pandemic hit, and all trips were canceled. We signed up for a trip to Iceland the next year, but Violet was not permitted to go without a Covid vaccine. Her cardiologist forbids it since a small percentage of teens develop pericarditis after the vaccine. But it was okay because we could go and visit Haleh and Bobby and oodles of cousins in California.

Bobby is in the Army and Haleh has her CPA license and works for an accounting firm. They have a beautiful little daughter named Paisley Rose. I spent seven weeks with her after her home birth with a midwife.

The Salvador Dali Museum in Monterey is totally worth seeing. Cousin Chris in Santa Cruz took us on a marvelous sailing trip to Monterey and back. Then we toured San Francisco. I had lunch with an American friend I knew in Germany. She makes films and gave me two DVDs of her best that had won awards. We visited Cousin Kathy east of Sacramento. That was very happy. Her daughter Bonnie and daughters drove four hours to be with us. It is a blessing that my cousins and their children have a close bond with us. We are daily in touch and providing each other a lot of support and love, laughter and fun photos.

I went to Greece and Turkey with Road Scholar for a dream come true. That beautiful country is so peaceful one does not want to leave. You do not find homeless people because families are so close and compassionate and loyal. In my opinion, there is no ocean as beautiful a blue as the Aegean Sea.

If you visit an island that has no motorized vehicles, Amazon delivers large boxes on donkeys, not kidding. The scenery and history are something else. The food is so delicious and healthy, and they have interesting bakeries and candy stores. The island of Santorini with white buildings and bright blue rooftops is epic and other world pleasurable. Ephesus in Turkey is inspirational. All over Greece the little shops are intriguing. You will not find fast food restaurants. Greeks demand slow, fresh clean food!

I do not mind getting older, and proudly share my age numbers. I appreciate each day that is given to me, and take it with a side of humility. The snow-white hair does not hold permanent color anymore, so can't be a suicide blonde any longer. (Dyed by her own hands) Mumsie had snow-white hair, so I wear it proudly as my crown of wisdom. My crepey skin may look like Rip Van "Wrinkle," but that's alright. I declare that crepey skin is better than being a miserable old sack of cellulite. Being mellow and content are good and desirable.

I have asked the Dear Lord to let me live to a ripe old age of one-hundred-fourteen. That way I can see and experience what the grandchildren will do and become. The fact that Haleh came and was such a healthy, bright baby when we were forty-six is virtually a good sign. It shows that the genetics are marked for at least a century of life or more. We shall continue to eat fresh clean food and stay physically very active. Fitbit, you can expect around nine-thousand steps per day from me. Plus, there is California nouveau cuisine: three beans and a glance at the chicken!

Incidentally, dancing reduces dementia by around 47%. You ask me why? There is a very concrete physiological reason. Dancing creates new neural paths in the brain when one is memorizing the steps or remembering them. This includes making rapid decisions about which step comes next. I dance every day almost without fail. It's good to dance to songs that have a lot of meaning and feeling for you. That way you feed your mind, will and emotions while strengthening the muscles and bones. Firm muscles burn more fat even when you are sitting or lying down. Who knew? Strong muscles help coordination and which obviously prevents falls. Doesn't hurt to do a little Tai Chi to improve balance. Yoga is too slow for me and thus too boring. I have to get my stretching in other forms of exercise like doing the short girl stretch to reach things in cabinets.

If a physical symptom appears and medical help is needed, I tell the doctor: Oh, well, I have that condition called TMB. When they look bewildered and worried that they missed that one in medical school, I explain: That stands for Too Many Birthdays, and we all get a good laugh. Since we have as many neurons and dendrites in our guts as in our brains, and the gut can communicate with the brain, there are plenty of times when one can give an ailment a couple of days until you have the "a ha" moment. You then realize a way to use food as medicine or rebalance the intake of nourishment. One must first have a basic knowledge of super foods and inner body inflammation. You don't want to "rust" from the inside out.

I can go years without having a headache and have not had a cold since February of the year 2012. I was in a beach house in Belize with eleven sick people, and they finally wore me down. However, we are from in IBS family. Crank up a weekly bellyache? No problem! We usually don't have genetic disorders that can kill you, but things like allergic rhinitis nasal issues and food allergies could probably worry you to death. Mahmoud is the Grand Puba of accident survival. He went to the Nine Lives Olympics and got a gold medal, leaving the cats in the dust! They know us at the ER at Northside, Piedmont and Emory hospitals. Usually they say, "We don't know why he is not dead from this fall or gash or head trauma."

I need to design a coat of arms for my family. The Latin inscription at the top might be:

<u>AUDENTES FORTUNA IUVAT</u> (Fortune favors the bold) or
<u>ME VEXAT PED</u> (Like a pebble in the shoe) or
<u>MULGERE HIRCUM</u> (Attempting to milk a goat)

There would be pictorial icon representations of IBS, allergic rhinitis, reflux and a mule for stubbornness for sure!

There is a gift inborn in me from my creator. I can teach and preach to most any age group like there is no tomorrow! Put an object in a paper bag and give it to me, and I will teach a twenty-minute lesson about it, secular or spiritual, adding songs, poems, scriptures, anecdotes and examples to make a point.

So, Pandora, what else do you have in your box? One early July morning I was on the sidewalk by the front steps. Seemingly out of nowhere, a stinging insect came up from behind me and got me on my lower right cheek. I swatted at it, but nothing fell. It appeared that it had retreated backward like a reverse SCUD missile and gone. I went in the house and went upstairs to get some Benadryl, Zyrtec and Flonase that has steroids. On the way down the steps my hands and feet swelled up like balloons and started to tingle. I began to hallucinate seeing bright white, pink and purple fireworks.

Nothing like this had ever happened to me, but I realized I was in deep trouble. I made it to the phone and dialed 911. Thank heaven we live in a county with wonderful paramedics! They arrived in under five minutes and started working on me. They said I was five minutes from death. The reaction was so violent that I was coughing up cups of foamy pulmonary edema and could have drowned in my own fluids.

The ER doctor felt that it might have been a guinea wasp since they are more poisonous. The hospital planned to keep me overnight, but I told them I would be in my own bed that night. Seven hours later they let me go home with a myriad of antihistamine and steroid prescriptions for the next seven days.

This terrifying event led me to do some research about insect repellents. I am a great believer in essential oils and read that certain ones repel flying nuisances. Don't want to kill them because they have good purposes in nature. I formulated a repellent that I call "Not 2 B." It also works for mosquitoes. It has a light, pleasant fragrance.

Chapter 26
A Fruit Salad of Extra Thoughts (From That Busy Astrodome Frontal Lobe, I Call My Forehead)

Nil desperandum! Do not despair!

Avoid people who majored in guilt with a minor in crazy. They will make you feel like you are the star of the 'I'm So Tired' show! You can lead a horse to water, but… you cannot keep them from being a horse's behind! I have had to say to certain individuals, "You have sent me on so many guilt trips, I have enough frequent flyer points to go all the way to hell and back." I like the Latin phrase: illigitimi non carborundum. It means don't let a certain kind of people get you down.

Most people are basically rational, but there are those who think they were abducted by aliens or are lost on this planet. If your knight does not have shining armor, love your knight who is in sensible armor. Avoid those who want you on tap like a mug of Guinness Stout. At times life will be so hard you will be sweating like the pig who knows he's dinner.

Avoid fanatics. People who are off the deep end tend to worship at the Shrine of the "Immaculate CONTRAPTION." This is not healthy long term.

There may be other accusatory, inflammatory, demanding souls who even trash you behind your back after you help them emotionally and cash flow wise and try to be a cheerleader for them. They need to hear: Baby, you need a kite to fly. Name your favorite, box kite or regular kite-shaped, and I will provide it in the color, fabric and design of your preference. I will even take you to a field where you can fly it. Please do not make me any madder, or it will be a mine field! Sometime bad treatment simply comes from that green-eyed monster named jealousy. Plus, today's third planet from the sun often tends to hate people who love Heaven. Put that in your smoke and pipe it!

There will always be bullies. They formerly took your lunch money, called you stupid or pushed you down for a snack of dirt or sand. You did not get to take your marbles and go home, because they took your marbles to their home. They find one of your weaknesses and harp on that. Today with texting, email and social media, they send you "nastygrams." When I asked my Daddy about harassment law suits for slander and libel, his wise reply was, "Darlin', don't aggravate yourself. Just ignore, ignore ignore! The earth is billions of years old, and you do not have to do but a hundred of them. Fifty years from now it won't make a BIT of difference!"

You may be a funky-junky messy-Bessie, and if not, you are probably married to one. Find a happy balance between tolerance and giving insanity consequences instead of trying to argue with it. Try your best to be ladylike or gentlemanly like with your speech. My dear friends Richard and Lori heard me call someone a Pillsbury Doughboy Son of a Biscuit. They laughed and said, "I bet that is one of the dirtiest things you have ever said." I replied, "Yes, that is fairly accurate. I have also called some people hiney crevices." My kids know when I shout, "Ding dang it to the holy caramba," they better duck and cover!

There are poor souls who keep choosing to be hollow inside like the Tin Man. They probably can't help it. Most likely some hurting person hurt them, and they have not had the proper mental health treatment or pastoral care ministering to synchronize their body, mind, will, emotions and spirit. That's where we have to stand in the gap for them like Moses did with the Israelites. If they finally do seek and accept help, the world heaves a collective sigh of relief.

We must all guard our thoughts. Marcus Aurelius said, "The soul becomes dyed with the color of its thoughts." The apostle Paul said here and there in his writings, "Whatsoever things are lovely, think on these things. Guard your thoughts. Put on the mind of the Lord. God has not given us a spirit of fear but of power and a sound mind."

Some people are very anxious and intense and a bit fearful. They typically constantly check the weather and the temperature. Myself, I just tell them, "Look at the sky for the weather and put your hand on the window for the temperature." I tell them to simmer down and pump up their faith. I suggest they celebrate their blessings once in a while with a glass of beer's hifalutin cousin, Champagne. I tell them to put on their big kid britches and get over their little sweet selves!

I read that recently a vegetarian woman on a plane had a fit on the lady sitting next to her who was eating a hamburger. She read the lady an excrement essay and told her to stop eating it because it was making her nauseated and upset and disgusted. Not sure what I would have done if I were the Burger King Beauty, but militant vegetarians might need to wear a Covid mask scented with essential oil of Brussel sprouts. The world is full of unpleasant odors. Adjust your nose.

The roof and windows and gutters will leak from time to time and cause you great consternation. Then along comes the roof repair handyman who gives you the name of a skilled window installer with a reasonable price. That's why the Good Book says, "Evil means itself for evil, but the Good Lord will use it for good." Your loved ones and friends may have illnesses and accidents that make them holy terrors from time to time. You will ask yourself, "Is that psycho baby from hell? Is someone going to drop a house on them?" Simply spoken, that is just your golden opportunity to learn forgiveness and forbearance. There have been times when I had to say, "Father forgive them even though they KNOW what they do, the little brats!"

If someone says "Machu Pichu," say GESUNDHEIT! If you feel like you are in grave danger, just give someone your blood type with a list of relatives willing to donate kidneys and such. If you have to drive on Interstate 85 or 20 or 285 N, S E or W, have terrycloth towels, paper towels, food, water, Depends and essential medications. Our governor says the 18 wheelers of America come to Atlanta to have accidents. How many times have I sat for hours when a tractor trailer flipped over and burned enough to melt the freeway?

People familiar with the harsh unfair never-ending difficulties and traumas of my life history ask me why I do not take medication for anxiety or depression. It's very simple. A wonderfully nice man was cleaning my gutters and saw me sweeping my sidewalk. He said, "Hey Senora, my wife come cleana' you house." I said, "Pablo, if you wife come cleana' my house, it will kill me!" I told him when I am sweeping, I am getting out all my anger and frustration. I whap the crap out of the sidewalk or driveway or kitchen floor and say, "Take that you miserable, lousy dirt ball!" I believe there were fewer divorces and spousal murders and child abuse when women were doing more sweeping, scrubbing and dusting.

I learned this from my Greek neighbor, Mrs. Poulos on the street behind us. She spoke very little English, so we communicated with gestures and doodle art symbols. She had had the trying life of an immigrant being left in Greece for years while her husband got established enough to send for her and the children. She swept her back steps and patio every day. Another neighbor who hired yardmen was constantly agitated and as irritable as a sore-tailed cat in a room full of rocking chairs! How many times when something went wrong did I hear her shout, "Damn, damn, damn, dammit it all to hell!" But I am not judging her. I am too busy working on my own sins, faults and hangups to criticize anyone.

I never heard my Grandmother Hazel gossip or condemn or judge others, and she was perhaps the most peacefully content member of our family. If she heard gossip or criticism, she simply said, "Oh well, to each his own". She shouldered all of her own responsibilities and was vacuuming and dusting the week she died.

If you go to a Moroccan restaurant that has a belly dancer, and your son-in-law tells the dancer that you like to dance, and she grabs your hand: I HOPE YOU DANCE!!!

If you spend the night in a hospital, and they tell you to walk a lot around the floor with your IV pole in a backless gown, just say: I did not sign up to be a pole dancer, but let's do this until my Fitbit makes happy noises!

If you say to a distraught person: I hear what you are saying, and I understand how you feel. It goes miles and miles toward making that person feel heard. It develops trust and removes antagonism and ire.

Our family is not perfect. If we leave our closet doors open and get up at 2am, we will probably hear some bones rattling in there. So, we aim for fewer mistakes!

Be thankful for each day, and live it to the fullest. Focus on your blessings. Love with all your heart. Skip the regrets. Open up your brain and let the light in and push the wrong thoughts out. When you are knee deep in poo poo, it does not matter who pooped it or who scooped it, just keep on muckin'. Some days you may feel so squirrely that the squirrels in your head are juggling knives, but just ignore. It will pass. Stay on the sunny side of the street but don't put on emotional sunblock! Remember Fred Astaire's inspiring song and dance about failures. "Just pick yourself up, dust yourself off and start all over again." Life is harsh, unfair, complicated and uncertain. Choose love, joy, peace, kindness, forgiveness, faith. Listen to my favorite saying:

LIFE IS SHORT. HEAVEN IS LONG. WE CAN DO THIS!